FOR SUCH A

Time

AS THIS

The Life of Senator James Forrester
and the Story of His Fight for Marriage in North Carolina

Mary Frances Forrester

Rebecca Anthony

Trilogy Christian Publishers
A Wholly Owned Subsidary of Trinity Broadcasting Network
2442 Michelle Drive
Tustin, CA 92780

For information, address Trilogy Christian Publishing
Rights Department, 2442 Michelle Drive, Tustin, Ca 92780.
Trilogy Christian Publishing/ TBN and colophon are trademarks of Trinity Broadcasting Network.

For information about special discounts for bulk purchases, please contact Trilogy Christian Publishing.

Manufactured in the United States of America

10 9 8 7 6 5 4 3 2 1

Library of Congress Cataloging-in-Publication Data is available.

ISBN 978-1-64773-410-7 (Print Book)
ISBN 978-1-64773-411-4 (ebook)

Endorsements

As I have had the privilege of reading this work, it is without question a rich testimony to the life and work of Dr. Jim Forrester. It won't take the reader long to see this man's life can be summed up in two words: servant leadership. From his earliest day even to his untimely departure from this earth, it is clear that his destiny was to be a servant leader.

—Pastor Mark Harris of North Carolina

Dr. Jim Forrester was an amazing leader and visionary, brigadier general, legislator, physician, wonderful father, and friend to so many. A modern-day William Wilberforce, he courageously spent fifteen years in the North Carolina legislature shepherding a vote upholding "a union between a man and a woman" as the biblical definition of marriage. *For Such a Time as This* clearly depicts the sacrificial service of this incredible servant-leader and the vital support of his outstanding spouse, Mary Frances. You will find this to be an inspirational read that reveals what it looks like within the political system to stand in grace and truth with Jesus Christ.

—Tom Phillips, vice president
Billy Graham Evangelistic Association

Mary Frances Forrester is a powerhouse. She beautifully tells the story of her husband, Jim Forrester, who dedicated his life to his family, his patients, his nation, and the principles in which he believed. Much will be written in history about Dr. Forrester's career—it is important for Mary Frances to share her story.

—Penny Nance, CEO and president of
Concerned Women for America

Mary Frances Forrester has captured the essence of a true American hero, her late husband, Jim Forrester. *For Such a Time as This* tells the story of Jim's journey from being a poor immigrant boy with a single mother to becoming a noted doctor treating the needs of the sick, serving his nation as a flight surgeon, and being elected to the state senate, where he led the effort to protect marriage as the union of one man and one woman, as God created it. More than that, however, it shows what a life dedicated to Jesus Christ produces if lived as an act of worship and how a marriage built on Jesus Christ exemplifies the holy institution the Lord Jesus inspired Jim to protect in North Carolina's constitution. His life is a testimony of James 3:13 (NIV): "Who is wise and understanding among you? Let them show it by their good life, by deeds done in the humility that comes from wisdom."

—Tami Fitzgerald, executive director
of NC Values Coalition

In loving memory of Mary Paige Forrester (1966–2018)

She entered the title page of this book on my computer desktop as a gentle daily reminder to tell this story. Here's to you, my baby girl.

Brigadier General, NC Air National Guard, US Air Force, the Honorable NC Senator James S. Forrester Sr., BS, MD, MPH, Honorary Knighthood in the Order of Royal Brotherhood of St. Michael of the Wing (KSMA), initials denoting it was conferred by HRH Dom Duarte, Duke of Bragança, Portugal. Jim's response to formal introductions was always: "Just call me Jim."

Acknowledgments

To James Summers Forrester and Agnes "Nancy" Williamson Forrester (Glasgow, Scotland), who gave life to this story of courage, perseverance, and accomplishment on both sides of the Atlantic.

To our children and grandchildren, who have a legacy to live by, raised with firm roots and strong wings and who continue to soar in this land of opportunity.

To Don Brown, for his foresight, encouragement, and advice.

To all those countless friends, patients, fellow Guardsmen, and political associates who helped us tell Jim's story.

He was never one to sit down and tell his own story.
—Representative John Torbett

Contents

Part 2

Part 3

Prologue

Agnes "Nancy" Forrester stood on a dock at Wilmington, Delaware, hesitant to set foot on the gangplank of the lumbering freighter ship. The salty wind off the water bit into her cheeks. On her left side shivered her nine-year-old daughter Sheila. On her right shivered son Jim, five years old and possessed of eyes the color of a highland loch in autumn.

It was early morning. Spring, 1942.

The freighter, whose name is now lost to history, was bound for Glasgow in Nancy's native Scotland. There, her remaining family waited. Not far from them, her husband James lay buried in the black earth of a centuries-old cemetery. His headstone bore no epitaph, just his name and the years he walked the earth. A third child, Lillian, also waited in Scotland. Lillian, limited by congenital disabilities, could not physically endure the transatlantic voyage to America the previous year. She'd been happy to stay behind, safe and sound in the home of her beloved Aunt Jennie.

Nancy struggled with indecision. The ship was slated to depart within the hour. She mustn't delay.

But her feet were weighted to the dock, and her stomach was tied up in an apprehensive knot. The Atlantic was a perilous place, and German U-boats lurked like hungry sharks.

Do not board the ship......

She pressed the children close to her and watched the other passengers ascend to the passenger deck.

The thunder of Japanese bombs that had decimated Pearl Harbor only weeks before still reverberated through the collective American heart, stoking outrage and determination. The "sleeping giant" had been awakened. America was at war, the same costly war that had already wrecked the map of Europe and soaked it in blood.

Since the attack at Pearl, Nancy had been frantic to book passage home; and the aged dual-service vessel before her was the quickest, cheapest mode of travel to be found.

The moment of departure had now come.

And her feet would not move.

Do not board…

Perhaps it was an odd second sense peculiar to her sea-bred Scottish stock that whispered the warnings in her head. Or maybe it was that elusive maternal intuition that would awaken countless other mothers in the wartime nights to come with the stark knowledge that a husband or son had just died among the gentle hills of Italy or in some steamy Pacific jungle.

Or was it something else warning her?

Do not get on…

A firm but unseen hand urged her to turn her back on the ship. She yielded.

Her sister Peg—with whom she and the children had been enjoying a comforting, protracted stay after the loss of Nancy's husband—was shocked to see her sibling reenter the front door after the tearful goodbye exchanged just hours before.

So it was that Nancy's frantic arrangements to return home to Scotland came to nothing. She would remain in America, the future shrouded in the murky, impenetrable mist of war.

No one could say just what, or *who*, altered Nancy's decision on the dock that chilly Delaware morning. Not even Nancy. Yet one thing *is* certain.

The freighter was torpedoed by a German U-boat a few days later, to the loss of many souls.

Part 1

June 18, 1996

Against all odds, Senate Bill 1487 had found its way onto the day's agenda. The *Defense of Marriage Act* would finally be heard on the floor of the North Carolina Senate. James Summers Forrester—Jim—was confident. If he could persuade his Senate colleagues to embrace the proposed statute, he maintained a cautious optimism that the House would follow suit, ensuring final passage. The wording of the statute was simple: "Marriages, whether created by common law, contracted, or performed outside of North Carolina, between individuals of the same gender, are not valid in North Carolina." It defined marriage as the exclusive union of one man and one woman. That the issue should be considered "controversial" was a travesty. To Jim, traditional marriage was set in biblical stone.

Allies had been sparse in the preceding weeks. Like-minded fellow legislators of both parties had urged Jim to back off. Their excuses varied:

"It's too controversial for an election year."

"*We don't really need it.*"

"Let's not address that issue right now."

"It's a waste of time. You'll never get it to the floor."

All the arguments amounted to the same thing—abandon the marriage issue.

Jim would do no such thing. To abandon the marriage "issue" would be abandoning marriage itself. Three years prior, in 1993, the Hawaii Supreme Court had ruled that denying marriage to same-sex couples constituted discrimination based on sex and violated the right to equal protection guaranteed by the state's constitution. In other words, refusal to grant same-sex couples marriage licenses was now discriminatory in that state.

The court's ruling disturbed Jim, for it revealed deep cultural implications for the future and exposed a slippery slope that would lead to a place far beyond homosexual unions themselves. Action had to be taken before the gay marriage push in North Carolina mushroomed into an irreversible legal assault which would find an accommodating ally in the form of a liberal judge. His Defense of Marriage statute was a necessary stop measure, a preemptive strike on behalf of the people of North Carolina, who overwhelmingly opposed same-sex marriage.

Yes, he had told naysayers, as a conservative, he recognized the procedural obstacles to getting the marriage bill to the floor, much less ratified, with a solidly entrenched Democrat General Assembly standing in opposition. *Yes*, he understood the potential political flak for those involved. What did that signify? Politics must bow to principle, and the principle of traditional marriage could not be deferred. The cultural and legal winds were shifting too fast.

Unsurprisingly, Jim's endeavors to pass the Defense of Marriage Act had sparked the ire of lesbian, gay, bisexual, and transgender (LGBT) groups, who launched angry rhetoric and pointed accusations in the media. Small darts compared to the poison-tipped arrows destined to fly later.

Some Democrats supported Jim's measure on an ideological basis but refused to do so on a political one. For that matter, so did some Republicans. Still, a few souls were willing to stand with Jim and be counted when gratification of conscience was likely the only thing to be gained.

Wherever individual members might stand personally on the matter of gay marriage, and whatever their subsequent willingness to affirm or deny those convictions in the critical glare of public light, they couldn't vote on a bill they were never allowed to hear. So Jim watched, frustrated but persistent, as his Defense of Marriage bill repeatedly circled the committee carousel, trapped in a purposeful legislative whirlpool to nowhere. It was the quintessential bureacratic doom for Republican legislation that Democrats wished to kill.

But now, by some gracious nudge of Providence, his bill had made it to the Senate floor. Its chance of *passing*, however, remained slim.

Jim, as primary sponsor, would speak to the bill first. He cleared his throat and rose to his full height of six feet one. Hardly had he begun to speak, however, when a flustered page entered the chamber and rushed straight to Jim with a message. Curious eyes looked on.

"There is an emergency in the House," Jim began.

Everyone had already guessed it was a medical emergency as Jim was the General Assembly's de facto physician. But they also knew how important the legislation at hand was to him. His statute bill would not get another chance.

"I'm a physician first," Jim continued without hesitation. "I will go to the House, and I yield my time."

Between Countries

We can do it!
> —Rosie the Riveter, from the iconic
> WWII recruitment poster

Nancy was now a legal alien in the United States, and her nation of Great Britain was also its wartime ally. Bill Curran, Peg's husband, the port captain in Wilmington, Delaware, helped Nancy secure a spot as a "Rosie Riveter" electrician in a nearby shipyard.

Supporting the Allied war effort was noble and gratifying, but the ever-present need for money did not defer to patriotic sincerity. The body selfishly demanded food on a daily basis and a doctor's care when it was sick. The children refused to stop outgrowing their clothes. The cost of living was steep, and there was little to set aside for the future at each month's end.

Return and Return Again

Remember those who help you and always reach back and help others.
—Nancy Forrester

When the raging of nations receded in the closing months of the war, Nancy returned to Scotland. But it was not a hopeful or happy homecoming. The misfortunes of war, and a few self-serving in-laws, had confiscated most of what the little Forrester family had once possessed. Things would never be as they were.

Still children must be reared and educated. In the short-lived suns of a Scottish winter, young Jim began his daily trek to school before sunrise, often returning in the dark of early evening. He made good use of the long school hours. A natural scholar, he sought academic achievement as a way to "fit in" and gain the respect of peers. He even missed his maternal grandmother's funeral because he was "head of class" that day, a title that conferred upon the bearer special recognition, rewards, and responsibilities.

He managed to adapt to the new reality, as children do. Not so his mother. Nancy's spirits were low, her days restless. She grieved still for James, and in Scotland, everything reminded her of their happy, prosperous years together before his sudden death. Emotionally and economically, life was too much to bear. What once was a garden was now a field of stones.

America shone across the Atlantic, beckoning, welcoming the destitute and industrious—welcoming the forlorn. Nothing of any real worth remained for her or her children in Scotland. Feeling a bittersweet mix of resignation and hope, Nancy decided to immigrate to the land of the free. This time, they would stay.

A few months later, on a bright June day in 1946, the USS *John Ericsson* slid into New York Harbor beneath the soaring form of Lady Liberty. The flame in her torch was welcoming and reassuring, like a candle in the window of one's cottage promising refuge and rest. And hope.

Nancy leaned over and squeezed the hand of nine-year-old Jim, curly haired and inquisitive. "Son," she said, "this is your new home. You're going to become a citizen, and you can do anything you are willing to work hard enough to do. But there's two things I want you to remember always. Remember those who help you and *always* reach back and help others."

The words, uttered in the massive shadow of Lady Liberty, were seared into his soft young heart.

A Physician First

Statesmen tell you what is true even though it may be unpopular.
Politicians tell you what is popular, even though it may be untrue.
—Anonymous

The medical emergency in the North Carolina House of Representatives was soon under control. Representative Theresa Esposito from Forsyth County had been suffering severe chest pains.

Mary Frances, listening to the session on her computer, had heard only that there was a medical emergency in the House, nothing more. Her initial reaction was skepticism. Had her husband's political opponents contrived a "heart attack" to get Jim and his thorny bill off the floor? Such diversions and delaying tactics were common in the legislature. Jim, on the scene in the House, knew this was not the case. Esposito was a Republican, after all, and her suffering proved all too real. He accompanied her to the hospital.

While it must have been emotionally excruciating, having to drop an ideological pearl of his legislative career like a muddy potato, Jim had no choice. He would not gamble with human life.

The upshot was that Jim did not return to the Senate floor before the session's adjournment. When he did, he was astonished to hear that his statute had been ratified. Forty-two votes had been cast in favor, including those of Democrat senators Mark Basnight, Roy Cooper, Joe Hackney, David Hoyle, Beverly Perdue, and Tony Rand. Jeanne Lucas cast no vote.

Democrat senators Charles Albertson and Charles Dannelly were absent. "Maybe they didn't want to vote it down in front of you," Mary Frances theorized afterward. "They have too much respect for you, on both sides of the aisle."

The Defense of Marriage Act was now sent to the House, where it passed the following day.

"I think they understood," Mary Frances later recalled. "They had accused and questioned why he wanted to stir up social issues unnecessarily. God used that moment to show that Jim had no ulterior motive and that he wasn't just trying to stir up a hornet's nest. He felt strongly about what he was doing. He did the right thing because it was the right thing to do."

In retrospect, one wonders how Jim's selfless actions regarding Esposito had touched people's consciences. Was it simply that he had not hesitated to put someone else above a bill they knew was important to him?

That day, Jim had done the right thing, and his efforts were rewarded. It would not always be so.

The Defense of Marriage Act was ratified by the North Carolina General Assembly on June 20, 1996. It was now state law.

Immigrants Find Their Feet

To live under the American Constitution is the greatest political privilege that was ever accorded to the human race.
—President Calvin Coolidge

America was a land of opportunity, but the immigrant existence was no Fourth of July picnic. From the outset, work was life, and life was work. Nancy found a position with Dr. Paul Black, a local ear, nose, and throat physician, as receptionist and bookkeeper. Weekends were spent tallying the books at O'Crowley's Dry Cleaners in Wilmington, North Carolina.

Thanks to her heavy workload, Nancy's two children were often left to shift for themselves. Jim was a latchkey kid long before anybody coined the phrase. As emotionally hard as his mother's long absences were, he was too busy working himself to dwell on them.

At ten, he landed his first job when he strode into the *Wilmington Star News* and requested not one but two paper routes, morning and afternoon. The editor was taken aback, noting the boy's arrival on foot at the door.

"Do you even have a bike?"

"I will have," Jim replied.

At the bicycle shop, he found a serviceable specimen and struck a bargain with the shop owner. Jim would give the man his full weekly wages from the morning paper route until the bike was paid for. The shop owner, admiring Jim's spunk, agreed with a smile and a handshake. Verbal agreements meant something back then. To Jim, this was a binding oath.

When the bike was paid off, all the proceeds from his afternoon paper route supplemented the Forrester grocery fund.

Paper routes were the first of many jobs that filled Jim's non-school hours. As soon as he was old enough, he delivered soft drinks for Coca-Cola, served up sodas at the drugstore, and sold Bibles door to door for Southwestern Publishing during the summers. He even held the ignominious, smelly job of janitor at Regal Paper Mill. There, on one random spring day, a tiny foreign particle found its way into his eye as he swept the floor. A speck of wood? A tiny metal shard? No one knew for certain, but Dr. Black took the usual steps to prevent infection, slapped an eye patch on Jim, and sent him on his way. The unknown particle, like the proverbial grain of sand in Cromwell's kidney, would twist the trajectory of Jim's own history.

Among today's youth, virtues such as gratitude and industry have given way to a mindset of passive entitlement. A modern teen in Jim's financial circumstances might resent having *one* job, much less several, especially if his earnings were earmarked for the collective family needs and not his own material interests. To nourish any hope for college, he must earn a large scholarship.

But Jim felt no resentment over the lack of spending cash or the pittance he saved for his own future. Family was the overruling concern, and he embraced his duty to it as a natural responsibility. His father's death had left him man of the house. Thus, his family must come first. *Others* must come first. It was the rule by which he would live out each and every one of the 27,275 days that God granted him on this earth.

Nonetheless, Jim nurtured his own ambitions and dreams. While his humble jobs were not lucrative, they were necessary stepping-stones on the road to achievement, workshops to prepare and shape him. Each opportunity was a chance to better himself and his condition. The duties of the present were heavy, but they were nothing compared to the limitless promise of the future.

On December 16, 1950, at the age of sixteen, Jim became a naturalized American citizen.

Cracks in the Foundation

Evil preaches tolerance until it is dominant, then it tries to silence good.
—Archbishop Charles J. Chaput

It is sad when one must justify oneself when stating obvious truths, both biological and societal, that have been obvious for millennia. Yet that is what Jim found himself called upon to do. To him, the definition—the essence—of marriage was not a superficial question of civil legality or social recognition. Marriage was intrinsically, *by nature*, the emotional and physical union of one male and one female. Similarly, "family" included a mother, a father, and whatever biological children they create together and which bond them more closely.

The very phrase "gay marriage" was an internal contradiction, a literal absurdity. One could not parse out the inherent characteristics of marriage and rearrange them according to desire or convenience. A machine only fulfills its designed purpose when it possesses all its essential parts, *and* those parts are configured in a specific way. Deviation from this pattern—whether via divorce, infidelity, fatherlessness, or homosexuality—can only yield dysfunction, barrenness, and emotional and psychological pain for those involved.

Author Orson Scott Card said in his 2004 essay "Homosexual 'Marriage' and Civilization" that "just because you give legal sanction to a homosexual couple and call their contract a 'marriage' does not make it a marriage. It simply removes *marriage* as a legitimate word for the real thing."

Jim held to the biblical worldview that traditional, natural marriage was the only viable building block for civilization and the stability of any society. It must be protected. He would not allow five thousand years of self-evident social and biological truth to be tossed to the rubbish heap like last season's baseball schedule.

Worse, the legalization and civil recognition of gay marriage would pave an inevitable and dangerous legal path to more radical definitions of the institution. Other fringe groups would use the legitimization of gay marriage as precedent and would adopt all the same arguments. If traditional heterosexual, monogamous marriage is nothing more than a mere "social construct," then why can an individual not redefine it as he or she chooses? If the only criteria in a marriage is love, who is the state or society to deny marriage to anyone based on where he or she chooses to bestow affection and devotion?

Of course, this natural logic was casually dismissed by gay marriage advocates as nonsense and fearmongering. It has since been acknowledged by some as a valid warning based on psychological and sociological fact.

From the beginning, champions of gay rights had a great deal going for them. For one, they had money. Lots of it.

They also had good strategy. They reaped the benefit of courts that were becoming increasingly stacked with liberal-appointed activist judges. Thus, framing their cause as a civil rights struggle would incur immediate sympathy among many inside the courthouse walls, whatever the law or constitution may or may not say.

The gay-rights proponents waved the ever-popular banner of civil rights not only in the legal arena but in the cultural arena at large. This was vital to winning public sympathy and support. They employed all the attendant civil rights terminology. "Discrimination" against gays was "hateful" and "social injustice." All they wanted was "equal protection." Such terminology in and of itself resonates with Americans, for it appeals to deeply cherished republican ideals and hearkens back to the nation's previous struggles for justice for women and African Americans. Unfortunately, few citizens today can or *will* recognize the physical and constitutional discrepancies between race and sexual behavior. It is, and always has been, a faulty comparison.

Words can be used to clarify or mislead. In December of 2015, Dr. David Deming, professor of arts and sciences at the University of Oklahoma penned an article for *The American Thinker* called "The Gay Agenda and the Real World." In it, he stated,

> The most significant tool for promoting the gay agenda was the introduction of the word *homophobia*. A phobia is an irrational fear. Thus the use of the term homophobia automatically implies that any aversion or objection to any facet of homosexuality is irrational. The beauty of this is that it removes the burden of argument. The speaker or writer who uses this term presumes to speak from an already established moral high ground. Control of language is control of thought.

Gay activists were sure to capture and exploit the inherent fair-mindedness of Americans. Marshall Kirk and Hunter Madsen, in their book *After the Ball: How America Will Conquer Its Fear and Hatred of Gays in the Nineties*, laid out the basic key to victory. "It is necessary to portray gays as victims, not as challengers but as victims in need of protection so that straights will be inclined by reflex to assume the role of protector." Gays would be this generation's downtrodden class. How could anyone with a heart not champion their struggle? The naive and simplistic "Love is love!" was the new battle cry.

The gay movement enjoyed a host of willing handmaidens in every bastion of public communication and information dissemination—mainstream media, public schools, universities, and pop culture. These were necessary to reform public opinion and attain the normalization of the homosexual lifestyle. Images of gays and of gay relationships must be always positive, innocent and beautiful when put before the public. "Love is love!" and that was all that mattered. Persons opposed to homosexuality, fictional or real, must wear the black hat of villainy. Words like *sodomy* and *pervert* were strictly forbidden, unless it came from the mouth of a bigoted antigay antagonist whom viewers were expected to hate.

Human nature is easily manipulated. Win small doses of acceptance at a time, and people will eventually become anesthetized to deviance. Familiarity still breeds contempt. Perhaps Kirk and Madsen themselves put it best: "Almost any behavior begins to look normal if you are exposed to enough of it."

Childhood in the Land of the Free

Kids have a hole in their soul in the shape of their dad.
And if a father is unwilling or unable to fill that hole,
it can leave a wound that is not easily healed.
—Roland Warren

Immigrants were not always met with open arms by the native-born. Nor were they always received well in their adopted land if they were a little different in habits and speech.

After his permanent immigration to America in 1946, Jim still found himself a target for school bullies and mean-spirited peers.

"I was called *Yankee* by the kids in Scotland and *sissy pants* in America!"

In the new world, as in the old, he fought to earn respect and acceptance. Like a young wolf surviving in a new pack, Jim did his best to claim his rightful place, to prove to his new country and his schoolmates that he *belonged*, that he was every inch an American. He even took elocution lessons, hoping to lose the vestiges of his Scottish lilt.

It wasn't about just pleasing his new countrymen, though. However he was viewed by others, Jim was bred from good Scottish stock. His father, James Summers Forrester, had been a professional golfer, whose reputation and name is recognized in Europe to this day. His father's accomplished and famed life, however short, was something the young Jim was determined to live up to. It mattered not that James was dead. Jim harbored a deep, abiding need to make his father proud.

Nancy fought her own battles to survive. While no one ever replaced James in Nancy's heart, she eventually remarried when Jim reached high school. It proved an unhappy arrangement for everyone. The new husband was by no means the surrogate father Jim longed for.

The closest thing to that was in the person of Dr. Black, Nancy's employer. Black liked Jim and followed the boy's academics and extracurricular pursuits with interest. He encouraged him to exercise diligence and praised him when he achieved good things. Jim's admiration of Black was amplified by gratitude. The doctor gave him precious pieces of attention and guidance that his own father would have given had he lived.

Nancy soon divorced Carson Davis and remarried again several years later, only to realize that this next husband was little better. The man's two teenage girls had lost their own mother that same year, and they vented their envy and bitterness by making life difficult for their father, their new stepmother, and her two children. This marital union also was doomed.

Sheila, less academically inclined than her little brother and exhibiting a stubborn adolescent rebellion, could sometimes be a discordant note in the family harmony. At sixteen, she eloped with her high school boyfriend, an action that may have been a need to fill the void of a father figure. It may also have been an escape from her family's financial hardships.

Her departure only increased Jim's emotional and economic burdens. The empty shadow of his father's death, war's ravages and the loss of the Forrester fortune, his uprooting back and forth from Scotland to America, Sheila's elopement, and his mother's failed marriages all conspired to widen a void in Jim. He longed for a "whole" family, one whose foundations were firm and whose endurance was certain. He longed for the dear, valuable things of this world to last, to *stay*, and he would forever struggle with a latent apprehension that they would slip away from him or break beyond repair.

Perhaps this is why he clung fast to things, even small material things, to a fault. It fed a sense of security in the greater possessions. Similarly, family gatherings would become the happiest times for him through the years, for they reassured his soul. He could look about and know that all he valued and loved was *still* with him, intact and healthy.

In another part of Wilmington, Mary Frances All, Jim's future wife, was experiencing her own unorthodox childhood. Her father, Walter William "Bill" All, was station master for a series of Atlantic Coastline railroad depots; and her mother, Frances, was a private-duty nurse. Thanks to their irregular hours and late-night shifts, Mary Frances led a pillar-to-post existence divided between train stations, emergency rooms, and the nearby beach.

Bill was six feet four and smoked two packs of unfiltered Lucky Strikes a day as he tapped out train routes, schedules, and other sundry Morse Code communications on the telegraph. Mary Frances trembled, breath caught in her throat, whenever he stood beside a passing train with his message hoop raised high, a tiny telegraph note attached to it, as the pants of his dark suit flapped in the artificial wind created by a speeding juggernaut of iron and steel.

But the train would always pass, and her father would still stand safe and sound, leaving her to return to her own devices for entertaining herself.

Alongside her mother, Mary Frances spent many a night in the hospital, sleeping on a gurney tucked away in an equipment room with a nervous eye on Mary Jane, the creepy dummy used for resuscitation practice. Yet Mary Jane was one of the nicer things Mary Frances's tender young eyes saw in those cold clinical halls and rooms that reeked of alcohol and ether. The worst was the body of an inebriated man severed in two after he'd fallen asleep on a train track. The unnatural juxtaposition of his upward-facing torso and downward-facing legs was a memory she would never shake.

The world was full of ugly realities, but there was beauty too. At twelve, she began taking classical ballet lessons. Frances, a proper Baptist lady, disapproved of dancing, or at least the pursuit of it, but she allowed it. It helped that her own sister Lillian, a devotee of the arts, was happy to foot the steep studio bill. Aunt "Lil" was convinced Mary Frances was the next Ava Gardner and took delight in living vicariously through her young niece.

July 1961

Illinois repeals its sodomy laws, becoming the first state to decriminalize homosexuality.

February 1972

National Coalition of Gay Organizations (NCGO) adopts a "gay rights platform" outlining its policy goals, including the following:

- Amend all civil rights laws to prohibit discrimination on the basis of sexual orientation
- Permit homosexuals to serve in the armed forces
- Decriminalize private sexual acts between consenting "persons"
- Repeal any legal restrictions on the sex or number of persons entering into a "marriage unit"
- Federal encouragement and support for pro-homosexual sex education courses in public schools
- Repeal all laws governing the age of consent
- Federal funding for homosexual advocacy groups
- Immediate release of all sexual offenders now incarcerated for crimes relating to sexual orientation
- Allow the immigration and naturalization of homosexual aliens

High School Days

If you had a question, Jim had the answer.
—Barbara Hailey, high school classmate

Jim's academic marks were high despite his jobs, extracurricular activities, and household duties. Being naturally bright helped, but it was a ruthless work ethic that squeezed the last ounce of productivity from every waking minute. He was far more than "conscientious" about his studies. He was *driven.*

His experiences in ROTC had fostered an enthusiasm for the military. Military service was a boon to any cash-strapped family since it offered the financial wherewithal for a college education. For Jim, there was an additional motivation for a military career. What better way to prove his devotion to his adopted country than by serving in her armed forces!

Initially, he set his sights on the Navy. Perhaps it was a manifestation of the saltwater in his genes. His Scottish forbears on his mother's side had been seafaring men, after all, and Jim had heard his share of nautical yarns about their adventures.

Thus, the future looked especially bright when, in early 1954, he received an appointment to the United States Naval Academy in Annapolis, Maryland.

Mary Frances was not so driven academically. Artistically, yes.

With her mother working long nocturnal hours, Mary Frances became a de facto nurse at home, housebound with her invalid father for prolonged periods. She prepared his meals, assisted him from sofa to bed to bathroom, and picked up half-lit cigarettes he left lying around. His disposition and unpredictable temper, worsened by declining health, were trying to her patience. All the while, she yearned to be away, engaged in fun adolescent pursuits.

She resolved never to become a nurse like her mother and Aunt Lil. It was a burdensome, demanding chain that would only enslave her.

Ah, but the *theater*.

If the military was Jim's escape from small-town conventionality, the theater was hers. It offered *freedom* wherein she could assert her individualism, forge her own path, and explore the wide world beyond the confines of Wilmington, North Carolina.

Young Love

Where does the family start? It starts with a young man falling in love with a girl. No superior alternative has yet been found.
—Sir Winston Churchill

The romance between Jim and Mary Frances conjures mental images of a Rockwell illustration. The year: 1953. The setting: Futrell's Drugs at the corner of Second Street and Princess Street in Wilmington, North Carolina, near a bus stop. Mary Frances is the pretty, popular cheerleader; Jim, the grinning soda jerk sporting a ridiculous white paper cap and skinny black bowtie.

Girl is hopelessly smitten; boy is painfully shy. A ham sandwich and vanilla milkshake lie untouched on the chrome-lined countertop. Clean-cut figures adorn the background as "On the Boardwalk" and "Blueberry Hill" emanate from the jukebox. The first decade of rock 'n' roll is in full swing.

From the first moment she saw him, Mary Frances was drawn by Jim's tall good looks, quiet manner, and slim, masculine hands. She squandered precious bus fare on endless sodas so she could talk to him as he filled orders.

The *jerk* in "soda jerk" was not a derogatory term then, merely colloquial. This did not stop Mary Frances in later years from teasing her husband often that she had "bought all those sodas and then married the jerk." Jim, good-natured and proud of his fine catch of a wife, would only chuckle or occasionally joke in return. "We're happily married. Mary Frances is happy, and I'm married."

Though only a year older than his freshman sweetheart, Jim was already an academic senior at New Hanover High School, its band drum major and ROTC captain.

When Mary Frances turned fifteen and was allowed to double-date, he began to come calling at her home, in a borrowed car and without a driver's license. Frances disapproved. Jim's immigrant status automatically stuck him in a different class. The Alls were a respectable middle-class family in a genteel pocket of Southern tradition, sprung from solid historical roots dating back to the Revolution. The Forresters were outsiders, foreigners. "Who are his *people*, Mary Frances?" Did anyone really know?

In truth, Jim's background was more impressive than her own. If Nancy's husband, James, had not died, he would undoubtedly have continued as a successful pro-golfer, keeping his family in comfortable ease and enviable social standing. Had her future not been so altered, Nancy might have ended up visiting America for a pleasure trip in a private yacht rather than immigrating to it on a cramped immigrant vessel.

However, it was not merely an objection to Jim's obscure social status that Frances All harbored. With a staunch preference for the practical over the sentimental, there was her daughter's financial future and security to be considered. Mary Frances's confession that "I could really see myself marrying him someday" prompted the universal maternal question: "What does he plan on doing for a living?"

At fifteen, Mary Frances had no specifics to give her mother, but of one thing she was quite certain. "As long as it's not military, politics, or medicine, I don't care," she declared, uttering forth her own doom.

Numerous times over the next fifty-one years, she would contemplate her doctor/senator/brigadier general husband and shake her head at the irony of youthful declarations. But she contemplated them with humor, love, and a willingness to help him achieve his American dream.

As for Jim, Mary Frances was the only girl he ever took home to meet his mother.

December 1973

The prestigious American Psychiatric Association's 1973 decides to remove homosexuality from its catalog of mental disorders. The change is more than symbolic. The homosexual contingent gains its first respectable ally, one that assures them and the world that homosexuality is normal, not deviant.

October 1973

The American Baptist Association, American Lutheran Association, United Presbyterians, United Methodists and the Society of Friends (Quakers) launch the National Task Force on Gay People in the Church.

September 1977

Actor Billy Crystal, in *Soap*, plays one of the first openly gay characters in a recurring role on prime-time television.

October 1979

The first National March on Washington, an event promoting gay rights, draws up to 75,000 and 125,000 individuals.

College Days

*College has taught me one very important
thing: naps are essential for survival.*

—Unknown

Jim never made it to Annapolis. The unknown particle that had invaded his eye at Regal Paper Mill returned to wound him once again. His military vision test was failed. It was a deal breaker, and it broke Jim's heart to boot.

But life has a way of going on, however we may feel, and Jim was consoled with the first drum major scholarship ever offered at Wake Forest University. So in autumn of 1954, Jim found himself waving the Old Gold & Black pennant in Winston-Salem rather than memorizing nautical terms at Annapolis.

Academically, he remained studious. Recreation was rare and sporadic as he was usually tinkering in the lab, haunting the library into the late-night hours, or pulling working shifts in the cafeteria. His industry paid off for others as well as himself. A fraternity brother joked that "Jim helped raise the grade point average for the fraternity. He was never a party boy."

Still Jim's popularity with his college peers cannot wholly be attributed to scholastic contributions. He was congenial and full of humor, possessed of a quiet confidence and charm that drew people to him. A gentleman to the bone.

His original course of study was prelaw, with an eye toward criminal practice, but this became fraught with misgivings over the inevitable ethical conundrums that pop up in the legal profession. In the end, he eschewed the law.

"I could never defend a guilty man," he told Mary Frances.

The next option was business. Friends and family thought this a fine fit as he manifested a canny astuteness necessary for the profession, and his wide range of prior jobs, however humble, had prepared him accordingly. Besides being a math whiz, he could quickly assimilate information and devise solutions, a talent that would serve him well in making medical diagnoses later on.

Still his passion for a calling could not find its home in business any more than it could for the legal profession.

His interests gravitated increasingly toward medicine. This hearkened back to the influence of Dr. Black. Long before the eyepatch episode, Jim would sometimes go meet his mother at Black's medical office, where she kept the account books. Observing and interacting with the good doctor had given him a taste of the medical profession and planted a seed of interest in helping ailing people.

As if affirming this route, Providence, in the form of the North Carolina Medical Care Commission, smiled upon Jim. It had a contract program that extended a tuition loan for medical school in exchange for a student's commitment to practice in an underserved community for four years upon graduation. Jim thought this a worthy exchange, and through it, he could become a worthy doctor. Thus his searching passion, his innate *com*passion, found their true home in medicine, where Jim came to rest with a deep and abiding satisfaction.

But the particulars remained to be sorted out. Specialization in medicine was still an infant concept. Options to focus on a particular area or system of the body were far fewer than today.

There was pediatrics. More than anything, Jim wanted to be a pediatrician. He adored babies! But pediatrics training would take longer and was notorious for the stress it placed on a doctor's family.

Radiology, perhaps? Oh no! A radiologist could end up sterile. Jim would do nothing that might keep him from having babies of his own.

Teachers and advisors urged him to pursue a career in psychiatry because he was "such a good listener." But this prospect, however intellectually stimulating it might be to poke around in the human psyche, did not appeal to Jim as a profession.

Well, he would be a family physician. A family doc was specialized in a little bit of everything, including pediatrics. It was a nice fit considering Jim's multifaceted interests and enthusiasm for solving new and diverse problems. No two patients were ever the same, and that was just fine with him.

Long-Distance Love

Distance is just a test to see how far love can travel.
—Unknown

Mary Frances, stuck in her senior year of high school, was contemplating her own career path. Jim was already in his junior year in college. Most of the females in her life were either teachers or nurses, but that meant nothing. The classroom was not her cup of tea, and she remained firmly set against any door leading to the medical field.

She was an artist, a ballerina throughout every limb and sinew. She was born for plies and pirouettes, not pills and pathologies! She would dance, beautifully, and she would achieve success at it.

Her romantic ambitions still sat ill with her conservative Baptist family. Dancing as a profession was an immodest, menial pursuit. And it paid the dancer pittance.

Her mother, Frances, Baptist but pragmatic, reacted like many an anxious parent whose child expresses longing for an artistic career. She informed her daughter baldly that "you'll never make a living at it." As for attending an exclusive performing arts conservatory, that was out of the question. Mary Frances would enroll in a standard four-year college. That was final.

As for ballet, she relented strategically. "Well, go on then and get it out of your system," she told her daughter, convinced Mary Frances would soon grow weary of ballet. Aunt Lil, by contrast, remained starry-eyed over her dancer-niece and nurtured high hopes for her future fame.

As Mary Frances scoured the all-knowing Blue Book of Colleges at the local library for an affordable school with a dance program, her eyes landed on Jordan College of Music at Butler University in Indianapolis. Now here was a likely prospect. Jordan was a reputable arts program, and better still, it was far away from Wilmington.

So in early autumn of 1957, she boarded an Indiana-bound train. The only thing she had qualms about was the increased distance from Jim, still in Winston-Salem. He had begged her to stay in North Carolina, to come to Wake Forest instead. But her mind was set on Butler.

When she was gone, a disappointed Jim buried himself still deeper in his studies. But this only made him think of Mary Frances more!

Up in Indiana, to make up the deficits in school tuition and expenses, Mary Frances was spending her off-school working hours as a photographer's model, a role for which her dancer's form was fit.

Nevertheless, woven in and out of busy days and nights were phone calls and correspondence between the sweethearts. Letters flew like crazy back and forth. Dormitory phone booths, coveted bits of real estate for college kids in those days, became second homes.

Jim visited whenever he got the chance, which was rare. Mary Frances made as many trips south as the semester schedule and finances allowed.

The road of romance was bumpy and rutted. So much separated the two young people—geographically, financially, and emotionally. Jim's studiousness, while admirable, could stir a well of frustration in Mary Frances when they were together. It was an ever-present competitor for his attention. She didn't visit Winston-Salem to twiddle her thumbs while his nose was stuck in a textbook! Exasperated, she confided her frustration to Raymond Farrow, Jim's fraternity brother.

Raymond's response: "Jim just wants you here."

She strove to paint herself as a party girl back in Indiana, a popular coed with legions of friends and male admirers. The last thing she wanted was for Jim to become complacent in her attachment. He must know she was not pining away in longing for him.

She felt she was on a seesaw, never quite certain if he nurtured serious, long-term intentions. Once, he had even encouraged her date other guys.

But to Jim, this was simply a matter of gentlemanly honor. It was wrong to tie Mary Frances down when his future was unsettled and his education incomplete. How soon would he even be in a position to take and support a wife? He could make her no certain promises regarding the future and could not, in good conscience, withhold her from better marital candidates.

This did not keep the two of them from cuddling up in an oversized chair and dream of the future.

"One of these days," Jim would say, "we'll grow old together, just sit and rock, and watch the sun go down."

Mary Frances's heart would quiver in happiness.

"But that's a long way off," he would add, matter-of-fact. "We can't think about that right now."

And so it went. He wooed, then retreated. There was nearness, then distance. Still he eventually bestowed his fraternity pin on her, in those days an offering fraught with marital implications.

Long-Distance Love Succumbs

To get the full value of joy, you must have someone to divide it with.
—Mark Twain

"Mary Frances, come home. Come back to North Carolina." It was Jim's constant refrain.

But to Mary Frances, the future looked too bright from where she stood in Indiana.

Until life interrupted her plans. During her sophomore year, her father, Bill, suffered his second heart attack and died. His passing birthed more than just grief. Worries over the future flooded her mind. With her father gone, how would she get by?

She retrieved all her money, the balance of next semester's tuition, currently banked in the college safe. It was needed for the trip home, the funeral, and the trip back. If she did come back.

She did return to Indiana, but the year that followed was tough. Each time Jim and Mary Frances managed a visit to each other, it was increasingly difficult to part again—especially for her. The Indiana winter was more harsh and dismal than ever. How it chilled her Southern blood! She dreaded the prospect of returning north after the Christmas break. All that awaited her was the bitter cold, exams, and an exclusive three-year modeling contract awaiting her signature.

Three years. An eternity to a twenty-one-year-old girl who's in love and separated from the object of her devotion by six hundred miles!

Still missing her terribly and grieved by her misery, Jim pleaded yet again, "Just come *home*. Come home for *good*."

She heard this plea with some suspicion. Jim often said such things when he believed he was falling short academically. "Did you just flunk a quiz?" she asked.

He had not flunked anything. He was just impatient and worried, contemplating his own imminent future. In a few months, he would be drowning in round-the-clock rigors of clinical rotations, his hours eaten up by the hospital. If he did not marry Mary Frances before summer, he would hardly see her for two years! Would she still be waiting for him at the end of them? Did she *want* to wait?

Over and again he begged her, unsuccessfully, to return to North Carolina. To Winston-Salem. To *him.*

Maybe a firm offer of marriage would do the trick. He could not see himself marrying anyone else anyway.

His proposal in January of 1960 failed in romance but excelled in honesty. "I've never had a family," he said. "I want a family."

Mary Frances, torn between love of Terpsichore and love of Jim, pointed out the obstacles, her mother being the chief one. Frances would not approve.

"I'm not asking to marry your mother," Jim stressed. "Do you *want* to be with me?"

"Yes." *But…*

"You can transfer to Wake Forest for next to nothing as a student wife."

Still Mary Frances hesitated. One of her chief life objectives had been to get *out* of North Carolina. There was no school of dance at Baptist Wake Forest. To muddy matters further, she harbored a deep aversion to Jim's medical aspirations. A doctor's wife was a pitiful human specimen, always playing second fiddle to patients and to legions of assorted medical demands.

In the end, she was persuaded to do what her instincts and her heart had already chosen. She and Jim had been together seven years, and their maturing relationship had thus far weathered the limitations of distance. What if she rejected his proposal and he met someone on the rebound? She would not risk that, nor had she any desire to find another fellow. Who could replace Jim!

"Okay," she told him. "You call your mother, and I'll call mine."

Mary Frances hung up, only to stare at the phone, thinking. She was still in disbelief, expecting Jim to call back after a while with a changed mind or at least a changed plan. He did call back, only to inform her that he had related the happy tidings to Nancy, who was surprised but pleased.

Mary Frances phoned her own mother, who was thrown into a good old Southern "tizzy" by the news. Her parting maternal command before hanging up was terse: "Come home, and we'll talk about it, Mary Frances. Do *not* bring your clothes."

Mary Frances flew to Winston-Salem first to discuss matters with Jim over a shared vanilla milkshake—not enough money for two—before returning to Wilmington to face Frances.

Jim telephoned Frances himself, exercising every tool of persuasion he could muster to win her blessing. All for naught. Frances remained opposed to this foolhardy leap into premature wedlock. Her daughter would stay right where she was—single, in college, and destined for a shining career. In ballet, if nothing else!

Hoping her child would heed the voice of spiritual authority, she even arranged for their church's minister to meet Mary Frances at the Wilmington airport. Perhaps *he* could dissuade the girl!

At the outset of this gentle confrontation, the minister was sure the romance was mere "infatuation" and that Mary Frances would be guided by his wisdom. By the end of their conversation, he was convinced it was true love, neither shallow nor transient but the stuff to forge a lasting union.

Mary Frances was never sure what the minister reported back to her mother. It might have been, "She's old enough to make up her mind," or "She's determined, so you should just make the best of it." Whatever it was, Frances became resigned to the situation and started planning a wedding.

Mary Frances insisted on a church ceremony, and there remained only a few short weeks to plan one. Circumstances conspired to frustrate the proceedings. Mother Nature sent snow three Mondays in a row. Mary Frances's clothes got lost somewhere between Indianapolis and Wilmington, so she hustled about town making arrangements in her future mother-in-law's wardrobe.

Poor Aunt Lil wanted nothing to do with nuptial planning. Her grand hopes for her gifted niece lay in tatters.

Jim was still sensitive to his prospective mother-in-law's lingering concerns about her daughter's future, agreeing it was best to think with one's head as well as the heart.

"She *will* finish school," he reassured Frances. "I'll see that she does. I will make you proud, and I will be a good husband to her."

Upon turning twenty-one in 1959, Mary Frances Forrester had registered to vote as a Republican in Indiana. That must change, Jim said, when she returned to North Carolina. Life was just easier for Democrats down South. She reluctantly complied, giving up the elephant for the donkey—the things we do for love!

Money-wise, the couple had nothing, and it was enough.

Marriage

Marriage is a union between a man and a woman, whose sanctity
and historic importance to our social fabric must be protected.
Marriage is, by definition, between a man and a woman.
—Jim Forrester

"MARY F. ALL WEDS J. S. FORRESTER IN BAPTIST RITES" was the
newspaper headline, followed by an eloquent and detailed wedding
write-up of a variety that has long since followed the Dodo into non-
existence. It ran like this:

> The bride wore a gown of bridal taffeta with a
> bolero effect of Chantilly lace. A bow formed a
> back bustle which ended in a chapel train.

It was a beautiful creation, thoughtfully designed and metic-
ulously sewn. Not mentioned in the article was its total cost: nine-
ty-nine dollars. Mary Frances paid for it herself.

> Her halo lace cap, edged in scallops, was trimmed
> with seed pearl and sequins. A fingertip veil was
> attached to it. She carried a prayer book with a
> white orchid and a shower of small white flowers.

March 12, 1960—the wedding day. The only thing more
resplendent than the bride was the pristine blanket of snow outside
Winter Park Baptist Church. It was beautiful but worrisome. The
usher did not show, so a "phantom usher" had to be recruited on the

cuff. His identity mattered far less than his size. He had to fit into the rented tux. Fate supplied an obliging salesman from the Life of Virginia Insurance Company, Nancy's employer.

Before God and men, Jim and Mary Frances exchanged wedding vows they had written themselves. The bride, nervous and flustered, jumbled her part. Jim just smiled in amused affection. In the end, the two were just as married.

"I give you Mr. and Mrs. James Summers Forrester," pronounced the minister.

Aunt Lil sat at home, boycotting the wedding. She had encouraged all her friends to do the same. Her mind stewed with images of all Mary Frances was giving up. It would be ten years before Aunt Lil came around.

The wedding guests were greeted and thanked. The couple embarked on their weekend honeymoon to Myrtle Beach and Charleston. Mary Frances did not return to Indiana afterward.

Having children was out of the question until Jim finished medical school, not that pregnancy would be an issue anyway. Mary Frances had been assured she would have difficulty conceiving due to physical limitations.

Early Days

The first bond of society is marriage.

—Cicero

Most college lads today seek fun and frivolity on spring break. Marriage, a commitment of sobriety and permanence, is not a near goal on their radar screen, if it's a goal at all.

Still, even in the more mature 1960, Jim Forrester's friends were shocked when he returned to Winston-Salem from spring break married.

For fifty dollars rent a month, Aunt Ruby and Uncle Buck offered their attic efficiency apartment as a newlywed nest. It consisted of a combined living area and kitchen as well as a bedroom, in total 375 square feet. Its cramped dimensions mattered little as neither Mary Frances nor Jim would ever spend much time there. Another medical wife, on the snooty side, more than once observed, to Mary Frances's extreme annoyance, "I don't know how you live there. I just *couldn't*!"

In June of that year, Jim began his grueling internship North Carolina Baptist Hospital, but there remained the issue of Mary Frances's formal education. In her third year at Butler when she married, she was now told that Wake Forest would not accept her dance credits. Their loss would relegate her back to sophomore status. This was unthinkable. "I'm not going to sacrifice a whole year of college just to go to Wake Forest," she told Jim.

Jim had promised her mother she would finish college, and he now saw a solution. If she took a semester of science courses at Wake Forest, she would qualify for a fellowship at Bowman Gray in cytotechnology, a new field pertaining to the study of pap smears. It would earn two hundred dollars a month. This, along with Jim's book allowance, helped pay living expenses.

The newlyweds had little time for each other. "I saw you more *before* we got married," Mary Frances lamented more than once.

She still modeled on weekends, a pursuit frustrated by her habit of falling for many of the beautifully designed apparel she wore. The most tempting creation was a black cone-shaped turban of swirl felt, modelled for the upscale Thalhimers Department Store in down-town Winston-Salem. It was a Mr. John hat worth a full fifty dollars, a whole month's rent. She went home and raved about it to Jim.

Her pleadings did not make a dent. "The hat's expensive," he said. "We're poor."

In the first few months of marriage, Jim discovered that his new wife talked in her sleep and would even respond to questions. This was useful, especially in trying to extract the identity of gifts—and other nuggets of useful information—from her unconscious brain.

The poorly heated, drafty attic apartment could be a miserable place in the winter months, and Mary Frances was grieved to watch her studious husband shiver through his studies in the late-night hours. She bought some fabric and made him a robe with an EZ-Y pattern and Aunt Ruby's assistance.

As Christmas drew near, Jim let slip a remark about the robe he was getting.

"How did you know that!"

"You talk in your sleep." Years later, he added a confession. He had *asked* what he was getting.

"What did you get Jim for his birthday?" was his soft-spoken query.

Her sleep-soaked brain had responded, "Well, I'll tell you if you won't tell Jim."

Mary Frances had observed that her husband wore articles of clothing until they became almost transparent. His old overcoat was one, so she took herself down to Babcock, a men's clothing shop, and entrusted a handsome double-breast creation of fine navy-blue wool. She had by now become chummy with the layaway ladies, so she entrusted the garment to their safekeeping, paying $2.50 a week throughout the summer and fall months.

Beaming, she presented it to her husband that Christmas, gratified to see he looked every bit as handsome in it as she had expected. Unfortunately, time would reveal that Jim still preferred his old gray-speckled nubby coat, fit only for burning in Mary Frances's view.

Jim was on call that same Christmas, so Mary Frances planned to spend it with her mother. Jim sent her home to Wilmington with his boxed gift and strict warnings not to open it before Christmas Day.

When Mary Frances finally unwrapped it and raised the lid, she gasped. It was the costly black turban she had wanted so bad!

Jim refused to tell her where he had gotten the money for it. She could only theorize that he sold his plasma, like many a cash-strapped medical student. It was a poignant, tearful moment, knowing that whatever he had given up was a sacrifice.

Mary Frances made other marital discoveries during the first few years of wedlock.

Jim was a man whose eyes were always looking up, forward, focused on his end goal. But the individual steps to *get* there were sometimes overlooked.

One evening during his pediatric rotation, he strode into the hospital nursery to check the newborns. With tender care, he unpinned the diaper of each tyke, checking for rashes, infections, and missing pinkies. He finished the last tiny patient and walked out of the nursery, leaving every last baby bereft of his or her diaper. He had not bothered to repin even one. The nurses later told Mary Frances, shaking their heads over his obliviousness to the necessity of doing this. He just assumed someone would come along and take care of the details.

"He was the ten," Mary Frances summed it up. "Not the one through nine." Time would vindicate him, though, as he learned to delegate the "one through nine" with great discernment and thoroughness throughout his life.

There are calendars we keep on our walls and desks and refrigerators, and then there is the calendar life keeps for us. In June 1962, Mary Frances discovered she was pregnant, which wasn't supposed to happen. Doctors! What did they know!

Pregnant, she continued to work long days and nights—there was no choice—to maintain her fellowship obligations. When the eighth month rolled around, she stashed an expectant-mom suitcase under her microscope-laden desk.

The happy day arrived, and a nervous Jim drove Mary Frances to the hospital and checked her in as Mary Frances All—to Mary Frances's horror!—and promptly left for the night. "You're probably going to have a long labor," was his reasoning. "I'll come by and check you in the morning and make sure everything is okay."

Mary Frances was miffed. "I better not have this baby, and some intern or resident—your classmate—delivers me, and then I have to ride up and down the elevator with him. I don't want to be their specimen for the day to talk about over lunch."

Six weeks before the close of Jim's internship, on March 14, 1963, the stork delivered his first child. He examined his baby with the diligence of the doctor he was and the emotional euphoria of a first-time father.

"Her name is Wyndi," he declared. *Lori Wynn Forrester.* "And she's perfect!"

That very day, he went out and bought a camera and an insurance policy; and for months, he walked around with a grin wider than a Scottish moor.

He was a *father*. At last he had his own complete family!

Father, mother, child. *Together.*

Bound for a Small Town

*She was snatched back from a dream of far countries
and found herself on Main Street.*
—Sinclair Lewis

Mary Frances had grown used to the taste of irony in her own words, so often was she forced to eat them.

"I will never marry a doctor."

"I'm going to have a hard time getting pregnant."

"I'll never live in some small town with a railroad track running down the middle."

To fulfill Jim's obligations to the Medical Care Commission, the couple, upon graduation, would have to reside in an underserved community for four years. The chief of obstetrics at Bowman Gray, when he learned Jim was on the commission, informed him that his father-in-law was an industrial "mogul" of Gaston County International Textiles located in the small community of Stanley, North Carolina. Jim should check it out.

Jim did and decided Stanley was the ideal place to launch a medical career, as the executives of four major industries demonstrated their commitment to utilizing his physician services not only in a corporate capacity but for the sake of their individual employees and families. It was a great deal of people in need of a doctor, which would certainly help him build his practice.

Mary Frances shed streams of tears upon forsaking Winston-Salem for little Stanley in July 1963. Jim sought to comfort her by way of admonishment. "Dear, you can be happy anywhere if you decide to be happy. Or you can be miserable. Besides, it's only for four years," he reminded.

The first thing to meet Mary Frances's eyes when they went to visit Stanley was the train track down the middle of town.

Only four years? Mary Frances wept harder. She was a city girl with a city heart. She wanted culture! Thank goodness Winston-Salem and its North Carolina School of the Arts were only an hour and a half away.

"It's close to Charlotte," Jim pointed out. "You'll find plenty of culture there. There's basketball and NASCAR."

Not the culture she had in mind. Jim advised her to read *Main Street* by Sinclair Lewis in the hopes it would educate her about life in a small town and help her acclimate to small-town life and culture—and to the bucolic mindset that often goes with it.

A New Calling

Tomorrow to fresh woods, and pastures new.
—John Milton

In the early '60s, Vietnam began exploding as President Lyndon Johnson committed thousands of American troops following the assassination of John F. Kennedy.

Jim had already applied to be a reserve Air Force physician when he received his army notice. As a physician, he was eligible for the draft until age fifty-five. With the army reserves, he could be stuck anywhere, far from his practice and his four-year commitment to the Medical Commission.

Congressman Basil Whitener helped him keep his North Carolina Air National Guard (NCANG) appointment. The guard unit in Charlotte was a medical transport group in sore need of a flight surgeon. Jim accepted a commission as a first lieutenant on the grounds he would attend a nine-week flight surgeon training, after which he would accept the NCANG appointment as a captain.

All in all, Jim was happy as the proverbial pig in the mud. At the age of twenty-six, he was on the cusp of private medical practice. He had a family of his own and was serving his country and his fellow men.

Setting Up Office

A friend in need is a friend indeed.
—Benjamin Franklin

Despite frugal living, the Forresters had debts, so it was a boon when one of the local textile executives offered Jim his first office rent-free for three years. Jim also secured a bank loan, his signature being the sole collateral required, with which to set up independent practice.

Hopeful and confident, he headed to Texas for his nine weeks' flight surgeon training at the School of Aerospace Medicine at Brooks Air Force Base, now Lackland, in San Antonio. But he would learn far more than the ins and outs of flight-surgeon duty. He was experiencing his first tastes of military camaraderie, not to mention practical jokes in the context of local culture, along with his buddy Harry Daughtery, a Charlotte heart surgeon.

On the first morning they sat down at the Base's BOQ, Jim noticed a pile of dark-green objects on Harry's plate and frowned. "What are those?"

"Oh, just a kind of sweet pickle," said Harry, a native Texan.

Jim loved pickles and was game to try this exotic new variety. He popped one in his mouth and began to chew. Two seconds later, his face was scarlet. The "sweet pickles" were jalapeño peppers!

Harry, who munched jalapeños like popcorn, rolled in laughter as Jim sputtered and spat for ten straight minutes. It was a favorite Texan joke on the unsuspecting outsider.

The two comrades got a much-needed break from the BOQ when Harry's roommate, an African American army colonel, another doctor, kindly invited them and two others to dinner at an upscale restaurant at Fort Sam Houston. It was not a common thing in those days to see four white men out celebrating with one black man, but neither Jim nor Harry gave a rat's bum for a fellow's skin color. The colonel was interesting and likeable, and his hospitality to the lowly trainees was never forgotten. "We were treated like generals," Harry recalled.

Six states away, back in Stanley, Mary Frances was readying the new "office" for patients upon Jim's return from Texas. It was an absurdly tiny, humble wood-frame house on Plum Street. The bedrooms were transformed into examining rooms, and the living room served as waiting area—unconventional, but it would serve.

All the necessary furniture and equipment, mundane and medical, had been ordered from a medical supply company. It was shipped by rail to the train depot a short distance from Plum Street and temporarily stored.

Out of the blue, Mary Frances received a call from Vick Gilmore, the railroad dispatcher, warning her that the railroad was on the cusp of a strike. If she needed the equipment anytime soon, he informed, she must make immediate arrangements to come get it out of storage as soon as possible. Otherwise, there was no telling how long it would be before they saw it.

Mary Frances knew nobody in town, no one she could appeal to for help. So with baby Wyndi glued to her hip, she hastened to the depot in desperation, pleading for assistance and exercising every feminine wile in her arsenal.

She proved irresistible. Between the dispatcher and the police department, she secured the aid of the local rescue squad. Load after load of equipment was transported via firetruck, ambulance, and gurney to Jim's office. It made for a ridiculous scene, and would probably be illegal today. But it was *done*. And Mary Frances had made her first friends in Stanley! Vick Gilmore became a patient and golf buddy of Jim's.

Back in Texas, nine weeks was creeping by too slowly for Jim, so he caught a red-eye flight on a military-transport plane, making an overnight haul to Charlotte, surprising his wife and daughter in the wee hours of the morning.

Mary Frances heard a soft knocking at the front door. She glanced at the clock: 2:00 a.m. She got up and cracked the front door, peering cautiously over the chain lock.

It was Jim.

"He looked like a little boy standing there, playing dress-up in somebody's flight suit," she recalled. "His face was so homesick and forlorn. It was pitiful."

"What are you doing here?" she asked him. "How'd you get home?"

"I decided to play hooky and hitch a flight back. I've got twelve hours."

He was too proud to *say* why he had come home, but his woe-begone countenance told all. He missed his little family too much to stay away.

North Carolina 2004

I'm not sure that it's right to view this as excluding a particular group. When the institution of marriage developed historically, people didn't get around and say, "Let's have this institution, but let's keep out homosexuals." The institution developed to serve purposes that, by their nature, didn't include homosexual couples.
—Chief Justice John Roberts

In February 2004, President George W. Bush issued a call for an amendment to the United States Constitution that would prohibit same-sex marriage.

"There is no assurance that the [present] Defense of Marriage Act will not itself be struck down by activist courts," Bush said. "In that event, every state would be forced to recognize any relationship that judges in Boston or officials in San Francisco choose to call a marriage."

His call came on the heels of two pro-gay victories: one, Texas's repeal of its sodomy laws; two, the legalization of gay marriage in Massachusetts. Both court decisions proved a source of empowerment for gay-marriage forces.

Cries rose in outrage against over Bush's call. Legal action must be taken!

A few weeks following Bush's call, Richard Mullinax and Perry Pike, two gay men in Durham County, North Carolina, applied for a marriage license and were denied, as they had known they would be. They filed a prompt suit, represented by Durham attorney Cheri Patrick. The legal work was already prepared.

Unsurprisingly, a push to repeal North Carolina's 1996 Defense of Marriage statute soon followed.

Gay-friendly local officials in liberal municipalities, some of whom had already approved votes to extend health benefits to the same-sex partners of their employees, chimed in the debate. Chapel Hill's openly gay councilman Mark Kleinschmidt asked his town council to consider a resolution supporting the repeal of the 1996 statute. Similarly, Carrboro mayor Mike Nelson, the first openly gay mayor in North Carolina, promised to put the matter to his board in early April.

Chantelle Fisher-Borne of Durham, an organizer with Triangle Freedom to Marry Coalition, was optimistic about the direction of the same-sex marriage cause. "We're moving toward more justice for gay and lesbian folks. We know we're on the right side of history."

"President Bush's willingness to write discrimination into the US Constitution has really brought this to the forefront," commented Ian Palmquist, executive director of the Raleigh-based pro-gay political-action committee Equality North Carolina. "Everything we do to get images of committed gay and lesbian couples before the public, the better off we'll be."

As Dr. Warner Doles puts it, "Repetition reduces resistance."

It was about normalization and parity. The message: "We're just like heterosexual couples!" Speak the message loudly and boldly as if it is already true, and people will soon accept it as such.

Director of Government Relations for the NC Family Policy Council John Rustin countered the pro-gay opposition's attempts to frame the debate as a civil rights matter:

> Marriage, by definition, is between a man and a woman. It is a complementary union between people of the opposite sex. It creates children and the opportunity for them to be raised in the optimum environment. Homosexuals have every right to be married, just not to someone of the same sex. They have disqualified themselves by engaging in a same sex relationship.

Homosexuals already had the freedom to associate or cohabitate in any domestic arrangement they chose. But that was not enough. They wanted legal legitimacy and special recognition.

The Durham lawsuit, along with the Texas and Massachusetts developments, and the ensuing threats to challenge the current law made it abundantly clear to Jim that the marriage statute in North Carolina was far too vulnerable to legal challenges. All it took was one activist judge to override and uproot it.

The statute wasn't enough. There would have to be an *amendment to the state constitution*, with the legal definition of marriage defined clearly therein. A constitutional amendment would also bolster the current statute by ensuring that North Carolina would not be legally required to recognize same-sex unions from other states.

"If we wait for a federal amendment, that could take years," Jim said.

In a May 11 press release, he stated that "all citizens should be able to enter into contracts for any reason, but marriage is a union between a man and woman, whose sanctity and historic importance to our social fabric must be protected." He added that "the most compelling reason for states to have laws regarding marriage is to protect the welfare of children."

A three-fifths majority in both chambers of the North Carolina General Assembly is required to ratify a constitutional amendment referendum for a statewide ballot. This is not an easy majority to reach in any case. For the minority party, it is nigh to impossible.

The legal wording of Jim's proposed amendment was critiqued down to the last article and preposition. "It's got to be ironclad," he said.

The language that resulted was as follows:

> Marriage is the union of one man and one woman at one time. This is the only marriage that shall be recognized as valid in this State. The uniting of two persons of the same sex or the uniting of more than two persons of any sex in a marriage, civil union, domestic partnership, or other sim-

ilar relationship within or outside of this State shall not be valid or recognized in this State. The constitution shall not be construed to require that marital status or the rights, privileges, benefits or other legal incidents of marriage be conferred upon unmarried individuals or groups.

The bill had fourteen cosponsors, including Senators Austin Allran, Phil Berger, Andrew Brock, Virginia Foxx, John Garwood, R. B. Sloan Jr., and Jerry Tillman. David Hoyle of Gastonia was the lone Democrat in the bunch.

Expressions of disgust were prompt from gay-marriage defenders. "The amendment is a tragedy," bemoaned Reverend Jack McKinney, a Baptist pastor from Raleigh and cochairman of NC Religious Coalition for Marriage Equality. "To think that in the twenty-first century, we're proposing amendments to the constitution that codify discrimination against some of our citizens."

Jim was accused of having ulterior political motivations. He was just trying to rile up conservative voters in an election year, they said. Cheri Patrick, the Durham attorney representing Mullinax and Pike, the two gay men denied a marriage license, claimed, "This is all about the election."

Nothing was further from the truth. Also untrue was the absurd charge that Jim harbored hatred against gay people simply for being gay. Jim did not live on a deserted island. He had gay and bisexual patients, gay colleagues, and gay family friends. He rented property to one gay gentleman who proudly flew the rainbow flag on his porch, a habit Jim never challenged. There was only good will and liking between the two men. The tenant even offered a contribution to Jim's senate campaign.

Jamie Scarborogh, a bisexual and close friend of the Forresters, was another enthusiastic campaign supporter of Jim. Considering herself one of their extended family, she was always quick to express her appreciation for the unfailing kindness and concern Jim and Mary Frances both were wont to show her in rough times and still refers to Jim affectionately as "the Senator."

Jim responded to the "it's just political" charges by pointing out that the same-sex marriage issue would "rile up" liberals every bit as much as conservatives. "Yes, it would bring people to the polls. We want more people at the polls," he told the *Winston-Salem Journal*. "But that wasn't my intent."

To be sure, having a constitutional marriage amendment on the ballot was the last thing gay marriage advocates wanted because they were well aware their cause lacked popular support. If it reached the ballot, it would likely pass. That was bad enough, but a defeat would also frustrate the pro-gay propaganda campaign. Once the will and disposition of the people was revealed through a statewide election, it would be harder to spin the issue and claim public opinion was on their side. It was better to keep the fight in the courts, where allies are more numerous, more politically correct, and where victory is more likely. The citizens of North Carolina must not have a crack at it.

Executive director of Equality NC Ian Palmquist was dedicated to stamping out the bill. "We don't believe that the NC Constitution is the place where we should be writing discrimination into our laws," he told the *Gaston Gazette*. "Equality NC is going to be working through our professional lobbyists and through our grassroots network across the state to encourage legislators to oppose this amendment."

Again strategic language was vital. The charge of "writing discrimination into our laws" forgets that, ultimately, the people retain the prerogative to determine what their constitution will or will not define as legal discrimination.

John Rustin of the NC Family Policy Council pointed out that "every individual who is of legal age can marry under the provisions that have been set out in state law." He was referring to the provisions for age, the degree of blood relations, and the distinction that it is between a man and a woman. "People who are seeking to marry someone of the same sex simply disqualify themselves from a valid and legal marriage under our laws."

In the legislature, Jim tried to gather support for a discharge petition, a measure requiring thirty senatorial signatures—three-fifths of that body—to force SB 1057, the latest marriage amendment bill, out of its committee quagmire and directly on to the Senate floor. In the end, the petition gained twenty-eight signatures, twenty-three Republicans and five Democrats. Jim's attempt failed by two votes.

Senator Charlie Albertson (D-Duplin) did not sign the petition, questioning the necessity of a constitutional amendment. Though an opponent of same-sex marriage, he had been absent for the 1996 DOMA statute vote. "I can't believe that the people sitting on the Supreme Court in North Carolina are going to overturn that law," he now said. "If it were to become necessary, I think we could go in and amend the constitution."

John Kerr (D-Wayne) also believed that the 1996 statute, for which he voted, was sufficient. "I have full confidence in the law that we have," he stated. "I have full confidence in the Supreme Court."

Whatever their claims, Jim knew that many antigay marriage Democrats would not sign the petition for self-interested reasons. "I think they're fearful that the amendment will hurt them politically to have it on the ballot," Jim told the press. A constitutional amendment, if it did make it onto the November ballot, could impact Democrats negatively in other races. They would not risk that.

Nonetheless, for the Democrat majority leadership, this latest try by Jim and the other amendment proponents to get the bill to the Senate floor was a little too close for comfort. The next year, they raised the number of required signatures for a discharge petition, essentially locking that door against any future attempts.

"I just want the people of North Carolina to have a chance to voice their opinion," Jim would say, frustrated. "If they vote it down, so be it."

Every year for *eight* consecutive years, Jim would file a state marriage amendment bill in the Senate. It was never allowed to get a just hearing on the floor, much less make it to a ballot. It went from committee to committee, only to die in the end. Many Assembly members came to view it as the proverbial bad penny.

It was trying, to say the least, but Jim did not give up. "I'll get my bill, and then I'll come home," he reassured Mary Frances more than once. "We'll sit on the back porch, listen to the birds, feed Miss Lily tuna and cream, and travel."

Miss Lily White was the cat.

Unfortunately, "getting" his bill would take almost a decade—and a huge political shift.

Guardsman

When we assumed the soldier we did not lay aside the citizen.
—George Washington

From the first, Jim took to guard life like the proverbial duck takes to water or, more appropriately, like a bird takes to air. The 156th Air Transport Squadron of the North Carolina Air National Guard (NCANG) and its 145th TAC clinic certainly took to him. He was only a "kid captain," a youngster in the pack that had formed the unit back in 1948 and included the formidable General William "Bill" Payne. "Those guys were getting to the end of their era," said Brigadier-General Fisk Outwater. "A wave of new guys was coming in." The nation and the world were on the cusp of great change, and the Charlotte NCANG unit was on the cusp with it.

Still, being a new kid on an old block did not intimidate Jim. He was too enthusiastic, viewing his military calling as a way to give back to the country that had been so good to him. It was a good fit for everyone else too. Because Jim was a family practitioner and not specialized, he was well-acquainted with all areas of ailment and treatment.

But there were other reasons Jim loved the Guard.

"He enjoyed the diversion of it," observed Jerry Lathan. It was a completely different environment from his everyday routine, both medically and socially. He was surrounded by women in his physician's practice and at home. By contrast, the Guard in those days remained, apart from a few dedicated nurses, a network of males, and it served as a refreshing break from all things feminine. Lieutenant

Colonel Al Rose empathized, "It's a military thing. It was a whole different set of friends. An escape."

Jim was as popular with his fellow Guardsmen as he had been with his college mates. He was interesting to talk to and, with a few glasses of wine, could even be persuaded to unleash his inner Scot along with the crisp Gaelic tongue he learned at his mother's knee.

Jim would witness and facilitate the positive evolution of the NCANG through the Cold War years, racial integration, women serving in the military, and in the words of Fisk Outwater, "the transition from the Guard being a backwater force to being a full-time partner with the active Air Force."

Jim was low on the totem pole at the Air Guard TAC clinic when he joined in 1963. Ten years later, he commanded it.

A Small-Town Doctor
Finds His Way

I get the whole family. And they stay with me.

—Jim Forrester

Jim relished his role as a small-town physician, particularly the perk of delivering successive generations of one family, caring for each member through all stages of life. It was satisfying to watch the babies he delivered develop from infant to child, adolescent to mature adult. It was gratifying to see parental features and personality traits reproduced in their small faces and bodies. It was even beneficial to know and recognize the generational maladies parents inevitably pass to their offspring.

The tiny office on Plum Street stayed crowded, for need was indeed great in "underserved" Stanley and its geographical surroundings. Worries over having to "build" a practice were unfounded.

Jim hired a sharp young girl named Rachel Armstrong as bookkeeper, confessing that his account books had never been done. Though he was zealous about paying bills on time, deeming it a matter of honor, he had little time for accounting. His shock was evident when Rachel told him after only a few days of work that the books had balanced perfectly. Rachel, along with Lou Sipe, Jim's first nurse, would remain with him until retirement in 1989.

Medicine is a profession comprised of servants, but in the '60s and '70s, a small-town family doctor was a downright slave to his calling. Corporately, Jim's patients owned him. His life and his time were not his own, and he must never go where he could not be found.

Without the liberation of pagers and cell phones, he was stuck to the homestead when "on call"—a laughable phrase in the Forrester household. He was never really *off* call. There was no group practice, no round-the-clock coverage 365 days a year, certainly not in a small rural community. The "exchanged call" with another physician was rare. If Jim ventured out, he was sure to leave detailed information, worthy of a top-secret dossier, as to his physical whereabouts and *potential* physical whereabouts.

Jim accepted the natural burdens of his vocation with stoicism and did his best to plan his weeks, days, and hours accordingly. He would even see patients early Sunday mornings, hoping it would reward him with the luxury of making it through church services without interruption.

Mary Frances, never idle, embarked on a new pursuit. She befriended another dancer, Daiselle Williams Hunter of Hunter Dairies fame. Missing the ballet world, the two converted a cow barn near Charlotte into a dance studio and taught ballet until pregnant bellies and multiplying children made it unfeasible for them to continue.

In the meantime, Jim sprang the most momentous bits of news on his unsuspecting wife. In December 1965, he walked into their apartment with a grin to end all grins and announced, "I've bought you a Christmas present. We have a house!"

Mary Frances was astonished, though she shouldn't have been by now. It was typical of Jim, the big-picture guy who went straight to the ten and left the one through nine with her. But Jim was eager to spend that Christmas in the new house, his "present" to her.

Moving was a whirlwind. There was little packing and unpacking involved. Furniture and belongings were simply uprooted from the apartment and dropped unceremoniously on the floor of the new house. Dirty dishes went directly from one sink to the other, linens from bed to bed. The Christmas tree, already fully decorated, was transported in the baby's playpen, where it stayed until Christmas was over.

August 1980

The national Democrat Party adds gay rights to its platform.

1982

- The US Center for Disease Control and Prevention replaces the acronym GRIDS (gay-related immune deficiency syndrome) with AIDS (acquired immune deficiency syndrome). One year later, the human immunodeficiency virus (HIV) that causes AIDS is discovered.
- Wisconsin becomes the first state to outlaw discrimination based on sexual orientation.

1984

The Berkley, California, city council passes a domestic partnership bill granting equal benefits to long-term gay and unmarried heterosexual couples.

1985

The first test to detect HIV is licensed in the United States. Almost nine thousand people are diagnosed with the disease, half already dead. By the end of that year, six thousand die of AIDS, and twelve thousand cases are reported.

Early Guard Days

Even a pacifist should admire the military virtues.
—John Keegan

In the military, nearly everybody gets stuck with a nickname at some point. It is almost a rite of passage, even a bonding device among men.

The North Carolina National Air Guard (NCANG) was no exception. According to Lieutenant Colonel Al Rose, people took some pride in their nicknames, even when they were less than flattering. To name but a few, there was Donald "Dirty" Kirby, Sergeant "Pinky" Springs, a flight engineer dubbed "Jug Butt," and "Squirrel" Russel, who had a face that allegedly resembled said creature. High rank did not grant one immunity from nicknames but merely limited the scope and frequency of their usage. Even the formidable General William Payne was referred to as "Curly Bill" due to the texture of his hair. "Though no one would ever have said it to his face," recalled Jerry Latham.

As for Jim, he was simply "Doc" to his fellow Guardsmen, "Chief" to a few.

Whatever names the airmen went by, they accrued due honor to them during the Vietnam War. The conflict was a game changer for the military as a whole, and it changed much for the NCANG, which became an essential lifeline to regular forces overseas. Battling maximum demands with minimum resources, it exercised its growing muscle like never before and proved its full worth to the United States military.

Latham, who flew cargo missions into Vietnam, sums up the Air Guard wartime flying experience this way: "Hours and hours of sheer boredom sprinkled with moments of sheer terror." If it wasn't the enemy shooting at you, it was a failing engine, inoperable prop, or any one of a thousand other wild-card complications that imperiled one's existence.

The belly of the two-engine C-119, the loud and Spartan "flying boxcar"—or "flying coffin" to the more pessimistic airman—became a familiar home for Jim, who flew medical and medical cargo missions in and around Southeast Asia and Europe. These were "not ideally configured for the evacuation, treatment, and transport of sick and wounded military personnel," to say the least. The upgrade to the "Super Connies," the C-121 Super Constellation model, was a welcome change for everyone.

In 1966, Jim, now a senior flight surgeon, began flying frequent medical airlift evacuations out of Southeast Asia, transporting wounded and sick to Weinstein, Germany, a receiving point for the war theater, or back across the Pacific to the States. His flight missions continued through the grim, still-bloody withdrawal process of the early '70s. One risky mission found him transferring to a C-141 in Cam Ranh Bay to assist freshly wounded soldiers en route from a burning combat zone.

Wherever and whenever the mission during those awful war years, it usually meant a grim and bitter cargo of dead and wounded soldiers. Many of the latter would die midflight, denied a final "I love you" to wives, children, and parents. Those who survived the journey were marked forever, both physically and emotionally. Jim felt more than mere satisfaction in helping them get stateside.

Whenever Mary Frances grew weary of being left alone for long stretches to deal with the demands of everyday domestic life, especially as children started coming, Jim would remind her that "these guys might not live to see *their* wives and children if I don't go bring them home." Even in the postwar years, he would volunteer for flights during holidays solely so that other Guardsmen, who might not otherwise be able to get home, could spend them with their families.

Whatever the mission, wartime or peacetime, overnight or overseas, Jim's ongoing observations, insights, and recommendations contributed to implementation of management and practice standards, utilized to this day, for the safety and welfare of soldiers and flight staff. He maximized his less-hectic flight-surgeon hours, putting together a manual that determines what maximum level of mobility a patient requires before he could be flown from Europe to the States without a physician on board.

During his career as a flight surgeon, Jim logged over 2,400 hours of flight time, exceeding the minimum flying requirements every year. His expertise and dedication and all those "extra miles" in the air and out of it did not go unnoticed. In 1978, he was selected as Major Command Flight Surgeon of the Year for the United States Air Force. Simultaneously, he was awarded the Vietnam Service Medal.

Babies Galore

The littlest feet make the biggest footprints in our hearts.

—Unknown

Jim Forrester waited on babies. They rarely waited on him, especially at certain peaks in the lunar cycle. One can quote statistics to the contrary for days, but the everyday anecdotal experience of countless physicians easily trumps the conclusions of scientists in laboratories or statisticians in dusty cubicles. For Jim, a full moon meant a full delivery room.

"Don't plan anything around the full moon," he advised his wife periodically, referring to the spike in deliveries during that period. The hospital would fill with rounded mothers about to "pop."

Unfortunately, rooms were scarce, and staff stretched thin. It was not unusual to see a prospective mommy relegated to a hallway gurney until final transportation to delivery. To the delicate sensibilities of twenty-first-century moms accustomed to spa-like, self-contained private suites, such circumstances seem downright Spartan.

But the busy times were okay with Jim. Delivering babies was gratifying—a joy. Even when the timing was inconvenient, being called to go "catch the baby" stirred a pleasant anticipation in him. This was the happiest province of the medical field. Unlike the fruitless suffering arising from the prolonged illnesses and injuries he saw, the temporary struggle and pain of childbirth had a *point*, a positive and beautiful purpose. It presented the mother with a tangible and precious reward for all her suffering and labor.

Jim's role in seeing it all come about safely was its own compensation. What could be more significant than helping bring new lives into the world?

Sometimes he just couldn't contain his excitement. In earlier days, Mary Frances, lamenting the more negative aspects of marriage to a doctor, had been given a friendly warning by an older medical spouse. "If he wants to wake you up in the middle of the night and talk to you, you'd better talk—or he'll find someone who will. If he wants scrambled eggs at five, get up and make him scrambled eggs." This sounds silly and old-fashioned in modern ears, but Mary Frances took it as sound advice.

So she held her tongue when Jim woke her up once at two in the morning bursting with news. It had been an exhausting kid-ridden day, and she must soon rise to face another. But her husband was giddy with excitement.

"I just delivered twins!" It was his first set. "One of them was breached, but that woman had a pelvis big enough to drive a truck through!"

That was his news? He woke her up to tell her that!

"But we were a great team," he added. "She had a natural delivery."

His delight rose not merely from bringing a new child into the world. It was watching that child being placed in the welcoming arms of happy, tearful parents. He was helping them *build a family.*

Stanley, North Carolina, has about thirty-five hundred residents, and Jim delivered about that many babies during his career. One could say he delivered a town.

His love for his chosen calling was not lost on others as on the day a young African American woman in her early twenties came into the office for a prenatal visit.

The civil rights struggle was raging. Few white doctors in the '60s received African American patients into their practices, which made it difficult for the latter to find health care. Jim was one of only two physicians in the community of Stanley who defied this injustice, and he refused to segregate his practice. Patients of all races sat side by side in his waiting room.

Jim greeted the young mother and her two small sons—both personally delivered by himself—by name. Also with her was a bright young African American girl about twelve years old.

"What do you want to be when you grow up?" Jim asked her.

"A doctor," she replied.

Jim gave her a pleased smile. "What kind of doctor will you be?"

"A baby doctor."

"Well, it's a noble profession, and I think you'll be able to do whatever you set your mind to."

The two parted, unaware that they would meet again, twenty-five years later and in a very different setting.

The Other Woman

At the end of your life, you will never regret not having won
one more verdict or not closing one more deal. You will regret
time not spent with a husband, a child, a friend or a parent.
And who knows there may even be someone sitting out there
who will follow in my footsteps and preside over the White
House as the president's spouse. And I wish him well.

—First Lady Barbara Bush,
in a college commencement speech

The *Gaston Gazette*, circa September 1971, did a feature story on Mary Frances titled "The Wife of a Doctor." The caption "feminine role" beneath the central photo would itself be enough to set modern-day feminists swooning like fragile Victorian misses. The photo captures a poised Mary Frances dressed in a classic sheath dress and tastefully sized bouffant hairdo. Two children, yet to come along in our narrative, also appear in the photo. On Mary Frances's left sits a little girl with blunt bangs and a camera-loving smile reminiscent of the actress she will one day become. On her lap is a one-year-old boy who stares saucer-eyed and gaping into the camera like a deer caught in headlights. All adorable.

"I try to remember that I knew I would have to share Jim when I married him," Mary Frances tells her interviewer.

"Knowing her husband listens all day to the problems of others," the writer of the article, Elsie Hamilton, informs readers, "Mrs. Forrester is careful not to complain of a headache or to give an account of her daily troubles the minute he comes home. She looks after her husband's health by preparing good meals for him and taking phone calls while he takes a quick nap after lunch."

The article states later:

> Unlike today's feminists, Mrs. Forrester finds homemaking a challenging and rewarding role. "I'm not in agreement with the liberation movement," she says, declaring that she doesn't think women want to be equal with men. She prefers cooking to repairing the electric mixer.

Certainly, the article's idealized tone is humorous when read in a contemporary light as well as when one peeks behind the domestic curtain and into the real-life, nitty-gritty trenches of wifedom and motherhood in any generation.

Motherhood is the most noble and important calling, for it plants and nurtures a fruit that lasts a lifetime and beyond. It is the toughest job and biggest responsibility a woman can assume, and there is only one chance to get it right.

If Jim was a slave to his profession, Mary Frances was a slave alongside him. She was stood up for countless dinner dates, dropped like a sack of stones during emergency calls, and stuck with battling assorted family crises solo. Her marital "quality time" existed at the grace of thousands of strangers who never thought to thank her for her sacrifice. In those days, Jim's medical practice was the "other woman" in their married life.

The constant interruptions in family time and recreational hours never ceased to be an annoyance. Holidays away, even of a few days, were a rare treat.

Nor were sentimental special occasions safe. In 1967, she and Jim celebrated their seventh anniversary at the Ranch House in Charlotte in company with three other couples. It was an expensive place, but then it was a worthy occasion. The Forresters would treat.

The salad course had hardly commenced when Jim got a call about a pregnant woman, nine centimeters dilated, at the hospital. Mary Frances groaned. Babies loved to interrupt sentimental celebrations!

"Don't worry, this won't take long," Jim announced, confident. "She may even deliver before I get there. I'll be back by dessert."

He wasn't back by dessert. He wasn't back at all.

It grew late. Mary Frances's eyes flew to the door every other minute, hoping to see his large frame stride through. She prayed the maître d' would come tap her shoulder and say there was a Dr. Forrester on the phone that wished to speak with her.

It was all a very sticky wicket, for she had no money with her. She hadn't thought to bring any. She took the waiter aside and explained the dilemma, hoping for grace. She got none, so she confessed everything to her guests in a cloud of embarrassment, informing them they must pay their own way, and hers too.

Oh, and could one of them drive her home to Stanley, please? "Jim has the car."

But there it was. As went the doctor's life, so went the doctor's wife.

There was no sacred time and no sacred space, particularly in a world that did not yet enjoy round-the-clock emergency rooms and urgent-care offices. She would answer the kitchen wall phone and hear the voice of a frantic patient who could not get through to Jim. Within seconds, she was consigned to the role of de facto emergency-room nurse, fielding all manner of minor and not-so-minor complaints from headaches to hemorrhoids.

There were other thorns in Mary Frances's life in that slow rural community. Her privacy was on nobody's list of considerations. Worse, the very nature of her position as "a doctor's wife" tended to make her the subject of speculation and ignorant gossip on occasion. It was baffling that people could adopt such a casual attitude toward her good name and reputation.

Chronic gossips are usually content to tattle and plant seeds of dissent behind their subject's back, but some succumb to the urge to gossip straight to one's face. This is done with a "concerned" air, a pretense of selfless sympathy that doesn't fool anybody.

The Forresters figured out that the best response to tasteless comments or implications was nonchalance and a puzzled expression. They had occasion to use these often.

Age and a full calendar began to limit her for dancing, so Mary Frances took up tennis, which did not come easy due to a dearth of upper-body strength. George Willis, a good friend and something of a surrogate father, would go with her to the Gaston College courts and, with great patience, hit balls with her and help her work through her physical and technical issues. When summer came, they would go early in the morning to avoid the brutal humidity and afterward, hungry as desert horses, would grab breakfast, usually at the convenient Holiday Inn nearby.

It wasn't long before Jim was going about his own business in downtown Stanley one afternoon when a "concerned" gentleman approached him in the post office with information that he had "seen your wife" at an early hour at the Holiday Inn several Saturdays in a row.

Jim hesitated, donned a worried frown, then smiled. "Oh, that's just George," he replied in a gentle, "bless your heart" tone that implied how foolish the man was with his silly implications.

Some people could be nosy to the point of rudeness, especially when they calculated how close together the Forrester children were in age. One could hardly visit the bank or post office without a busybody remarking on the subject in inquisitive tones. "Hello, Mrs. Forrester. Oh my goodness, look at *all those children!*"

"Good morning, Dr. Forrester," said another tactless individual. "Is your wife expecting *again*? Are y'all Catholic?"

"No," Jim said with a grin. "Just passionate Protestants."

1987

Homosexual activist Michael Swift writes in the *Gay Community News* regarding the teaching of homosexuality to school children, "We shall seduce them in your schools…they will be recast in our image. They will come to crave and adore us."

May 1987

Representative Barney Frank (D-Massachusetts) becomes the first openly gay member of the US Congress. In 2012, he will become the first congressman to marry someone of the same sex while in office.

1989

Heather Has Two Mommies, a children's book written by Leslea Newman with Diana Souza, is published. Google Books calls it "the first lesbian-themed children's book ever published."

Bleeding Green

I can watch only so much golf—the tee-off and
the coming in on the eighteenth hole.
                                                    —Mary Frances Forrester

"There is always time for golf." Jim never said this, but it was certainly a principle he embraced once his medical practice was established. Wednesday was the favored day to head to Green Meadows in Mount Holly or Cowans Ford in Stanley. Whatever the day, any friend with the urge to play had little trouble getting Jim on to the green for an afternoon of drives and putts, birdies and bogies.

There was no trick or practice, short of dark spells and incantations, that he would not implement in an effort to improve his game. He would bring his golf balls to the office to clean, soaking them in warm water in the belief that this made them hit farther. On weekends, the bathroom sink at home, to Mary Frances's chagrin, was employed for the same purpose.

Rachel Armstrong and Juanita Martin (Jim's faithful nurse of twenty-eight years) both remember the afternoon of the exploding golf ball, which spontaneously blew apart one day as Jim sat at his desk consulting with a patient. The noise was so loud the people out in the waiting area jumped. Tiny bits of rubber were strewn over Jim's office. Eerie, to say the least.

Forest Armstrong, Rachel's husband, rang the Forrester line many a weekend. "Is Forrester home?" Everyone knew what *that* call was about. Joe Bumgardner, a school principal in Stanley, was another fairway friend. Juanita smiled to recall that if things were slow at the office and the staff had a hankering to go home early, they would make a proactive call to Joe to see if he wished to go play golf with Jim. If Joe did, the girls would ask that *he* call Jim and suggest the game. It usually went like this:

"Dr. Forrester, Joe's on the line."
Pause. "Is anybody waiting?"
"No."
Pause. "Well, I think I'll go play a round with him."

Jim couldn't help it. Golf was in his blood—and in the most real way possible.

As a young boy, Jim's father, James Summers Forrester, had been a lowly club-toting caddy at Cruden Bay golf course in Cruden Bay, Scotland. By the age of seventeen, he was the club's resident golf pro, an unheard-of feat not only due to his tender age but his lowly social position.

Golf, in the rigid class system of the day, was strictly a "gentleman's sport." If you were born into a particular social stratum, you stayed there. James's parents were respectable enough, but were mere working-class folk nonetheless. Only exceptional native talent and ambition could vault a man into the gentleman's sport. James had both in good measure.

He would triumph in the 1934 Northern Open and the Scottish Professional Championship in 1936 before receiving the plum invitation to succeed Henry Cotton as golf pro at the Royal Waterloo Club in Lasne, Belgium, near Brussels.

Life was as bonny as a heather-strewn meadow in May for James and his little family. That is, until June of 1938, when he walked onto the Royal Waterloo's verdant green and never walked off. His caddy and nearby witnesses rushed to where he lay. Leopold the Third, king of Belgium, sent his own royal physician to attend him. All to no avail. James's killer was a brain abscess, a complication from a recent appendectomy.

Thus, James Summers Forrester exited this world at the promising age of thirty-two. His son Jim, still in naps and nappies, was fatherless.

If circumstances had been otherwise, without his famous father's premature death and a world war, Jim would have ended up following in the paternal footsteps. In long-sighted anticipation, James had already had a child's set of golf clubs, custom-made signature tools, ready and waiting to play with his son when he came of age.

They would never play together, but James bequeathed to his son a fine golf legacy in the form of sheer natural ability. Chief Master Sergeant Terry Henderson, a fellow air guardsman, recognized this generational talent. "The apple didn't fall far from *that* tree."

Throughout a busy and packed life, there would be few places Jim felt as content and "at home" as on the shaved emerald turf of a golf course. But the game was more than rest and recreation. It was a way to connect, even bond, with the father he had never known. He thought of James many times as he made a stroke or putt, or thought, *I wish my father could have seen that*, as he sank a hole in one. He could even imagine James was there, watching in approval and affection.

Children Keep Coming

*Like arrows in the hand of a warrior are the children of one's
youth. Blessed is the man who fills his quiver with them.*
—Psalm 127:4–5 ESV

At 10:00 p.m. on June 10, 1964, Jim Forrester was in a plane flying at ten thousand feet somewhere over South Carolina when he received a radio message from the pilot informing him that he was now the proud father of a baby girl, his second child. According to fellow crew members, Jim's reaction to the news was a smile, a shake of his head, and the words, "I'm never going to live this down."

He was reflecting on the last conversation with his wife upon leaving the house several hours before. No, he was *never* going to live this down.

It must be mentioned that Mary Frances had been led to expect spontaneous deliveries. For her, false labor pains, long hours of contraction-ridden waiting and grueling labor were unlikely. "Don't ever delay," she had been told. "Head to the hospital at the first twinge." For her, birth coaching consisted of repetitions of, "*Don't* push. *Don't* push."

"Jim, please don't go flying tonight," Mary Frances had urged him that evening before he left. "Stay home. I feel a twinge."

He examined her belly, then shook his head. "You're not going to deliver today. This baby hasn't even dropped yet."

Jim should have known better. Perhaps one is most blind to the things in his own immediate circle. Doctors' wives are either over-treated or underlooked. It is not from neglect or lack of sympathy, merely that, like people in other professions, physicians dislike hav-

101

ing family life and "work" collide too much. So they might be a little slower to admit there is anything amiss.

"Jim, please," Mary Frances urged. "I'm asking you to stay."

"You're not going anywhere," he said with a sweet kiss, then added jokingly, "Don't you dare have that baby now just to spite me." With that, he was gone. The clock on the wall read 6:30 p.m.

By 7:00 p.m., a desperate Mary Frances was on the line with Lou Sipe, one of Jim's nurses. "You have to take me to the hospital. *Now.*" She placed a second call to the church, breaking up Wednesday-night prayer meeting, to summon her good friend Gaynell to babysit Wyndi.

The fuel needle in Lou's car pointed to "empty," so a pit stop at the gas station was nonnegotiable. "It's that or have your baby in my car!" she told her anxious passenger. Mary Frances, less than amused, worried she might just do that!

At 8:00 p.m., Mary Frances was wheeled into Gaston Memorial Hospital through the emergency doors. "I'm the father!" Lou joked to the attendants.

The mother-to-be filled out the paperwork, was admitted, transferred to Labor, and prepped according to procedure. Just in time. At 9:27 p.m., Gloria Ann Forrester was born.

While it is true that Jim never lived the events of that night down, he was too happy to care. Each new child was another cornerstone in building the family he had always wanted.

Still, child number two complicated the logistics of life.

Jim could not contribute much to the day-to-day childcare at home as he had little professional freedom or flexibility. With his running off to see patients, deliver babies at all hours, and respond to any one of a thousand assorted emergencies, real or imagined, Mary Frances was homebound with two needy infants. Life was a nonstop wheel of cooking, laundry, diaper changes, and attempts to sort out childhood squabbles.

The problem of *the children* reached a head when Mary Frances was pregnant with her third baby. In her second trimester, she was as sick as the proverbial dog, bedridden with a lung infection on top of pregnancy. In a sane world, she'd have been in the hospital, enjoying quiet solitude, pudding she didn't have to make herself, and the soothing ministrations of angelic nurses in white.

But the world is not sane. There were the *children.*

As with all his expectant moms, Jim was conservative in allowing Mary Frances medications. The smallest aspirin was a concession as he was concerned about the long-term health and well-being of mother and baby. Who knew what dreadful yet-to-be-discovered effects that even common drugs might possess.

So Mary Frances was miserable. Her third trimester loomed ahead, just in time for the stifling humidity of the Southern summer months.

Then Jim did something that was "very much a dad thing," in the words of daughter Mary Paige. He walked into Stanley Junior High cafeteria and announced with desperation to the staff that his wife was ill and needed immediate assistance. Was anybody willing to come and stay with her to oversee the children until she recovered?

Nettie Floyd was willing. She agreed to come for a few weeks and stayed forty years.

With Nettie's care and a hardworking rotary fan, Mary Frances suffered and sweated her way through her third trimester. On September 25, 1966, Mary Paige Forrester was born.

Finally.

Son and Namesake

*It's the third child that gets you. With two, you have a
hand for each. You can handle that. You don't have a
third hand, so that kid tends to get away from you.*
—Mary Frances Forrester

Jim adored his three little girls. Like most men, though, he longed
for a son and namesake to carry on the Forrester bloodline. Not only
for himself but his mother as Nancy had great emotional investment
in the prospect of a male heir for her beloved James. Jim also pondered how nice it would be to have another male around the place,
to talk boy things and pursue boy activities.

But his desire for a son went far deeper. He had been denied the
unique father-son bond as a son. Would he also be denied it as *father*?

Thus, when Mary Frances announced she was pregnant for a
fourth time, he was ecstatic, and hope swelled.

Mary Frances was torn. She knew how much Jim wanted a son,
and she knew all the profound and poignant reasons why. Still she
had thought her baby days were done. Three kids so close in age were
work enough! It was all they could manage as it was with Jim's multitudinous commitments and their limited time.

Besides, childbirth was not the sublime experience one observed
in the movies. Giving birth was an intense affair. As for the mechanics
of the thing, she could only liken it to "trying to birth a watermelon."

"If this one's not a boy, we're buying one," she remarked one
day, only half-joking.

Jim's eyes went wide. "Are you serious?" He would have had a
dozen children if he could!

Mary Frances felt the unspoken pressure to have a son—until a little unexpected bit of grace came to her one day as she pulled up to a railroad crossing to wait on a passing train. As the railcars rumbled across her vision, she felt a sudden compulsion to pray. And pray she did.

"Lord," she whispered, "you've given us three beautiful, healthy girls. If you give us another, I'll accept her with a grateful heart and with love. But *please* let this one be a boy for Jim. For his sake, let us have a son."

As the train's caboose rolled past, she felt a deep, abiding assurance that God would honor her prayer. She simply *knew* it. The child kicking inside her belly *was* a boy. Her mind and heart finally felt at peace about the matter.

But the boy would take his sweet time in coming.

Nancy came to stay around the due date, eagerly waiting the child's arrival. After three weeks passed without a grandson in sight, she gave up waiting and returned home to Wilmington.

On the morning of March 9, 1970, Mary Frances woke with contractions. "You may be in false labor, with Braxton Hicks contractions," Jim said. She'd had them before. "But we're not taking any chances," he added. Heaven knew he had learned his lesson on that score!

He donned a blue necktie for work. A superstitious invocation of good luck? No, but it couldn't hurt to think positively.

With an affectionate parting kiss, he settled Mary Frances at the hospital and headed to the office to see patients as usual. At lunch, he returned to the hospital and headed straight to the nursery, where he introduced himself to his new son, James S. "Jimmy" Forrester Jr.

He was overcome with smiles, grateful prayers, and a few stray tears as he gazed on his baby boy, whole and healthy. He had lost count of all the baby boys he had delivered, but this one was *his*. A whole new joy. If only his father, James, could be there to witness his legacy.

This was the ultimate hole in one!

Jim often teased, "Every child is a smile from God." On that day, God could not have beamed more brightly on him. He now had four beautiful children. Four pillars to build a sturdy, enduring house.

And there were still grandchildren to look forward to!

The baby crossed the Forrester threshold on March 14, Wyndi's seventh birthday. The little girl, though impressed with her new baby brother, was confused.

"Mother," she asked, "is this the only present I'm getting for my birthday?"

There was another small miracle that year. Aunt Lil, perhaps inspired or shamed by this wonderful birth, finally made her peace with Mary Frances's marriage and journeyed to Stanley to visit the couple for the first time since the wedding she had boycotted. The ten-year estrangement was over. Children are the best balm for healing family rifts.

1991

Three same-sex couples in Hawaii are denied a marriage license by the State Department of Health. They sue the state, contending that Hawaii's marriage law is unconstitutional because it bars gay couples from obtaining the same marriage right afforded heterosexuals, denying them equal rights.

December 1992

In New York, a Queens school board rejects an attempt by Chancellor Joseph Fernandez to introduce the "rainbow curriculum" into elementary classrooms. The curriculum included the books *Heather Has Two Mommies*, *Daddy's Roommate*, and *Gloria Goes to Gay Pride*.

Pearls and Perils of Fatherhood

The first 40 years of parenting are always the hardest.
—Unknown

The arrival of each child sent Jim out to purchase a better camera and a larger life insurance policy. He understood at least two things in the frightening odyssey that was fatherhood: one took lots of photographs, and one ensured that the wife and kids were financially safe.

He also recognized the broader duties to mold and refine the members of his long-anticipated brood and to "raise them in the fear and admonition of the Lord." Family was, he believed, the all-important microcosm of life itself, a crucial dress rehearsal for the ultimate play.

Still, as Jim had had no paternal model, the practical path of fatherhood was not clearly marked. Sometimes a man just had to rely on his instinct and temper discipline with discretion.

Like the day seven-year-old Jimmy spray-painted his brand-new bike and then tried to wash in a nearby creek to erase his crime.

"I'm telling your father when he gets home," Mary Frances vowed. They both knew what the consequence would be.

True to her word, she related the whole incident to Jim that evening while Jimmy stood on the kitchen floor, pale-faced and spouting excuses. Jim banished him with, "Go upstairs to your room and wait for me there."

A little while later, he entered Jimmy's bedroom and sat down on the bed. Jimmy shook with trepidation over the imminent whipping at hand.

His father proceeded a stern talking-to about what Jimmy had done and why it was wrong et cetera.

"Listen, I need to punish you some way," he said at last with a sigh. "Okay, listen, I'm going to take my belt off and hit the bed with it a few times. And when I do, you just give a yelp each time. Just a little yelp now. Don't overdo it, or your mom will know."

The plan suited Jimmy just fine.

Jim hit the bed once with his belt. Jimmy yelped in pain. Twice. Jimmy yelped again. Three times. Jimmy gave his last yelp.

"Now, that's your secret and mine," said Jim. "I'm going downstairs, and you just stay up here for a while." Long enough so that the lack of evidence—tears and a sore bottom—would not be suspicious. "Then come down and apologize to your mother."

Jim relished family life, and he savored the golden moments of fatherhood.

A few words, in the right context, can speak volumes. Jim received a note one day from Jimmy, following some infraction the boy had committed. It read as follow:

> Dad,
>
> I'm sorry about last night. I'm sorry about the things I said. I'm going to try keep my attitude in. One more thing, I love you more than anything in the world.
>
> Love,
> Jimmy

A simpler missive, formed with crooked letters and uneven lines, came from Mary Paige:

> Dear Daddy,
> I love you very much.
>
> Love,
> Mary Paige Forrester

Years later, after Jim's death, the note was unexpectedly found in the pocket of his favorite jacket and buried with him.

Sweet gems like these could bring the reserved and stoic Jim Forrester to tears, or at least close to them. Like Mary in the Bible, he "stored them up" in his heart.

Jim got another letter from son Jimmy, this one more mature but no less sweet. The handwriting is neater and the grammar nearly perfect.

> Dad
>
> I just wanted to say have a safe trip. Your very important to me, and I love you a lot. If I only had one wish, I'd wish to be like you, for I admire you more than words can say. I'm proud to be your son.
>
> Love,
> Jimmy

Jim loved to sing, and he was good at it. His favorite go-to song to the kids, especially in the car, was "You Are My Sunshine." They all recall his stint with the Doctor Peppers, a group of physicians who sang at a charity talent show. His was the high-falsetto part of "The Lion Sleeps Tonight," the old classic from the Tokens.

> In the jungle, the mighty jungle,
> the lion sleeps tonight.
> In the jungle, the quiet jungle,
> the lion sleeps tonight.

"Weeheeheehee dee heeheeheehee weeoh aweem away," Jim would croon loftily. "Weeheeheehee dee heeheeheehee weeoh aweem away."

Jim's kids learned lessons from their father they didn't realize they were learning—like not being a fair-weather fan. A ten-year-old Jimmy witnessed this deep-rooted loyalty when his father took him to a Wake Forest–Duke football game.

The weather was abysmal, a dead pour that began with the coin toss and never let up. Their seats were fifty rows up. To make things worse, Wake Forest was losing badly.

By the fourth quarter, Jimmy reckoned they were maybe two of a hundred Wake Forest fans still left in the stands. The only Duke fans left were those on the team.

But Jim Forrester stayed, and Jimmy stayed with him, sitting there in the midst of an empty stadium like two lonely bums, their soaking heads poking up out of makeshift raincoats fashioned from trash bags.

But Jim stuck with his team to the bitter end, to the last echo of the fourth-quarter buzzer. It was the principle of the thing: do not abandon your team, *ever*, until the game is over.

It was not only sports he was thinking of.

Giving Back

*Always remember those who help you and
always reach back to help others.*

—Nancy Forrester

"Always remember those who help you and always reach back to help others." The words of Jim's mother were a subliminal refrain in his mind, the principle by which he lived his whole life.

Giving back necessitated wisdom, and Jim was tenacious in doing good things the right way, with a healthy dose of prudence and practicality.

In 1971, he was president of the Gaston Medical Society, serving on the building committee for a new county hospital. In the words of Chief Master Sergeant Terry Henderson, "Jim was as responsible for the new hospital as anyone."

It was a desperately needed project. The present hospital, Gaston Memorial, could claim only 233 beds, and those stayed full. Garrison General Hospital had a mere 50. More beds, more space, was needed to accommodate the growing population.

The new facility would boast over 400 beds, with room for expansion. It would also attract more badly needed doctors and nurses to the area.

As the only doctor on the building committee, Jim possessed experience and knowledge that was crucial. He had the right vision for the future too, which was to prioritize patient access and care.

First of all, this meant acknowledging the basic necessity of private single rooms. It was not a popular idea with many on the committee, but it was nonnegotiable to Jim. He had served in hospitals all around the world. He knew how germs traveled and had witnessed how quickly and insidiously infections can spread. For the same reasons, he insisted that each patient have a private adjoining bathroom as well. By the standards of the day, neither of these was the rule.

Despite opposition from some committee members, Jim was firm. "They'll have to walk all over me to change my mind," he told Mary Frances. His Scottish stubbornness paid off when a majority of the committee was at last persuaded.

His efforts proved a spearhead for modernization of American hospitals and for Gaston Memorial Hospital to be named in honor of World War II veterans. Opening its doors in 1973, it became one of the first medical facilities in the nation to offer single rooms with an adjoining private bathroom. Now, as CaroMont Regional Medical Center, the facility has accrued numerous awards to date, including being named by IBM Watson Health as one of the nation's 100 Top Hospitals.

Giving back was volunteering at the Gaston County Public Health Department's family-planning clinic. The phrase "family-planning clinic" held a far more humane meaning that it does today. Jim's patients there were mostly local mill folk and minorities of meager means. Jim received no reimbursement, but then he sought none.

He assisted infertile women and treated those who had diseases or conditions that threatened a safe pregnancy. Especially close to his heart were the babies of unwed mothers, fatherless little ones, some of whom he saw safely placed in adoption or foster-care families if the mother were unable to care for the child. These too were "his babies," and their welfare and future were important.

His experience at the public health clinic was partly what inspired him in 1976 to pursue a master's degree in preventative medicine.

He had developed a special concern for the mill people, considering the unhealthy conditions many faced each day, the damage of lint-clogged lungs, and hearing loss due to brutal decibel levels.

But it went beyond just the personal health of individual workers. In those days, a mill was a self-contained, enclosed environment, often lacking windows. Poor ventilation, combined with the close-working ranks of employees, made it a fertile ground for contagions to flourish and spread. Jim disliked the risks and did his best to prevent illness, encouraging the company executives, many of whom were also his patients, to improve working conditions.

He was one of the first doctors in the region to enter the mills and other industries to administer flu shots, attending each eight-hour shift change—round the clock—to ensure each worker had a chance to be inoculated. He gave auditory evaluations often to monitor hearing acuity.

Giving back, Jim in 1984 became certified in preventive medicine via training through his military service. It helped prepare him to tackle crises in public health among local populations in war zones, from battling germ pandemics to establishing field hospitals to countering chemical warfare among soldiers and citizenry.

Giving back was delivering outdated hospitals the United States military gifted to other countries. In 1989, as a brigadier general, Jim was part of a state-sponsored Air Guard delegation who boarded a cargo plane destined for a little pin prick on the map called Ayo Ayo in Bolivia.

The plane carried in its big metal belly the contents of a full army field hospital—operating tables, x-ray machines, and host of other hospital apparatus. The things were considered outdated in the States but were clean, functional, and highly valuable. Especially to a poor third-world people rife with illness, disease, malnutrition, staggering rates of infant mortality, scant prenatal care, and undrinkable water.

The people in the little village of Ayo Ayo almost didn't see the first Band-Aid. Initially, the trip was cancelled and rescheduled five times. Then at the stopover in Quito, Ecuador, the pilot grounded the plane due to malfunctioning gear. A larger C-141 was called in to ferry cargo and crew to La Paz, Bolivia's capital. From there, it was airlifted over the Andes to a grateful Ayo Ayo, where the humanitarians were met with street celebrations and thick clouds of confetti.

"When I got back to the hotel," Jim later told a reporter back home, "I even had confetti in my underwear!" On a more thoughtful note, he observed, "You learn to appreciate the freedom and security we have here and the advantages. True poverty—we just don't have that kind of poverty here in America."

Giving back meant providing pro bono physicals for high school football players and serving as team physician for East Gaston High School and Stanley Junior High for over twenty years. "You can't have your baby on Friday night," he liked to joke with his pregnant patients.

Giving back meant tending to smaller things, like advertising for used band instruments in the local paper, then buying them for students and band directors of local schools. Someone had done that for him once, and the result of their kindness had been a ticket to Wake Forest via a drum major music scholarship.

Giving back was not wanting his child to go on a grade school field trip if the whole class couldn't go. "He slipped my teachers money for kids who could not pay," daughter Gloria recalls. Jim had been the student left out of many extra class outings growing up. No one understood better how the feeling of noninclusion can carve a deep fissure in a child's heart.

Giving back, in 1985, was founding the Gaston County Commissioners School of Excellence, a two-week residential program. Its practical function was to educate students through seminars, field trips, and hands-on exercises in the structure and workings of Gaston County government, delving into local current issues, community service and involvement, technology, arts and culture. The program's overarching aim was to prepare students for future leadership roles, a crucial need for Jim Forrester. The program would eventually be renamed in his honor as the James S. Forrester Commissioners' School of Excellence.

Giving back meant befriending the orphan. While children in Stanley were playing baseball, bemoaning homework, and scarfing barbecue at the church picnic, all within a safe radius of loving parents, a little four-year-old boy named Su Ju languished in a South Korean orphanage seven thousand miles away.

Jim and Mary Frances supported the boy through an international charity organization. They wrote letters, sent him clothes, school supplies and other gifts, and supported the general running of the orphanage. In return, they received updates, photos of Su Ju, and translated messages.

Suddenly there came a long lapse in communication. Concerned, the Forresters wrote to inquire why. The orphanage authorities sent a simple, cryptic reply informing them that Su Ju had reached the age of twelve, and "as an adult, he has been released from our orphanage." That was all. The Forresters had been given no prior notice, no opportunity to exchange goodbyes or well wishes, and no information as to how they might continue assistance to the boy. Nothing.

Often Jim and Mary Frances would sit together in wonder and worry over what had become of Su Ju, turned out on the streets to fend for himself. The photographs stuck to the refrigerator faded, but prayer for Su Ju continued for many years to come.

Giving back was done in a thousand other little ways that went unmarked and unheralded—and sometimes unappreciated. But Jim did not care. To give back was his honor and his joy, a reward in itself.

November 1993

President Bill Clinton signs the "Don't Ask, Don't Tell" legislation prohibiting openly gay individuals from serving in the military. It also prohibits harassment against homosexuals who serve but are not openly gay.

January 1994

Philadelphia, a film depicting a closeted gay man dying of AIDS, is released. It wins two Academy Awards.

November 1995

The Hate Crimes Sentencing Enhancement Act takes effect, allowing a judge to impose harsher sentences if there is evidence showing a victim was targeted due to race, color, national origin, ethnicity, gender, disability, or sexual orientation.

Children Grow

*Every child should have a father who tells them the world
is a beautiful place and that they are worthy of it.*
—Wynn Forrester Maxwell

The Forrester children learned early what it meant to be a doctor's kid. They understood, in a vague intellectual sense, that lots of people needed Daddy and that they must share him, like Mother did.

But sharing a parent one loves is hard. The heart, especially a little one, craves constant reassurances. Jim's children sought reminders that Daddy loved them, and loved them best.

When small, they would climb on his lap and complain about their little aches and pains and show him "boo-boos," both real and imagined. He would then "treat" them, and they would know they were his favorite patients. In those short, full moments, Daddy belonged only to them.

Jim understood that one act of love can swallow a thousand words about it.

In elementary school, he let Gloria walk to the office after school and ride home with him that evening.

Mary Paige, with her father's generous nature, delighted in passing out lollipops to the children in Jim's waiting room. She felt sorry that their heads were stuffed with colds, or they were awaiting their dreaded vaccinations. Her generosity was a bit too much the day she raided the candy cache and began passing out lollipops before the kids were called back for examination. It robbed Jim of useful leverage. Little Johnny and Sally had no desire to see the doctor when they'd already gotten the long-promised treat!

When each child reached a certain level of maturity, Jim would take them to the hospital during his rounds, letting them sit in the doctors' lounge with a book, crayons, and the promise of an ice cream later for good behavior. How special they felt to join Daddy in his grown-up world.

Shared family time was a rare commodity. If Jim couldn't come to Mary Frances and the children, they went to him, whether it meant lunch in the hospital cafeteria or a fast-food feast on Sundays when he had rounds. Holidays were subject to unorthodox observances, like Thanksgiving at the Holiday Inn thanks to a mother-to-be on the cusp of delivery.

Friday nights in autumn meant football games, and Jim would take a kid or two along with him. The game was nice for them, but the best part was Dad himself. It was a thrill to sit in the stands or in the ambulance and watch him on the field or sidelines treating injuries and monitoring players' physical well-being.

"That's my daddy," they would boast. And Daddy was important!

And when a mother or father approached Jim with profuse thanks for his care of their son, their little blue eyes would shine with pride.

Boundless was their faith in his healing abilities. There was no creature Dad could not fix. At least that was the assumption in Jimmy's mind one Saturday when Mary Frances pulled into the garage after driving him home from swim practice. They heard an awful shriek of feline pain. Leaping from the car, they saw the General, the family cat, writhing in agony beside a back tire.

Mary Frances was aghast. "Good Lord! I've killed him!"

Jimmy too was horrified but slightly more clear-headed. "Maybe not, Mom."

He rushed inside and phoned his father. "Dad, Mom just ran over the General. Can we bring him to the office?"

There was a quiet pause as Jim absorbed the suddenness of it all. "But, son, I don't *do* cats."

"Dad, *pleeeease.*"

There was another pause, a longer one. Then his father's reply. "Well, all right, but bring him through the *back door*, understand?"

Jimmy ran back to his shocked, crying mother, who still stood staring down at the suffering animal she had crushed.

"Come on," he told her. "We're taking him to Dad."

The boy's confidence calmed Mary Frances, who managed to contrive a sling out of a bath towel. At Jim's office, the General was x-rayed, his wounds cleaned, and his broken leg set in a neat splint made from tongue depressors. Well, Jim had always said he liked the unpredictability of medicine, that no two patients were ever the same!

Prognosis: "He'll live."

And live the General did, in the caring bosom of his guilt-ridden human family, becoming a pampered pet with a high cholesterol count from the pure cream and canned tuna in oil the Forresters frequently fed him. It was the least they could do.

Valleys

Parenthood is as much pain as joy, and there were days when Jim and Mary Frances thought it would swallow them whole, far beyond the minor crises of injured pets and skinned knees.

One grim emergency occurred in April 1964. Jim had taken one-year-old Wyndi to church, leaving an exhausted Mary Frances, seven months pregnant, at home for a much-needed rest.

Long before the church service should have ended, Jim rushed in the house. "Get your purse! We're going to the emergency room. There's been an accident."

Mary Frances cried out in horror when she looked down and saw her child's foot, wounded and bloodied. Wyndi was screaming in pain and shock.

"You hold her," commanded Jim, his voice urgent. "I'll drive."

Wyndi had been in the church nursery while Jim was singing hymns in the sanctuary. A nursery worker, severely lacking in judgement, had left a baby-bottle warmer on the floor in the middle of the nursery room.

Wyndi, seeing only a yummy bottle of milk for the taking, went straight for it and promptly turned over the warmer. Boiling water poured over her little foot. The frantic nursery worker began to take off her sock and shoe, pulling off a patches of tender flesh with it.

Jim was summoned. Heart pounding, he grabbed Wyndi and sped home, a few blocks away.

Now Mary Frances held the traumatized Wyndi atop her bulging pregnant belly, trying to keep the screaming child from grabbing her wounded foot. It was the longest eight miles of the Forresters' life.

Halfway through the trip, the unrelenting pressure on Mary Frances's stomach was making her nauseous and giddy.

"I think I might faint," she told Jim. "You have to hold her. I'll drive."

"Can you drive?"

They pulled off the road and swapped places as Mary Frances inhaled deep breaths and regained enough equilibrium to take the wheel, struggling to stay calm and focused. The mind of both parents was assailed with every possible tragedy.

They made it to the emergency room, where Jim accompanied Dr. Charles Morgan, the surgeon on call, to attend the patient. Mary Frances managed to get to the nearest restroom before vomiting. When that was done, she went to collapse in the waiting room, clutching her huge belly, where little Gloria moved about restlessly, as if knowing something was amiss.

Nearly the whole of Wyndi's foot was affected.

"We'll do everything we can to save her foot," Dr. Morgan said after she had been stabilized. "She may lose her toes."

Jim and Mary Frances shrank at his words.

"But remember," added Morgan, "babies are resilient. And we can graft skin from the buttocks."

In the midst of crisis, the words failed to encourage.

"Let's be optimistic," Morgan added. "Just know it's going to be a long healing process."

Mary Frances cried all the way home.

Jim tried to console her, and himself. "Dear, we have to look at the positive," he admonished. "It could have been her face."

Dr. Morgan had told Mary Frances, "I'm worried about you. You have to focus on your baby."

It was hard. For the last two months of Mary Frances's pregnancy, Wyndi lived on her mother's hip, never set down during waking hours.

A toddler understands nothing when he or she is in pain and tends to be a complication rather than an aid to her own physical care. Thus, Jim and Mary Frances were forced to tie Wyndi's hands and her undamaged foot to the bed frame at night so she could not yield to her natural impulse to rub her foot or work off the bandages.

Every three days, the foot was soaked to soften the bandages for easier removal. Then salve was reapplied and the dressings replaced. Each time Jim and Mary Frances carried out the process and saw blood running profusely from the tiny foot, all the horror of the incident returned.

Jim monitored the condition of his little patient every chance he got, checking the wound and following all proper medical protocol just as if they were in his office. "She's going to be all right," he would reassure Mary Frances.

Jim was her "rock" during those trying months. Even so, she could see the pain and helplessness in his face when he looked at his little girl, wishing he could take her anguish on himself. As every doctor knows, professional objectivity is strained to its limits when the health and wholeness of one's own child is at stake.

"I'm so pleased at how well she's healing," Dr. Morgan said after a year's passing. "Her foot will be okay. Probably a stiff ankle and a scar will be the only lasting effects."

As Wyndi grew, her body continued to repair itself. Her ankle was not stiff, and the scar never became the horrible disfigurement everyone expected.

Ten years later in 1974, a four-year-old Jimmy fell dreadfully sick one night, consumed with a fever approaching 105 brutal degrees. Mary Frances believed he might be having a seizure, but Jim assured her this wasn't so. When early morning dawned, they rushed Jimmy to the pediatrician, Bill "Bo" Abernathy. Abernathy advised them to "get him to the hospital without delay."

The hospital medical staff immediately put Jimmy in isolation. They suspected viral meningitis, which is contagious, but could not be sure.

Mary Frances stayed with Jimmy, exchanging calls with Jim for updates and returning home only to wash and change clothes. The phone rang in the middle of her shower. It was a nurse at the hospital. "Mrs. Forrester, you need to come back now. Your son is in a coma."

She rushed back to the hospital, sure the worst was befalling them.

Jimmy's illness was revealed as Rocky Mountain spotted fever. Two other patients in hospital had it also, a ten-year-old and a thirty-three-year-old. Jim and Mary Frances guessed that their child had contracted the disease from a tic on Snoopy, their pet beagle. Their son must be given massive doses of tetracycline.

The minister was called. Mary Frances was in turmoil, despair, and confusion. She and Jim went into the hospital chapel, knelt, and prayed their breaking hearts out. "Lord, you've given us this son, Jim's namesake, and we don't understand. Please, Lord, don't take him."

Mary Frances stayed by Jimmy's side, losing count of the hours and days until, finally, his condition "turned." Slowly he got better, until a pediatric specialist declared him well enough to be discharged.

The ten-year-old and thirty-three-year-old never went home.

Overcome with relief, Mary Frances drove Jimmy back home. On the way, Jimmy spontaneously began to sing: "He's got the whole world in His hand. He's got the whole wide world…"

His mother frowned, bewildered. "Jimmy, I've never heard you sing that song. Where did you learn it?"

Jimmy shook his head. "Mommy, it's in my heart."

His declaration stopped time. Mary Frances hit the brakes and pulled off the road. All she could do was offer thanksgiving to God for saving Jimmy's precious life and promising as never before that she and Jim would raise him "in the nurture and admonition of the Lord."

And the calm, ever-stoic Jim Forrester was overcome with emotion and gratitude whenever he reflected on Jimmy's illness. God was good and had answered their prayers.

And then there was Mary Paige, plagued with constant kidney and urinary tract infections and on constant antibiotics until puberty. Though hospital rooms were familiar spaces, she was often treated at home by Jim. One night, a solitary and distraught Mary

Frances, wracked with worry, found herself rocking Mary Paige back and forth and offering up prayers that the high fever plaguing her little girl would subside.

She needed Jim so badly, needed his support and help. But he was out tending a mother in the throes of a difficult labor, and Mary Frances could not help but feel resentful. Her husband was off "holding another woman's hand"—another mother—while she was alone nursing and fretting over their own sick child.

Suddenly the little body in her arms moved, and Mary Paige's tired eyes looked up, full of concern over the tears silently streaming down her mother's face.

"Mommy, it's gonna be okay," she said. "I'm gonna be all right."

Mary Frances was torn between tears and laughter at the irony. Here was her sick, feverish four-year-old trying to comfort *her*, telling *her* it was going to be okay!

And it was.

Experiences of a Doctor

We make a living by what we get. We make a life by what we give.
—Winston Churchill

Dr. Jim Forrester was the ultimate professional. His lab coat was kept spotless as a Roman's senatorial toga, hiding a crisp white shirt and clean tie underneath. He presented himself always as the competent and collected physician he was. Even when, in practical terms, it didn't matter a fig what he had on.

As it often did, the Forrester phone rang in the middle of the night once, its shrillness shattering the sleepy domestic peace. Jim grabbed it and heard the voice on the other end inform him that a mill worker on the graveyard shift had sustained a deep cut and was losing copious amounts of blood. He jumped out of bed and, trying not to disturb Mary Frances, fumbled in the dark for his white shirt and tie hanging off a valet stand.

"Oh, just *go*," Mary Frances grumbled at having another sleep interrupted in the wee hours. "They won't care if you don't have on a white shirt. It's two o'clock in the morning for heaven's sake! You could wear a gunnysack and nobody'd care, least of all a bleeding patient."

Jim froze for a moment at her words, then dropped the shirt. "You're right," he said. "I'll be back as soon as I can."

Professionalism was paramount, but so was being personal. He didn't want his patients to feel rushed, like one unit on an assembly line. So he took his time with them, building a close rapport. His sincere bedside manner and the quiet concern in his voice invited confidences.

Jim knew his patients' names on sight, and he took an interest in their lives beyond the physical. Still, with so many patients, keeping track of everyone's personal details and evolving circumstances was tough. Yet he was good at it. Juanita helped out by scribbling little notes in a patient's medical chart before Jim saw him or her. She might have learned something through friends or simply by reading the announcement section of the paper that morning—or something the patient might have told her upon entering the office a few moments before.

"Don't you have a new grandbaby, Mrs. Blake?" Jim might say as he walked into the exam room. "Congratulations."

"I declare, Thelma, don't you look nice today with that new perm."

"Frank, good to see you! How are you liking your new job?"

There were perks to practicing in a small community.

Things could be a bit more complicated when it came to poor or uneducated patients. Occasionally, some, presumably on hard times, would covertly help themselves to the contents of the office storage room, filching bars of soap, toilet tissue, and to Jim's extreme annoyance, lightbulbs. Jim never said anything. Understanding to a fault, he felt that if the culprits were desperate enough to take food, he would not begrudge them.

Though he gave his patients the benefit of the doubt, he was unapologetically honest with them.

Enter Bill, a passionate lover of motorcycles who came in periodically with some new bodily ailment or injury incurred from his driving hobby. Jim grew increasingly worried for him.

"Bill, there's not a bone you haven't broken over the years, not a place that isn't scarred," he stated bluntly to his reckless patient. "I'm not sure I can put you together next time." He would not sympathize with the physical risks Bill deliberately continued to take. After doing his best to patch Bill up, he walked into his house that night vowing to everyone within earshot that "my children will never get on a motorcycle."

Unfortunately, he said nothing about his wife. He didn't think he had to. Mary Frances had to learn her own lesson when her brother

Tom, a daredevil, convinced her to take a motorcycle ride with him. Within moments, she was speeding down Stanley's main drag, digging her hands into Tom's sides and holding on for dear life. Worse, everyone in town saw her.

It is true that, in the words of country music singer Miranda Lambert, "Everybody dies famous in a small town." Thus, Mary Frances, knowing her excursion could never be kept secret from her motorcycle-disapproving husband, preempted the tongue-wagging and called Jim directly.

"Jim, when it gets back to you that I was speeding down the middle of town on Tom's motorcycle, don't worry. I'll *never* do it again!"

One of the things Jim loved about general family practice was the variety of complaints he was confronted with each day, everything from in-grown toenails to severed veins. No day was ever the same, and he loved the challenges and unpredictability of it all. His brain loved going to work on a completely new malady.

His abilities as a diagnostician were uncanny. Like a genius mathematician solving a complex equation, he could add up a set of symptoms, complaints, a test result or two, and a whole lot of natural intuition and come up with the right diagnosis. "He was the ultimate diagnostician," said his sister-in-law Sally.

An epidemic of any stripe—measles, chicken pox, flu—took a nasty toll on a community, descending like a locust plague and leaving a sleep-deprived and exhausted Jim in its wake. There were not enough physicians to go around, so the burden of seeing patients was especially heavy. Still, in the midst of exhaustion, he reaped a curious satisfaction in making so many sick well.

Adhering to a long-standing tradition, ministers and other clergy were treated without charge by Jim. This tradition arose from a historical reverence for the clerical calling in general, but in a medical context it suggests that physicians and ministers share many commonalities and a unique kinship. They both pull inconvenient hours, both draw the critical eyes and gossiping tongues of the very people they seek to serve, and both are charged with bringing relief and comfort to the sick and dying. In both cases they—the good ones, anyway—acknowledge that healing, whether physical or spiritual, comes ultimately from the hand of a gracious Providence. Perhaps this is why physicians and pastors alike tend to believe in miracles. That, and the fact that many have witnessed a miracle or two in the course of their careers.

One such episode is recounted in an e-mail written by Robert R. Gittens IV:

> In 1997, my dad, Pastor Robert R. Gittens Jr. of Revival Tabernacle Inc., collapsed in the office area of the church upstairs. 911 was called, and the paramedics arrived to find him with no heartbeat and not breathing. Dr. James Forrester, who was his doctor, was also called. He arrived after the paramedics. The paramedics did CPR, electric paddle shocks, and they worked on him quite a while; and at some point, Dr. Forrester told the paramedics to stop, that he was gone, and he was going to call the time of death. At this point, my mom, Rev. Ruby Gittens, who had been present the whole time, asked them frantically "if they were through and, if so, get out of the way."
>
> I guess they thought she was just going to say goodbye or something, but she jumped on my dad and started praying and said in the last part of her prayer, "You are not going to leave me in a mess! You get back here right now in the name of Jesus!" At which time, Dad's eyes popped open, and he breathed on his own again and almost scared the paramedics half to death. My dad later told this to numerous people that when he collapsed, his spirit left his body, and he was through the roof of the church but able to see and hear clearly everything that went on for all that time. He was able to recall everything that was said and who all was there and even what

everyone was wearing. He said that when Mom said that last part—"in the name of Jesus"—his spirit went back into his body like being sucked in by a vacuum.

This is a true and accurate story, retold here July 7, 2015.

Reverend Robert R. Gittens IV

Jim knew a dead man when he saw one, and Pastor Gittens had been dead. Jim did not—could not!—fail to acknowledge divine intervention, saying simply, "I guess the Lord's not through with him yet."

March 1996

A Gallup poll finds that 68 percent of American adults oppose gay marriage while only 27 percent favor it. Twenty years later, the same poll would reveal a radically altered sentiment.

May 1996

A film by Debra Chasnoff and Helen Cohen titled *It's Elementary: Talking About Gay Issues in School* is released and made available through Women's Educational Media. Intended for use in the classroom, the film presents lessons for educators on how to talk to children about lesbian, gay, bisexual, and transgender people for the purposes of addressing "antigay prejudice." Vice President for Concerned Woman for America Carmen Pate calls it "a training tool for breaking down a child's natural resistance to homosexuality."

The Asbury School Witch

You have witchcraft in your lips.

—Macbeth

In more innocent decades, every small rural community had a local "witch" that inhabited run-down houses and haunted the imaginations of frightened children on Halloween. Gaston and Lincoln Counties was no exception, except that their witch was extroverted, smiled a lot, and possessed singular flair.

Trained in theater, she knew the tricks of the trade. Her costume was thoughtfully planned—black tunic, orange-and-green striped socks, pointed hat encrusted with moss and fake critters, and lace-up granny boots. Her face sported warts and a hooked nose. On her belt hung a black bag packed full of spiders, snakes, and newts.

She was "born" October 31, 1971, and became known as the Asbury School Witch. Asbury Witch for short.

Her story goes like this:

Her husband was a doctor whose vocation made it impossible to plan trick-or-treat outings on Halloween as he was invariably on call and bound to the homestead. Even for the Asbury Witch, it was a scary venture to brave the neighborhood on the busiest night of the year with the sole charge of four sugar-high children to herd house to house. Babysitters on Halloween were *never* available, or she might have left the littlest ghoul at home.

To solve this dilemma, the witch and her husband decided to bring the whole compass of Halloween into their garage. They decorated every inch in mildly scary style and tempted passing neighborhood children inside with a generous array of candy treats and party favors.

The doctor, when there, distributed toothbrushes, sample vitamins, and other assorted healthy items to trick-or-treaters. These were not the most popular offerings, but then he had a reputation to consider, and he had seen too many cases of sugar-related health issues, from cavities to obesity, to feel good about encouraging bad habits and a careless disregard for nutrition. He teased his own children one year by declaring his intention to give out flu shots. What is scarier to a child than a shot?

"But, Daddy, nobody will come!" they cried, appalled.

Whatever they gave out, Halloween was a big night at the Forrester residence, and the Asbury School Witch was its star. So popular that she branched out, invited to appear at a host of events—school parties, festivals, church functions, Air National Guard dinners, and Jim's examining room by way of wifely pranks. Political fund-raisers would eventually come to be scrawled on her calendar, one of which would almost land her in hot water with the authorities.

The witch's children, not in the least afraid, loved to hold her hand and show her off about town. What other kid could boast an honest-to-goodness witch-mom! Jimmy remembers sitting at his desk at elementary school, having class as usual, when an unexpected chorus of squeals and shrieks would sound from a classroom down the hall. It would die down, only to erupt again a few moments later in another classroom, this one a little closer to his own room. The witch's modus operandi was hit and run: appear from nowhere, give a frightful scare, then vanish in a metaphorical *poof!*

The witch is coming, Jimmy would think to himself, burying his head in his hands. *Mama's here.*

Her doctor-husband enjoyed the novelty of being married to a witch and harbored no reservations about committing her, sometimes without her knowledge or permission, to both safe and socially perilous appearances. To these she preferred going incognito, her everyday identity strictly secret.

Superman-style, she could transform from everyday housewife into hero just about anywhere—phone booths, fast-food restaurants, gas stations, obscure clumps of trees. Octobers became such a busy season she borrowed a used dune buggy to get herself around with better stealth and efficiency. Brooms were for sweeping!

The Road to Morocco

Would you like an adventure now, or shall we have our tea first?
—Alice in Wonderland

Adventure tends to take one unaware and unprepared, as Jim and Mary Frances discovered in the early '70s on a nonworking, off-time guard trip. A party of NCANG guardsmen and spouses chartered a private plane and crossed the Atlantic, all to soak up the beauties and wonders of the Costa del Sol, the sunny coast of southern Spain.

Jim and Mary Frances had anticipated the excursion with excitement. It would be so exotic, so romantic! They had even set aside a longstanding pact never to fly together on the same aircraft, hating the idea of leaving their children bereft of both parents.

Not long after landing in Torremolinos, a whole new excursion took wings. "Let's go to Africa!" someone declared. Africa was so conveniently close, after all. What a waste not to cross the Strait of Gibraltar to Rabat, Morocco, for the day. Jim supported the idea, eager to stand on the African continent. Mary Frances too was drawn by the prospect of walking that mysterious and exotic ground.

The weather gods proved uncooperative and began to throw a vicious tantrum, sending brutal winds with currents that bent trees to the ground, like Persian slaves of old. The ferry over the strait was shut down, the operators knowing deadly conditions when they saw them.

Sensible tourist folk would have rescheduled the trip. Airmen are not always sensible. Flyers will fly in any conditions as their brains are wired to "complete the mission" no matter what. The day's weather was a minor glitch to them. No ferry? No problem! They would just hire a private plane instead.

Mary Frances balked at crossing the strait in a questionable-looking two-engine puddle jumper in stormy weather. "I'm not doing this."

"But you *want* to see Africa!" Jim reminded her.

Yes, she did—*before* the heavens exploded. Besides, apprehension was a mother's prerogative. "Who'd take care of the children!"

Every trip boasts one ringleader, mischief-maker, and comic. One "Pinky" Springs served on this venture. Ignoring Mary Frances's resistance, he and the other guardsmen formed a little ring around her and escorted her aboard the little hired craft, strapping her in tight.

"All will be well!" they assured her.

The journey proved every bit the rough and terrifying flight she expected. She held her breath during takeoff. Her tense muscles locked up whenever the plane butted heads with a pocket of turbulence, which was often. The forty-five-minute flight across the strait felt like forty-five days.

As they approached Morocco, however, the atmosphere calmed, and the gloom of the overcast sky dissipated before the glorious rays of an emerging African sun. The sight stole her breath away, and Mary Frances had to admit it was worth the nerve-racking flight.

Intent on making the day memorable, Jim and Mary Frances explored the markets and shops of the ancient Medina town, taking in the sights and smells of the Near East, both pleasant and not so pleasant. There were camel rides and the photos to prove it; a lunch of lamb, couscous, and fresh figs; and plenty of street vendors hospitably offering to relieve the Americans of their Yankee greenbacks.

Then Mary Frances saw it. The most beautiful Rabat rug, a heavenly vision in pure hand-knotted wool and vivid mosaic of blues and reds. Her heart fluttered. It must be hers, the ideal souvenir of their brief adventure in Africa. Ideal but expensive. The tag read $600.

"We can't afford it," Jim told her. "We're building a house."

"Yes, and that's why I want this rug. It's going to be perfect in the foyer!"

Their native guide, sensing her deep desire for the rug, approached the shopkeeper on the Americans' behalf. "I have brought these people here to your shop, that this lady really wants that rug. This is the off-season, and you need to give her husband a good price on this rug."

The shop owner gave Mary Frances a long, assessing gaze, then turned to Jim with a blunt, "I make you good bargain. I give you rug and three camels. You give me wife."

For a several moments, Jim's face registered astonishment. Had he understood the man right? Had something been lost in translation? Was the offer a joke, or did the shopkeeper really think Jim might trade his wife for a rug? Words failed him. All he could do was scratch his head, befuddled, and decide how to respond.

Mary Frances took Jim's protracted hesitance as consideration. *No, he wouldn't.* Would *he?* Was he actually entertaining the offer of bartering her away? *Lord, don't let me end up in somebody's harem!*

After a bit of nominal haggling between the shopkeeper and the guide, acting for Jim, a bargain was struck. It was a painful blow to Jim's wallet. He was always the frugal Scot.

Mary Frances had her rug, and arrangements were made for delivery. It would be carefully rolled and shipped to the beautiful American lady worth three camels and a fine Rabat rug. At least that was the promise.

"You do realize we'll never see that rug again," Jim presaged as they walked away from the shop. Ever a frugal Scot, he could be cynical when it came to his wallet, if nothing else. "Since he's already got our money!" he added. Shipping to and from third world countries was—remains—a gamble.

But it had been great day. Mary Frances had the perfect rug, and her children still had parents.

The Forresters' return flight to the States was another unplanned adventure, making the puddle jump over the Strait of Gibraltar feel like a walk in the park.

The night was black. Drenching rain and grumpy wind currents pounded the plane over the Atlantic. It only seemed to get worse the nearer they came to Charlotte. The crisis began when the hydraulic system for the plan's landing gear failed. The wheels would not drop, the pilot informed his passengers.

A shudder of apprehension rippled through the cabin. They had all seen the popular disaster movies of the day. Dysfunctional landing gear was always a preamble to tragedy!

"I *knew* we shouldn't have flown together!" Mary Frances whispered harshly to her husband.

Coming into Charlotte, the plane had to circle to spend its fuel. They might crash, but at least there would be no messy explosion. The luggage, extra weight, was next on the dump list.

An approach to the runway was made, but the landing attempt was aborted.

To further exasperate Mary Frances, the devil-may-care sergeant "Pinky" Springs, in the seat just behind them, began crooning in a lilting ironic tenor, "I beg your pardon...I never promised you a rose garden..."

Mary Frances was already shaking down to her toes in a terror and doing her best to be brave and keep calm. The sergeant wasn't helping. Her mind reeled, *The kids will be orphans after all! And I will never see my beautiful rug in the foyer!*

"Along with the sunshine...there's gotta be a little rain sometime," Sergeant Springs crooned on.

"Jim, can't you please ask him shut up!" she hissed under her breath. Fear made her irritable. Jim did nothing but remain his own stoic self in spite of their grim circumstances.

"So smile for a while and let's be jolly...love shouldn't be so melancholy...come along and share the good times while we can..."

Mary Frances, in a whirl of panic and aggravation, was already contemplating her death. Now her last act on earth just might be climbing over the seat and pummeling Sergeant Springs!

"You'd better look before you leap...still waters run deep...And there won't always be someone there to pull you out..."

The pilot's voice blared over the loudspeaker. "Okay, folks," he drawled, "we're gonna land the lady this time. But the emergency teams are standing by on the ground," he added, in an attempt to reassure everyone, "and the runway will be foamed. Everything's going to be all right."

As her hands gripped the armrests of her seat, ridiculous thoughts ran through her head. *I want those girls to have those red polka-dot dresses!*

She and Jim had just bought three red-and-black polka-dot flamenco dresses for the girls. So what if they were gaudy? Wyndi, Gloria, and Mary Paige would be cute as buttons in them!

The plane descended. Thankfully, despite a blown tire, the landing apparatus did not fail, and the plane dropped to the ground with a gargantuan thud, zooming down the landing strip amidst ruts and bumps before coming to an abrupt half. But without tragedy.

Providence had spared them.

Still, Jim and Mary Frances would not presume on God's grace. They never again flew together until after the children were grown. And "I Never Promised You a Rose Garden" became an oft-quoted reminder in times of hardship.

Providence was merciful yet again four months later, when Mary Frances's prized Rabat rug arrived in the small town of Stanley, where it graces the floor of the Forrester home to this day. Jim's inner Scot was mollified.

After the Morocco adventure, whenever Jim was peeved with Mary Frances over something, she would laugh and remind him of her high value. "Be careful. I'm still worth one oriental rug and three camels."

September 1996

The federal Defense of Marriage Act (DOMA) is enacted in large veto-proof majorities of Congress. It defines marriage "for all purposes of federal law" and protects states, under the Constitution's "full faith and credit" clause, from being forced to recognize as a marriage any "union" other than that of one man and one woman. The same day, Bill Clinton signs the bill into law. Perhaps worried about the fallout from a certain contingency of his political base, he refuses to hold a signing ceremony and allows no photographs of his putting his name to the document.

A rush of states enact their own DOMA-related laws.

December 1996

Following a ruling by Circuit Court, Judge Kevin S. C. Chang declares Hawaii's same-sex marriage ban unconstitutional and orders the state to cease denying marriage licenses to same-sex couples.

Jim the Boss

If a cluttered desk is a sign of a cluttered mind,
of what, then, is an empty desk a sign?
—Albert Einstein

As an employer, Jim required the highest standard of professionalism from those who worked for him. Punctuality was a sacred totem. As for dress, female nurses and administrative staff were required to wear skirts, in keeping with medical decorum of the day.

Still Jim was slow to change with the times. Rachel recalled the landmark day in the '80s when Jim conceded in letting her and her coworkers wear pants. "As long as you *look nice,*" was his firm condition. His reluctance might have sprung from a respect for modesty as much as modernity. As for the new baggy "scrubs" nurses were partial to, they were much too casual for the medical work environment in his view.

Beyond appearances, Jim expected much from his subordinates. Still he was always fair, as Juanita attests. "He never showed partiality among his employees." And while his demands were great, so were his rewards. Jim recognized the unique burdens of employment in the medical field and appreciated the sacrifices his employees, and their families, made to it—late irregular hours and long days of wall-to-wall patients.

In return, he was flexible and generous. That might mean a lengthened holiday, a long lunch to recover from an especially hectic morning, or the occasional dinner or theater show in Charlotte at his expense. One year, he even bought them their television set for office break room. Now they could watch *As the World Turns* or *All*

My Children during lunch on a slow day while Jim slipped home for his twenty-minute "snack nap."

He had a genuine concern for his employees' financial security and future. He gave them retirement benefits long before small and part-time businesses were required to do so, especially to women. He could provide no health insurance, but did extend profit sharing. His concern for his female employees' future can be traced to the economic struggles and financial insecurity of his mother, which haunted the back on his memory.

Jim's goodness paid off. His employees were loyal and stuck with him for many years—in spite of his untidy office habits.

"His desk was a disaster!" recalled Juanita, adding in wonder, "But he always knew where everything was."

Rachel remembered that his whole messy office was "not to be touched."

Tammy Johnson, who came to work for Jim in 2003, remembered that "if you touched anything on his desk, he knew it. And he never threw any mail away."

Assorted forms and reports, decades-old paperwork long since irrelevant and in duplicate copies, would pile up—as did drug samples and other medications he saved for missions and medical trips. "A little past the expiration date," he would say, "but still perfectly good."

He had been slow to make the transition from hard-copy records to electronic ones stored somewhere in the misty nebulous of cyberspace. At any rate, the mobile shred truck in the parking lot was kept quite busy.

To be fair, Jim's reluctance to discard things went beyond a mere personality trait. It was also a healthy exercise of caution as he was a favorite auditee of the IRS, an entity that seemed to particularly keen to penalize charity. He was audited by the IRS so often because of his multitudinous benevolent contributions (musical instruments to camp scholarships) that he felt impelled to cling to every scrap of paper. He even had to pay to have his books open for IRS auditors in training. Eventually, he engaged his CPA, Jim Hall, to contest harassment from the IRS, and in the end, they won the showdown with the feds.

But peek beneath the surface, and one finds that his pack-rat proclivities stemmed partly from a lack of stability growing up and his family's frequent moves. As with his threadbare overcoat in medical school worn down to translucence, holding on to things in perpetuity brought a sense of comfort, a feeling of endurance. Stir in a little Scottish thrift, and nothing was ever wasted.

Time especially was not to be squandered, even when he got calls summoning him to court to act as a medical witness in a legal case. This generally involved twiddling his thumbs in a hallway until the lawyers were ready for him. Jim had no patience with this waste of precious minutes and hours. It was not only his time, after all, but that of his patients.

"Just call the office when you're ready and I'll come," he would tell the court authorities and district attorneys. On one particularly hectic day, the judicial powers that be called and chided Jim for not being present at the courthouse. He was not *needed* anytime soon, but they wanted him there.

His response was blunt. "Look, I have an office packed with flu patients. Just call me when you need me, but give me thirty minutes to get there." He did not mean to be obstinate, but his patients needed him.

Nonetheless, a police car appeared outside a few moments later to collect Jim and escort him to the courthouse. He resented this high-handedness, and it frustrated him that they could not be sensitive to his position as caregiver.

If *they* were sick patients sitting in his waiting room, they would sing a different song!

April 1997

Lesbian comedian Ellen DeGeneres "comes out" on the cover of *Time* magazine with the words, "Yes, I'm gay." That same month, her character on her TV series *Ellen* becomes the first lead character to come out on a prime-time network show.

August 1997

The Provincetown, Massachusetts, school board votes to begin educating preschoolers about homosexual "lifestyles" and backs hiring preferences for "sexual minorities." "We are on a trailblazing path," said Susan Fleming, Provincetown school superintendent. Miss Fleming and Jeannine Cristina, the homosexual mother who pushed the initiative, said they hope to persuade other school system to adopt their "antibias" proposal.

December 1997

New Jersey becomes the first state to allow homosexual partners to adopt a child jointly.

November 1998

Two-thirds of Hawaii voters pass a measure to amend their state constitution to define marriage as a compact between a man and woman.

Humor in Stitches

There is a thin line that separates laughter and pain, comedy and tragedy, humor and hurt.
—Erma Bombeck

Day-to-day life in Jim's Stanley office never lacked a chuckle or two. It even saw the occasional prank. Not a bad thing. In the health-care environment, more than any other, comic relief is necessary for emotional survival, therapeutic for both patient and health-care provider alike.

An eavesdropping wall fly beside two doctors will enjoy the most bizarre anecdotes. There was, for example, the doctor who sat down to do a pelvic exam only to discover that his patient had dyed her pubic hair neon green. "My, aren't we festive today."

Jimmy Forrester, who followed his father into the medical profession as an electrophysiologist, remembers a woman who pierced through the fog of anesthesia to tell a joke.

"Knock, knock," said the unconscious woman suddenly from the operating table. Jimmy and all the other surgery participants, sterile and standing ready, jumped. Jaws dropped behind surgical masks.

"Who's…there?" Jimmy answered the woman in a tentative voice when his own heart started beating again.

"Iona," said the woman.

"Iona who?"

"Iona get outta here."

And then there was the muddled gentleman, still in drugged twilight following an operation, who lifted the sheet from his lower region and asked aloud, "Is it all still there?"

"Uh...yes, dear," said his astonished wife. "You had *back* surgery."

Jim had his own store of anecdotes, and he shared them if they were not inappropriate or a violation of patient confidentiality. Perhaps the choicest concerned "Billy," the four-year-old son of a respected deacon at a local church, who was brought into the office with a deep cut sustained from stepping on glass. "It's going to need stiches," Jim told Billy's mother.

Juanita injected a dose of Novocaine to the torn area with minimum resistance from the patient. But when Billy's eyes saw the needle and thread, all hell broke loose. He thrashed every which way, screaming as if the needle were a medieval pike and the thread barbed wire. He was too much for two people, so Juanita called Billy's mother in to "calm him down." This really meant *hold* him down.

None of this surprised anybody. Frightened children resisted and cried in Jim's office all the time. What was singular about this incident was the stream of explicit profanity that poured, unceasing, from Billy's tongue. Jim and Juanita were dumbfounded.

The mother's eyes widened in shock, her face red with embarrassment. "I just don't know where he got all that! I have no idea!"

No idea? Jim was skeptical. Billy was four and had not even started kindergarten.

For the rest of the day, Jim went about shaking his head in wonder. "I haven't heard language that salty since my Uncle Dan!" he told Juanita, referring to the rough and worldly merchant marine from northern Scotland.

In another episode, a miserable young Brian Miskelly was brought into the office claiming to be sick. His father, however, was all but convinced the boy was just trying to miss school. "If you're not sick," he had threatened his son, "if you're spoofing me, you're gonna get a whuppin'."

After examining Brian for a few moments, Jim asked with a smile, "Young 'un, how on earth did you make it here? Your throat's on fire, and those ears are terribly infected."

At Jim's words, Brian was vindicated, redeemed! His father hung his head and offered to buy his ailing son an ice cream on the way home.

Brian would always be grateful to Jim for the "whuppin'" he never got.

It wasn't just children that kept things interesting. Among Jim's not-so-bright grown-up patients was a middle-aged female who complained of terrible nausea, likely from a virus. Jim prescribed an appropriate drug that came in the form of a rectal suppository, a small dissolvable bullet-shaped object. "That should clear up the problem," Jim assured her, thinking no more about it.

Until he got a phone call from the woman a few days later. She was flustered.

"I'm not at all better!" she said. "I'm still vomiting."

"And the suppositories didn't help?" Jim asked, surprised. The treatment had always proved effective for that condition before. "How often did you use them?"

"I took them twice a day."

"Took them?" *Took them.* A light went off in Jim's brain. *Oh my Lord, she ate them!*

Trying not to lose his composure, he enlightened her as to why the prescribed course of treatment had not worked.

Jim laughed all the way home. Mary Frances laughed like crazy. They decided between them that the incident had been a *mis*-supposition of the worst sort.

Even the Asbury Witch stirred up some fun. Stuck between gigs one October day but having no time to go home in between, she headed to Jim's office. It was the season for tricks, and feeling mischievous, she conspired with Juanita to play one on the good doctor. Thus, an unsuspecting Jim entered an exam room for a routine pap smear and came face-to-face with the Asbury Witch, decked out in her full regalia, warts and all, her booted feet propped up in the stirrups.

"I needed to rest," she informed him, grinning. "Where else can a witch go to catch her breath?"

Jim just chuckled, rolling his eyes, when she gave him a kiss on the cheek. But he wore the imprint of her black lipstick all day, refusing to wash it off.

Compassion to a Fault

Compassion is a verb.
—Thich Nhat Hanh, Zen monk

The Roman philosopher and statesman Seneca the Younger had a maxim: "People pay the doctor for his trouble; for his kindness they still remain in his debt." Jim accumulated many, many debtors.

A shabby-looking African American gentleman was seen one day pulling a small Red Flyer wagon through the middle of town, apparently lacking any other means of transportation. Curled up inside lay a feverish, whimpering toddler. Gathering the child in his arms, he entered the Plum Street office.

"Doctor, my boy's very sick. Can you see him?" In his open palm lay fifty cents. "This is all I have."

"That's all you need," Jim said, proceeding with an examination. He did take the fifty cents, to spare the man's pride. The gentleman became yet another recipient of a paid-in-full Christmas receipt one year.

Doc Forrester accepted just about anything as reimbursement from patients who had no money or were mired in some economic crisis. Even animals—he loved God's creatures—were acceptable currency from time to time. He sometimes appeared at the back door hoisting a cardboard box filled with squirmy whimpering balls of fur, recalling to mind a simpler age when frontier physicians went home with a squawking chicken after patching up an injured settler.

Ignoring the appeal in his face, Mary Frances could only shake her head through the paned glass and mouth a silent but unequivocal *no*.

From time to time, Jim *bought* things from patients and counted the deal as payment for medical services.

"I bought an apple farm," he announced to his unsuspecting wife one day.

"You did *what*!" Mary Frances nearly dropped the plate she was drying and stared at him.

Jim launched into an explanation of how he had reached a mutually beneficial agreement with a patient in financial straits who was having trouble meeting the monetary obligations for his family's medical treatment. He proposed selling Jim an apple farm in the next county at Iron Station to settle the bill. Jim bought the property sight unseen.

His beaming expression reminded Mary Frances of a self-satisfied cat who drops a dead bird on the back doorstep, expecting human praise and gratitude for this generous offering that expresses his devotion. The owner's eyes see only a poor dead bird.

Was the man crazy? Did he have *no* sense of proportion! "Jim, I've been begging you for a washing machine. We've got two babies in diapers, and you buy a *farm*?"

It wasn't the first time he had made a big decision without consulting her. Still he was taken aback at her anger, unable to comprehend why she was so upset. In his reckoning, he had done a wise and wonderful thing for her, for *them*, and for their future. It was a prudent investment, or so he thought.

"It's good security, dear," he said. "Just wait. This farm will put the kids through college when the time comes. I paid a fair price, and it helped both buyer and seller."

Mary Frances was out of sorts for days.

A week later, a delivery truck rolled into the driveway. The driver informed Mary Frances with a congratulatory air, "Mrs. Forrester? I have your new washing machine."

Was this Jim's gesture of conciliation? Proof that her soft-hearted husband retained some sense? She sighed, happy to see the washer and dryer. As for the farm—at least they could enjoy plenty of fresh, ripe apples.

Alas, even that was not to be. She never tasted the first juicy bite. Someone always came under cover of night and cleared the ready crop before she could get any. All that remained were sad denuded trees. Well, at least the farm would help finance college tuition…

But no. By the time the older kids were ready for college, Jim announced that it was "not a seller's market," and they must keep the farm for the present. But nothing could dampen his long-term optimism. "When the right time comes, we'll sell."

Eventually, the apple farm *did* pay off, when Jim and Mary Frances built their last house mortgage-free.

Jim's compassion was a twenty-four-hour business with patients calling the house at all hours or just appearing without warning on the front doorstep. There were no emergency rooms and urgent-care facilities, so his medical office was never *really* closed. The lights might be off, the doors locked, and Jim and his tired staff preparing to head home after a long day. Then a knock would sound at the front entrance: a patient with hives or a parent holding a crying child who had sustained lacerations on his arms and legs.

"Can you still see us?" they would plead. "Please, we just can't wait."

Jim was no proof against distressed, pleading looks. "Let them in," he would respond.

Sickness does not discriminate among its victims, nor did Jim ever discriminate among suffering patients. Color was invisible, social status and political beliefs were immaterial, and sexual preference was irrelevant. No patient—male or female, black or white, gay or straight—was ever turned away.

"I treat them," he said. "I don't give them a sermon. They are entitled to the same concern and care I give all my patients."

Nonetheless, he never withheld appropriate warnings regarding the physical dangers, risks, and residual effects of any unhealthy lifestyle, effects which are borne out statistically. Medical ethics bound Jim to report the facts and not withhold information for the sake of sparing sensibilities. If they resented or misjudged him for his honesty, so be it.

Doctor-patient confidentiality and mutual trust were a sacred circle in which all Jim's patients rested secure, but he was especially careful to protect the privacy of his homosexual patients, particularly those who were HIV positive. This does not mean that medical ethics could not tug his heart in several directions at once.

On top of his regular practice, Jim did complete employment physicals for local industries and mills, including J.P. Stevens Company, Talon Inc., and Gaston County International Dying Machine Company. One afternoon, an applicant for J.P. Stevens named Zinny May entered Jim's office for a full employment physical, including a required breast check. A tall lass, she glided through the front door in a white lace dress, high heels, and thick blond wig.

While taking her blood pressure, Juanita's gaze was drawn to Zinny May's scrupulously manicured hands. "How tall are you, Zinny May?" she asked, curious.

"Six feet, flatfooted."

Juanita took the patient to an exam room to prep her for the physical, telling her to remove her dress and shoes and giving her a wrap for modesty. The patient was reluctant to undress but complied.

Juanita gave a parting smile, stepped into the hall, and called to Jim.

"Zinny May is a man," she informed him bluntly.

"*What?*" To be sure, the medical field never lacked for surprise. This was a first!

Uncertain how to proceed exactly, Jim went through the motions of the physical. It was awkward, to say the least. Still training and professionalism did not fail him, and he managed to keep a polite but neutral expression. Inwardly, he was bemused. Was the man consciously pretending or genuinely delusional in the belief he was a woman?

"I wanted to have implants, but they wouldn't do it," Zinny May informed him at one point.

Jim neither confronted nor contradicted Zinny May during the physical. Still, in their consultation later, he did offer a gentle warning. "You know, Zinny May...you might have difficulty getting the job you applied for."

When Zinny May had gone, Jim instructed Juanita to specify on his exam report that *"she* is a male" and then phoned J.P. Stevens' personnel director to share the truth about their prospective employee directly. Jim could not, by any code of ethics or patient confidentiality, participate in a deception.

The personnel director and other human resources guys at J.P. Stevens were baffled. They had shown Zinny May over the whole plant, opening doors for her—*him*—with gentlemanly care.

Through it all, Jim never mistreated or mocked Zinny May, to his face or behind his back. He was as kind to him as would have been to his own son. Moreover, whatever Zinny May's psychological or emotional state, he was physically sound. And for Jim, a whole and healthy human being was always cause for joy. Even so, thought the incident was bizarre and even comical at the time, it is an ironic peek into the controversy over so-called "gender identity" and gender-neutral restrooms raging today.

But for Jim, some days yielded no joy and no reward. They brought only a sense of powerlessness, the inescapable burden of a medical vocation. It was heaviest at the bedside of children, where "the least of these" suffered beyond remedy or hope.

There was the soul-wrenching day a ten-year-old girl with syphilis walked into his office. Overcome with astonishment and anger, he examined the child, made the bitter diagnosis, reported the case to the health department, and drove home with a broken heart.

In 1966, three-year-old Elaine Craig was walking home with her older sister when she pulled away and ran into the street. A car hit her.

Jim, knowing the little girl was "gone," accompanied her confused, grief-stricken mother in the ambulance to the hospital. Elaine was his patient, and Jim wanted to be near her even in death. And Eleanor, her mother, needed his assistance and comfort.

Jim, still a young doctor, had now been blindsided by the first great tragedy of his career, involving a *child*, and he faced the stark reality that he was, ultimately, helpless against the great enemy that is Death. Even the best doctors are only mortal.

But the tragedy of Elaine Craig was difficult for Jim to process for other reasons. He could not shake the recurring image of his own little girl tucked away snug at home, nor rid his mind of one terrible thought:

It might have been Wyndi.

It was the darkest day of his young career, and the night that followed brought no sleep.

Doctoring the Guard

I never saw him without a smile on his face. He had no mask.
                                    —Brigadier General Fisk Outwater

Jim was born with a good bedside manner. It was a natural gift, not something he had to "practice." And like his favorite stethoscope, he carried it everywhere he went in life—to his Stanley medical office each morning, to the TAC clinic at the Air Guard, to every hospital room he ever entered, and eventually through the halls and chambers of the General Assembly in Raleigh, where manners of any kind can be in short supply.

Even in the no-nonsense, unsentimental military environment, Jim's bedside manner was a welcome relief to many an ailing servicemen. Brigadier-General Fisk Outwater recalled his easygoing ways. "He had a gentle manner, gracious. He would sit and talk and positively reassure them. I had never seen that before and thought it unique."

Still, at the Guard, Jim could relax his professionalism just a bit and have a little fun with his calling. He would stand at the clinic door after finishing with one patient and, with an eager and diabolical grin, call out, "Next!" All Lieutenant X or Sergeant Y heard was, "Come on! You're my next victim!"

Flight physicals for pilots and crew members were his specialty. Jim had a great deal of say in determining who could climb into a cockpit and who could not. He combined a scrupulous duty to safety with much-needed common sense.

"Any of our members who encountered a problem," recalled Chief Master Sergeant Terry Henderson, "would want to see Doc

Forrester, especially if it could affect their flying careers. They knew how important those decisions were and trusted his expertise."

Because he was one of the few doctors qualified to do flight physicals, a special type of assessment, he was no less valuable in the commercial realm. He gathered quite a nationwide following among pilots who came to him for their physicals, originating from as far away as the West Coast and passing through Charlotte.

Brigadier General Fisk Outwater, flying commercial for United Airlines, experienced a terrible nosebleed the night before a trip. He managed to get it stopped and completed his trip, phoning Jim. Jim instructed Fisk to come in for an examination. "Here's what you're going to do," Jim said when the exam was over. Wanting a specialist to confirm his determination, he told Fisk to visit an eye, ear, nose, and throat doctor in Charlotte, a friend of Jim's, and instructed him to pay the doctor in cash, forget about receipts, and to send all the paperwork to Jim. Jim wanted a specialist's backup for his diagnosis but wanted to avoid the government red tape, though the final Federal Aviation Administration report would come from Jim.

The Charlotte doctor told Fisk that the dry air associated with flying, especially out west, for extended periods was causing the issue and that this would be a recurring problem for him.

Had Fisk first consulted another flight surgeon or the FAA, he likely would have been grounded and extensively "run through the mill of bureaucratic garbage" to clear something that everyone knew was not a real problem. It might have been a whole year before Fisk regained his flying status. Fisk was grateful to Jim, to say the least. Nonetheless, he is confident that "had it been a problem, Jim would have said, 'No, you're grounded permanently.'"

Jim loved doing flight physicals, almost as much as delivering babies. Perhaps that is why he was still performing FAA physicals two months before his death. It was the last thing he gave up in his medical career.

Jim, while concerned for the physical well-being of the guardsmen under his care, was also concerned for their spiritual well-being. Colonel Phillip Tillman, who met Jim in summer of 1979, when Tillman became NCANG chaplain, found in Dr. Forrester a strong advocate for the chapel program. "You didn't have to know Jim long to know he was a man that cared for you. For people."

Jim's sincerity and personality in the exam room won him a firm loyalty from friends and patients in the Guard, who often followed him into civilian life. Jim became Tillman's personal physician in the early '80s. Chief Master Sergeant Jerry Lathan and Lieutenant Colonel Al Rose both became patients, counting the drive from Charlotte to Stanley well worth it.

"Why do you go all that way to see a doctor?" Al's wife would ask.

"I like Jim," was Al's reply. "He talks to me as a friend, not just as a physician."

Doctors dread delivering bad news almost as much as patients dread hearing it. "But somehow," recalled Tillman, "Jim could make you feel comfortable and at ease even when the word *cancer* came out."

Bad news he gave in person, during a scheduled appointment, unwilling to leave the delivery of a negative diagnosis to a nurse or anyone else.

Compassionate but no pushover.

As in every field, there are those who try to game the system. When word got around that Jim was a family practice doctor in civilian life, Guard members began haunting sick bay with every possible ailment, many wholly unrelated to Guard service or its designated medical business.

To simply refuse people was bad form, but the trend must be curbed. In league with several other clinic physicians, including a proctologist, patients were informed that the "new procedure" was to perform a prostate exam on every male subject. Sick bay numbers fell quickly.

As in civilian practice, the occasional odd bird crossed the Guard clinic threshold. One such fellow begged Jim to write a prescription, for the benefit of the man's wife, that more sex was a medical necessity. At first, Jim thought it a joke, then realized the man was not kidding.

The overarching framework that encompassed all he did was his love of family. Of *families* military and civilian.

Chaplain Colonel Phillip Tillman would later relate an incident that took place when the 145th had been called up for duty in Kuwait. "In those tense, tearful moments of saying goodbyes, General Willian Lackey expressed his care and concern for those leaving. To which General Forrester replied, 'You're right, Bill, but let's not overlook the needs of the family members remaining at home.' This conversation displayed one of the general's deepest loves and one of the many shining salient traits possessed by him—namely, that the family was always in the forefront, no matter which hat he might be wearing."

Second, apart from his medical ability, Jim had a widely acknowledged gift for administration, and he made maintaining a full clinic complement a top priority. This meant *recruitment*. It helped that he not only knew all the medical specialties on the base at any given time but also all the good doctors in the area, such as Dr. James Mason, an optometrist from Gastonia.

Thanks to "Doc Forrester," the units at the clinic stayed fully manned. "He made sure there were enough and that they were *good*," observed Brigadier-General Fisk Outwater.

Soon after Jim's first retirement came the American invasion of Iraq known as Operation Desert Storm, when the 145 TAC clinic was all but depleted. Many of its doctors decided they didn't want to risk being called into long-term duty, possibly up to two years. This was disruptive to jobs and families.

The unit badly needed Jim and his crucial experience to recruit and train physicians to reman the clinic. Jim felt a duty to do so. So he did something few men would dream of doing, especially at an age upon which they could draw retirement pay. He surrendered his rank of brigadier general, his general commission, and reentered the Air Guard as a colonel until the clinic was back to full capacity. He "took off a star," said Terry Henderson, meaning Jim not only took a voluntary reduction in rank but in pay—simply to serve a need.

"A lesser man would not have done it," Colonel Steve Martin later wrote in the *Tar Heel Guardian*. "How many would willingly take a reduction in rank to best serve the interests of the organization?

Pride and ego would have gotten in the way of most, but Dr. Forrester did what was needed. The organization was bigger than his ego."

March 2000

California voters pass Proposition 22, restricting marriage to heterosexuals.

June 2000

The Supreme Court rules that the Boy Scouts of America (BSA) can bar gay scouts and troop leaders from membership, saying that as a private youth organization, it has the right to do so. Thirteen years later, under increasing pressure to change its policy, the BSA holds a vote on the controversial membership guidelines and lifts its ban on gay scouts.

September 2000

A same-sex union ceremony is performed in Wait Chapel at Wake Forest University, Jim Forrester's alma mater.

2001

The Evangelical Lutheran Church of America proposes Synod resolutions which would have terminated the ban on the ordination of sexually active gays and lesbians. A resolution is brought forth to create "a rite of blessing for same-gender committed relationships of lifelong fidelity," which would not be defined as a marriage. To avoid a serious division within the denomination, the church body instead starts a church-wide study of homosexuality based on biblical, theological, scientific, and practical considerations.

Holidays and Happy Hearts

*To many people holidays are not voyages of
discovery, but a ritual of reassurance.*
—Philip Andrew Adams

The Forrester calendar, like that of every other American family, was marked by holidays. They were anticipated with excitement and missed when gone. But for Jim, for whom holidays had been either nonexistent or humble affairs, they were an especially meaningful cause for excitement. He had to make up for lost time.

Every year on January 8, *his* birthday, the grown-up Jim would send flowers to his mother, Nancy. To a man who well understood the pain and sacrifice of childbearing and single parenting, it made perfect sense.

Of all holidays, however, Christmas was the one he savored most. He became a child again, determined to experience the Christmases he had longed for as a boy, the ones that *should* have been. Now he wanted to taste every morsel of the joy, fun, and family fellowship he had been starved of growing up.

He knew what constituted an ideal yuletide season, the camaraderie of a big, boisterous clan, the ritual of giving and receiving, the transformation of a common house into a shiny wonderland, and a dinner table spread with traditional American and Scottish dishes too special to serve any other time of year.

Not that he did much to make all the Christmas magic happen. In fact, he did as little as possible, happy for Mary Frances and others to shoulder the burden of preparation. It wasn't that he was selfish or indolent. Had he not sacrificed many a Christmas Eve flying home wounded soldiers or spent Christmas Day delivering someone's new baby?

No, it was simply that the work and stress and preparations spoiled the magic for him. No one understood this better than Mary Frances, and she bore no resentment. If he preferred to sit back and observe the transformation in wonder and anticipation, then she'd let him. He deserved it.

One Christmas, he gave new dolls to Wyndi, Gloria, and Mary Paige. All three dolls, of nearly identical cost, were adorable. But they were different. Seeing nothing *but* the difference, the girls took to fussing, each complaining that she had received an inferior doll.

Jim—a man accustomed to nuts, a few oranges, and a new quarter in his Christmas stocking growing up—was disappointed by their negative response, as well as the underlying assumption that they were entitled to *any* gift. Did a slight difference in dolls really translate in their minds as, *Daddy must love her more than me since he gave her a doll that was different?*

Jim was baffled. He could not comprehend this lack of gratitude, so he used the episode as a lesson in God's love and generosity. He may give His earthly children different circumstances and different gifts, but He loves them the same. They must be thankful to God—and their earthly father—for what they are freely given, which is not to be compared by small differences.

The Forresters did not restrict Christmas gatherings—any gathering—to blood relations. For widow or wanderer, there was always an extra place under the Forrester roof. A good thing too because Jim was highly prone to pick up strays. Lonely or displaced strangers, or anybody else who found himself alone during Christmas, were as natural a sight at the Forrester table as the Scottish hamburger, devilled eggs, Scottish trifle, and fresh strawberry pie—Jim's favorite dishes.

In 1974, Jim was headed to the post office about two in the afternoon when he spotted four men on the street in tartan sport coats. He approached them and learned they were a quartet of traveling gospel singers from Scotland touring the United States. His

Scottish blood thrilled, and he invited them home for supper that evening without a second thought.

The second thoughts, he gave to his "one-through-nine" wife when he called her a while later with what he had done. The conversation went something like this:

"Jim, it's already three o'clock!" Mary Frances cried. "I still have to pick up the children from school and take one to piano lessons. And what on earth am I going to feed those people!"

For Jim, there was only one answer to this: "Fix them Scottish hamburger. And a Scottish trifle."

"Jim!" Nothing in the fridge or pantry added up to Scottish anything.

"Oh, and you'll have to go pick them up and bring them to the house," Mr. Ten went on. "I'll try to make it home before dessert."

"But—"

"They'll have to eat early. They're singing at a church at seven and have to be there before then."

Mary Frances was fit to be tied. Apart from the food conundrum, they had just moved into their new house. All was still clutter and chaos, bereft of the essentials needed to entertain strangers. Sheets were serving as window drapes, for heaven's sake! She hung up the phone, mad as a wet hen, then rang neighbor Peggy for help. There was no time for a grocery run, but the two ladies managed to whip up a dinner with the resources of their combined kitchens.

It all came together in the end. Mary Frances, a good hostess, was outwardly cool and collected when she picked up the singers and brought them to the house. Jim appeared during dessert, eager to talk about the "old country" and savor a Scot-to-Scot kinship. He asked if they remembered his father, James. They had.

"What do you do about health care on the road, being from another country?" Jim asked, curious how they managed to take care of any medical problems.

"We have none," was the reply. "But we trust God to take care of us."

Jim got an earful from Mary Frances that night, but he just thanked her for all she'd done and told her not to worry so over the "small things."

A few hours later, the Forresters got a call. It was the Scottish singers. One of their number, Angus, was in severe pain.

"We didn't know who else to call!" they said, desperate.

"Don't worry," Jim said, then promptly phoned an internist colleague, Dr. Lloyd "Bud" Anthony.

"Take him to emergency room," said Anthony, who attended Angus until he passed a kidney stone the size of a Scotch egg. At least it felt like one to Angus.

Maybe it just needed a bit of Mary Frances's Scottish hamburger to get it moving.

Jim and Mary Frances could not help but reflect on the providential order of events that day. A perfectly timed meeting brought together an ailing singer in an alien land and a doctor who loved all things Scottish. God takes care of His children, they realized, and He does it through His *other* children. Mary Frances regretted her frustration with all those "small things" but expressed her reasons why impromptu dinner invitations deserve some consideration for the cook.

Nothing much changed about Christmas from year to year, except everybody's age. Jim still tried to wheedle the identity of his gift from Mary Frances while she slept (and got lucky on occasion). And he still liked his house and holiday table full, even after the kids were grown and had long since abandoned their own childlike eagerness with Christmas. His unspoken attitude was, *If God leaves me an empty chair at the dinner table or a vacant bed, then I am meant to fill it.*

It was a characteristic that his children emulated, bringing home roommates and friends from college who had no kin or were far removed either physically or emotionally from their family. Room at the Forrester Inn could get scarce.

"Wyndi, she is welcome to come for the *day*," Mary Frances told her daughter one Christmas when Wyndi announced to her parents that she was bringing her roommate Sarah home for the holiday. "But we're all out of extra beds."

Wyndi then explained that Sarah—bulimic, troubled, depressed—had received a curt letter from her mother with a less-than-kind message: "Don't bother coming home. We won't be there."

"Okay, bring her," Jim said. "We'll make room."

Guard Life Holds Steady

I wear this uniform so others can sleep well at night.
—Jim Forrester

Jim was proud of his Air National Guard uniform. On Fridays before guard duty, he readied it with meticulous and ritual precision. With a six-inch metal ruler, he measured every medal, bar, and ribbon down to the millimeter. Creases were razor sharp, shoes spit-shined to reflective glory. The immaculate garment, clean and pressed, was then hung carefully on the back of the bedroom door, ready for that 5:00 a.m. alarm to call it into action.

Mary Frances, heading to the bathroom in the middle of the night, would mentally salute "the Uniform" as she passed by, half in awe, half in wonder. Jim's fastidiousness with it was downright strange when he was so messy in other areas of his life.

But the Uniform was something apart, not to be touched by casual hands. Perhaps it evoked a sacred pride, reminding Jim of his prized American citizenship and the privilege of serving in his adopted nation's armed forces. He wore the Uniform, and all it represented, in a way most native-born citizens could not.

Still his assiduous care for the Uniform had another purpose, to set an example of excellence for peers and subordinates. Jim adopted this outlook in all areas of his life, but in the military, it was applied with double measure.

In years to follow, when appointed to adjudicate in the admission of candidates for military academies, he spent hours poring over student applications and files, giving opinions regarding the quality and shortcomings of competing applicants. If he were down to two or three equally qualified candidates and pressed for anything to differentiate between them, he would zoom in on the finer details—the haircut, the length of sideburns, the sharpness of the collar, the set of the head. A candidate's concern over such details in personal appearance might indicate an extra concern for details in military duties.

Jim was keen to cultivate the next generation of NCANG leaders. It was the duty of a good leader, a good officer, to find and encourage potential leaders for the future.

While a lieutenant colonel, he encouraged Juanita's son Steve Martin to enter the military, stressing it as a path that would return far more than college funds. It was a life experience of infinite worth, an experience to be gained nowhere else. And the North Carolina Air National Guard was the prime spot to start.

And there were practical advantages too. At the time, the Army National Guard had a much larger presence in North Carolina than the Air National Guard, a ten-to-one disparity. In the NCANG, Steve would have better opportunity for advancement.

Jim's influence in cultivating military leaders did not end with Steve. On March 29, 1980, a band of seven young men, all friends from East Gaston High School, enlisted in the North Carolina Air National Guard.

"Jim was responsible for all of them," Steve observed. Two chief master sergeants and a colonel eventually emerged from this band.

Jim followed the careers of his Gaston County boys and, barring clinic emergencies, always found time to stop and talk with them, on base or off.

Continental Guests

The exchange of students…should be vastly expanded…
information and education are powerful forces in support of
peace. Just as war begins in the minds of men, so does peace.
— Dwight D. Eisenhower

Jim's welcoming spirit was not limited to persons of any one hemisphere or continent, and the Forresters hosted a range of international exchange students over the years.

The endeavor was part of Jim's "giving back" but also as an educational vehicle to expand the cultural horizons of his own children, starting at a young age, as well as provide a safe environment for foreign students to discover the traditions, unique characteristics, and overall goodness of America.

In 1979, Roxanna was the first and, perhaps, the most beloved of their exchange students. In the six months she stayed, the Forresters grew to love the girl, and she them. Things were dark in her home country of El Salvador, torn by civil unrest and poverty. Brutal factions vied for power and had no respect for the age or innocence of the casualties they left in their wake.

For Roxanna, the daughter of a government official, circumstances were particularly threatening. Both private and public buildings were unsafe as bombings were a daily affair. Not even schools were immune to violence. Roxanna did not set foot outside her house without an armed escort due to the ever-present threat of kidnapping or other violence. She lived in constant dread that men would break through the front door and snatch away her father in the middle of the night.

It made for one terrified adolescent. Mary Frances was careful never to enter Roxanna's room or touch her, even gently, while she slept. She would jerk awake in fright, quivering, in the way of those who live in daily fear for their safety.

Tears flowed all around when Roxanna returned to El Salvador. Jim and Mary Frances would have loved to keep her with them always.

A few years later, the Forresters received their second exchange student, courtesy of Peru and an "Open Door" sponsorship. Her name was Yoko. She was Japanese, the daughter of a Sunoco Oil executive.

Yoko's mother and grandmother came to the States for a visit and were invited to dinner at the Forrester home. The evening began with cordial smiles and a host of customary Japanese bows. The aged, gray grandmother bowed nearly to the floor every time, causing worry the aged lady would flush, faint, or fall from the constant rush of blood back and forth.

Jim and Mary Frances struggled to understand what their guests were saying. Were they speaking Spanish with a Japanese accent or Japanese with a Spanish twist? Were they getting heavily accented snatches of English? Gloria Forrester, fluent in Spanish, did her best to bridge the language gaps.

If Roxanna was the most beloved of the Forresters' exchange students, Isabel of France—Isa, for short—was one of the more memorable. Her summer stay proved a unique cultural odyssey for everybody.

"We loved Isa. But she didn't want to take a bath." This was not a pleasant omission, especially at the height of a humid and sweaty North Carolina summer. Mary Frances, with genteel Southern discretion, constantly offered to wash the girl's clothes, especially her jeans. Isa would refuse with a carefree smile. "No, no. No bother."

Jim and Mary Frances swapped whispered realizations as to "just why the French wear so much perfume and why it's so strong." When the olfactory crisis reached its peak, Mary Frances ordered her daughters to take Isa down to the pool where Gloria worked as lifeguard. Maybe the chlorine would work some magic!

"And while you girls are gone, I'm going to wash those jeans."

A true daughter of Europa, Isa possessed its continental standards of modesty. These proved especially free on an outing to Lake Norman, where the girl cast off her bathing-suit top without a qualm before jumping in the cool water.

Isa's parting gift to the Forrester clan upon leaving was French perfume. It possessed base notes of humor with distinct hints of irony.

The '90s saw the Forresters welcome their final exchange student, Tatiana, a young Ukranian mother from Kiev trying to navigate a hopeful path in the wake of Perestroika. Leaving her son behind with relatives, she entered the States through an educational exchange administered by Belmont Abbey College.

Tatiana had her own cultural odyssey. She was overwhelmed upon first setting foot in an American grocery store. The endless full shelves and variety were too much for her.

At meals, she was shy about portions. She would pour a mere ounce or two of orange juice into her glass at breakfast and take only one or two baby potatoes at dinner. Second helpings of anything were beyond the scope of her comprehension.

"Tatiana, dear, you can have more," Mary Frances would reassure her at each meal. The foreign girl would always refuse. Whether from proper Ukranian manners or simple conditioning through years of want, Tatiana would not risk taking an excess of food. It was just too precious.

The kids observed their guest's humble frugality with something akin to awe, reflecting on the state of plenty they enjoyed themselves. "Mom, I'm ashamed of what we have," Mary Paige remarked.

"That's a good life lesson for you, Mary Paige," Mary Frances replied.

And yet, as is not strange for many people who experience want, Tatiana was generous to the American family who extended her hospitality. She first crossed the Forrester threshold bearing multiple gifts of the most colorful and unique Russian variety, such as a stunning array of painted spoons. Her bags contained more gifts for her hosts than clothes for herself!

She continued to correspond with the Forresters after her return to Kiev. In light of Tatiana's poverty, Jim and Mary Frances would send highly valued American goods and medicines for her and her son, much of which never reached her but ended up in the hands of corrupt Ukrainian customs officials. Disgusted, the Forresters began sending things via missionaries in the region.

November 2003

The Episcopalian Church consecrates its first openly homosexual bishop.

June 2003

The United States Supreme Court, in *Lawrence v. Texas*, strikes down a Texas law that bans private consensual sex between adults of the same sex. This invalidates sodomy laws in thirteen other states and legalizes same-sex sexual activity in every US state and territory.

November 2003

Massachusetts Supreme Judicial Court rules it unconstitutional for the state to deny marriage licenses to gay and lesbian couples; thus, Massachusetts becomes the first state to legalize same-sex marriage.

Guardsman's Wife

I love you, I salute you, but I ain't calling you sir.
—Mary Frances Forrester, to Jim Forrester

In the span of Jim's career as flight surgeon, he ended up in many far-flung pinpoints on the globe, from the Azores to Germany, from Iceland to Japan. If he were stuck somewhere due to mechanical issues or other obstacles, he spent his extra time collecting gifts for his bride back home. Oil paintings, furniture, china, silk fabric for sewing, and other assorted treasures found their way into Mary Frances's domestic kingdom. It was a perk of being a flight surgeon's wife.

A military officer's wife in the '60s and '70s could help or hinder her husband's career. She might even be the deciding factor in seeing a potential promotion come to pass. Military brass might ask themselves, "How will this woman represent her husband? How will she represent the United States military?"

Naturally, Mary Frances wished to be an asset to Jim, not a liability. But the honor of being an officer's wife brought its own pressures, some of them unexpected and unplanned. As she perused the drugstore in downtown Stanley one day, she noticed a strange man observing her movements a little too closely. After about ten minutes of this, he began asking her intrusive questions.

"Is this the pharmacy you use?"

"Where do you buy your groceries?"

"What church do you attend?"

"What's going on?" she asked Jim when she got home, describing her encounter.

"It's part of your security clearance, dear."

Jim was up for promotion to brigadier general. If he attained the rank, he would be privy to some of the nation's most top secret areas, places secured for times of national emergency or hostile attack. With higher promotion came greater obligation to his country and her safety. Wives also had to meet certain criteria and clear security checks before promotion could be granted to her husband.

Jim and Mary Frances apparently passed every security test, for Jim received the promotion, and the couple headed off to Washington for "charm school" with other generals-to-be.

There, husbands and wives received separate briefings, complete with closed-curtain meetings and guarded doors.

During the wives' instruction, Mary Frances realized with a sinking heart just how much was now expected of her—of Brigadier General Jim Forrester's wife. So many rules and restrictions when she was by Jim's side at military and other public functions. *Always*.

- She must be where she was expected to be at any given time. Never truant, never late.
- She must be appropriately and modestly attired.
- She must observe all proper protocol and fulfill her spousal duties like a soldier.
- She must remain calm and circumspect at all times.
- She must always make her husband look good!

There were more practical rules, though:

- She must clear any planned overseas trip through the State Department. The department would determine if there were any geopolitical concern or security risk that precluded her from traveling to her particular destination.
- She must not carry her military passport on her person except to military functions.
- She must never, in a foreign country, volunteer her nationality as American, much less her status as a general's wife. Jim would have information that other countries would be eager to possess. Even though Mary Frances herself was not

privy to that information, she must be careful not to jeopardize Jim's identity, military rank, or America's intelligence structure. Not even inadvertently or secondhand.

Some of the rules made her downright apprehensive:

If a uniformed Jim were in an official car in the States, his designated place was in the back seat on the right side. In another country, however, in the global shadow of terrorism and unrest, Mary Frances was told she must take this "hot seat" herself. She must remain the willing target for any hostile happenstance. She must always protect her valuable flag-officer husband.

This notion felt counterintuitive to Mary Frances, not to say frightfully unchivalrous to her Southern rearing. But she was a duty-minded patriot as well as a well-bred lady, so she would take the proverbial bullet if it were in her country's interests.

The first "charm school" class was barely out when Mary Frances declared privately, "Jim, I don't think I want to do this."

"Dear, at this point, you don't have a choice," was his blunt reply.

Both watched their *p*'s and *q*'s with rigor. Honesty and integrity mattered, even in the minutiae.

"Don't take any souvenirs with you when we leave," Jim warned. "Not the first pen or embossed napkin. Always leave a billet *exactly* as you found it."

Naturally, Mary Frances's grilling on security and intelligence precautions at charm school was nothing to Jim's. This manifested itself to her over the years at unexpected times and places, such as on one wintry November afternoon in London. Beneath its cheerful surface was a national tension thanks to the Irish Republican Army (IRA) and its recent spate of terrorist attacks.

Freezing, they descended some stairs into an underground pub for tea and toddies to thaw their blood.

Mary Frances had barely had time to decide between Pekoe and Darjeeling when Jim quietly said, "I'm going to leave some money on the table. Just get up and leave with me."

"What?"

"Just follow me."

Outside, he explained, "There was no other exit down there."

Exits were the first thing Jim looked for upon entering every place, old or new. Training forbade lingering in a room with no or limited egress, and he must respect and avoid the physical potentiality of being caught or trapped in the event of any attack or crisis.

It was a small incident, but a big reminder that a military member operates within a completely different mindset from a civilian, even when he or she is not in uniform or serving in a military capacity. The ever-present consciousness of the security, or lack of security, in one's surroundings is never turned off. Not in war, not in peace, not at work or on vacation, not on foreign soil or one's backyard.

Mary Frances walked arm in arm with Jim to countless ceremonies and functions, but metaphorically speaking, she was walking two steps behind. Everyone was respectful and kind to her, but Jim was the important one. He was the tribal chief, and Mary Frances was not co-chief but a lowly squaw devoted to making him look strong and capable. This was no easy position for one of Mary Frances's independent spirit, and on occasion, she felt this unspoken disparity keenly.

Her role as a subservient general's wife was often far more a burden than a boon.

Not long after the controversial 2000 presidential election between George W. Bush and Al Gore, Professor Pia, a member of the University of Rome faculty, invited Mary Frances to give a lecture to the school's United States History class on the Electoral College and the office of president. Jim would give a separate talk on the working of state government in North Carolina.

One evening, they returned to their hotel room and got a call from Gloria at her home in Peru. A crisis in that country was imminent. The bank for which Gloria's husband, Marco, worked had just been seized by a rogue government following a political coup by President Alberto Fujimori. This rogue government was unpredictable and ferocious in its zeal to gain power.

Gloria feared for her family's safety and wanted to return to the States with her two children without delay. Marco pleaded with Mary Frances to come to Peru instead.

"Just let us get back home to Charlotte, and I'll come," Mary Frances assured Gloria.

Back in Stanley, Mary Frances began a whirlwind of packing, her mind full of apprehension over flying into a third world county in the midst of political upheaval. But Gloria needed her! She grabbed the clean clothes remaining in her Rome luggage, added a few new items, and threw the whole bundle into one large suitcase of Jim's.

Within twenty-four hours, she was on a plane headed to South America. Upon arrival, her latent fears were validated as she hit Peruvian customs. It was discovered that the name on her passport did not match that on her suitcase tag. The tags read "Senator James Forrester," along with his credentials. In her haste, checking the names on the luggage tags had never entered her mind!

She was summarily escorted away from customs and sequestered in an obscure room in the airport. The armed government agents grilled her with the same questions over and over. Their eyes were full of suspicion, intimidation, and to Mary Frances, even an *eagerness* to find her guilty of some horrible capital offense.

"Why are you in our country, señora?"

"Why does your name on passport not match that on the suitcase?"

"Tell us, who is your husband? Why is he not with you?"

Mary Frances shivered in her boots. She would end up a political prisoner for sure!

Gloria, along with Marco, stood on the other side of customs, worried and ignorant of her plight. Her mother's plane had long since landed, but there was no sign of Mary Frances.

The "prisoner" did her best to explain things, treading the line between truth and reticence to avoid any traps. She could not, of course, give the real reason for her visit to Peru, and she avoided bringing up Marco's name and job for fear of risking the family's safety.

"I'm just here to visit my daughter for Christmas," she kept repeating. "And my grandchildren."

Then, without given any reason, the guards abruptly released her.

"We have decided you may go, señora," one said, opening the door and stretching an arm outward with a false smile.

Mary Frances just stared for a moment, surprised at this sudden change of heart.

"Your bags must remain with us, however," the other guard added.

That was fine with her!

She moved toward the door, almost more nervous than she'd been upon first being sequestered. Her heart pounded the inner wall of her chest, and her imagination entertained a host of possible scenarios—all of them unpleasant.

Was this some sort of trick? Would they grab her at the last second and haul her off to jail? Or even shoot her as she left, claiming she'd attempted to flee in her guilt for some contrived crime? She eyed their guns, fear blurring rational thought, and kept moving.

She was neither shot nor hauled away. Instead, she was met with relief by Gloria and Marco.

The authorities kept her suitcase for four days—four nervous days during which Mary Frances walked around in Gloria's clothes, unable to shake the distinct feeling the whole household was being watched, monitored. Worried questions as to what might happen next ran through everyone's mind. Might Mary Frances or Marco be detained? Was there a phone tap?

When Mary Frances finally talked to Jim on the phone, she shared what had happened.

"Just stay calm," he reassured her, ever unruffled. "It'll be okay."

Part 2

Wrong Ship, Right Destiny

Nancy Forrester and her two children had made it to America. Ellis Island was behind them. It was 1946.

They had barely stepped off one boat before they booked passage for another, one that would return them to Wilmington, Delaware, and the home of Peg and Bill Curran, Nancy's sister and brother-in-law. The Currans were now the Forresters' immigrant sponsors.

Unlike the ill-fated cargo ship, this vessel reached its destination safe and sound.

However, Nancy's exhausted eyes must have misread the schedule of ships back in New York, or she had followed signs to the wrong pier of departure, or the Unseen Hand tweaked things once more. Whatever it was, the little immigrant trio stepped off the boat, not in Wilmington, Delaware, but in Wilmington, *North Carolina*. It was a quaint town on the Cape Fear River, little more than a fishing village that had once been a strategic Civil War port.

There was no money left for passage back north, so the Forresters stayed where they had landed and set about making a permanent home. Nancy had packed few material possessions for the voyage, but she did make room for her greatest treasures: her wedding china, the swivel rocker in which she had rocked her three babies, and a cluster of photographs to remind her of happier days. She packed only half her heart. The other half remained buried in Hillfoot Cemetery.

It wasn't the first time the wrong boat had sailed someone to the right destination. In this instance, Providence had a purpose for Jim in the Tar Heel State.

Generous Love, Loving Gestures

Food is symbolic of love when words are inadequate.
—Alan Wolfelt

Jim loved his children deeply, but the phrase "I love you" did not fall easily from his lips. It was a mix of Scottish stoicism and his own native reserve.

It was more natural to express his love for his children in other ways: a ball game, singing to them, or splurging on a train trip to Disney World. Maybe it was slipping an unasked-for twenty-dollar bill into the pocket of their jeans.

But Jim's favorite vehicle for demonstrating love, for family or anyone else, was making sure you were fed and fed *well*. It is hard for modern generations of Americans, born into a world of relative plenty, to comprehend this mindset. To them equating a meal with love seems shallow or crass, but in the reckoning of previous, needier generations, it makes sense.

In days past, a husband and father who truly cared for his family provided it with food, the most essential form of sustenance, and did so even in economically strapped conditions and at great labor and personal sacrifice. Filling the bellies of a wife and children with nourishment was an expression of love every bit as sincere as a sonnet and every bit as open as a message written across the sky by plane.

Material need has diminished in our culture, but this mindset of expressing love through provision lingers in older generations. Thus, Jim was always concerned that there was plenty of food to be consumed. It was a concern for the ten-year-old paperboy and the seventy-year-old senator.

187

Besides, to feed a family member or friend afforded a sense of personal gratification, and Jim would not be robbed of the pleasure of paying for meals. If you wanted to pay for your own lunch or dinner, you had to plot with the waitress ahead of time. Fail once, as Jim's future son-in-law Thomas Blalock learned, and there would never be a second chance. Jim would be wise to you then.

On a simpler level, paying for another person's meal was a manifestation of Jim's generous heart, and it didn't discriminate. If he loved you, he fed you. If he *liked* you, he fed you. If he didn't like you, he fed you anyway. If you were a complete stranger, he just might feed you!

Jimmy recalls one clear example of this from his boyhood. He and his father had finished lunch at Morrison's Cafeteria and were headed to the checkout register when they stopped at the booth of a solitary, disheveled-looking man. Jim smiled and spoke with the man for several minutes while Jimmy's attention was elsewhere. When they were finished eating, Jim pulled out a twenty-dollar bill and set it down on the man's table. "Your dinner's on me tonight."

"Who was that man?" Jimmy asked while they were headed to the car.

"I don't know, son," said Jim with a shrug. "Just a man who wanted to talk to somebody and was eating by himself."

Nor was it strange for Jim, in the drive-through at a fast-food restaurant, to make the spontaneous decision to pay for the meals of the car behind him.

Yet there were times when Jim's magnanimity toward others was hard for his family to understand, as on the day Mary Paige had a fender-bender with a poor uninsured man. To her astonishment Jim paid to fix *his* car while Mary Paige was stuck with the bill for her own repairs. Mary Paige was angry. The other driver had been at fault!

Jim didn't waver. "I'm not going to fight over a bumper."

"Dad, it's the *principle* of the thing."

No one understood standing on principle better than Jim, but he understood grace too, and there were times when grace was the greater virtue.

Fed Up

There used to be so much charity.

—Jim Forrester

On a planet that screams for free health care, it is ironic that one can be penalized for giving it.

This was not always the case. In simpler days, good-hearted doctors such as Jim Forrester would work independently or jointly in pro bono ventures such as "well-baby" clinics, vaccination drives, and various health screenings. Such public offerings helped needy individuals but also contributed to a healthier overall community in that waiting-room crowds were lessened and widespread health crises often averted prevented.

Then, as if overnight, every eye check and throat swab must be religiously documented on an insurance schedule or government form, and the fee for it recorded in a great, nebulous computer database. The expanding "health-care industry" adopted a simple dogma: *somebody* must pay, and somebody must *be* paid, and it all must be in writing somewhere. "Free" was no longer a true option.

A sick and desperate patient named Philip came to see Jim one morning. Before Jim had even examined him, Philip expressed worry that he would be unable to meet his financial obligation for treatment. He was a working man of little means, but he needed help.

Jim told him not to worry about it. Philip's case necessitated treatment regardless. "Just pay me what you can," he said, treating Philip and sending him home. Simple.

At least it should have been.

When Christmas rolled around, Jim pulled Philip's file and wrote "PAID IN FULL" on the patient's account balance sheet and sent a copy to him with a cheery note saying "Merry Christmas!" Rachel marked it "gift" in the practice's accounting books. Jim did this every Christmas with at least one of his patients. But this time, because of a collection discrepancy in the paperwork, the regulators pounced. Jim was forced to make up the difference himself. Now charity would come with a price.

"I can't even give my charity to a needy patient," he lamented. "*I have to pay for it. It's not like I can just give it to them and keep it off the books.*" It rubbed a raw spot in his sense of justice and offended his compassionate nature. The high-handed medical powers that be apparently wished to make generosity next to impossible.

To Jim, this was wrong. A trained, competent, certified physician should maintain the prerogative to give his expertise and care away for nothing if he chooses. It was not merely a question of helping people in need but of *liberty*.

"They're tying my hands," he remarked often with disgust.

He grieved that there was increasingly less professional discretion allowed in the examination room, less freedom to modify treatment to fit the circumstances and needs of a particular patient. One of the most frustrating examples involved a pneumonia patient, a single father living paycheck to paycheck, who showed up in his examining room one afternoon.

"Richard, you need to go to the hospital," Jim told him.

It wasn't that simple.

"I can't," Richard replied. "I have kids at home. I've *got* to work!"

If anybody could sympathize with this, it was Jim. So he was flexible and offered a solution that would allow the man to fulfill his familial obligations *and* get well without risk of infecting others. "The only way you can stay out of the hospital," Jim told him, "is to come in here every day for a high powerful antibiotic injection and a chest x-ray."

It was reasonable, but reason does not rule in the murky, confused, and often greedy landscape of medical insurance. Jim was contacted by a self-important insurance representative that knew little about the patient's physical condition and nothing about his personal situation.

Jim tried to explain things to this "suit behind a desk" at the other end of the phone line, but the man's ears were stopped with wax, and his mind stuck in a rigid system of procedural dictates.

"Dr. Forrester, why did you give him this antibiotic when you could have given him an oral medication?"

"No, I *couldn't*," was Jim's terse reply. "He *couldn't* go to the hospital. And I saved you thousands of dollars on a hospital stay." The antibiotic injection was far cheaper at three hundred dollars per dose.

All his explanations fell upon stone in the end. The antibiotic injection would *not* be covered, he was informed.

But they would have covered a hospital stay? Ridiculous!

Jim's inner Scot refused to back down on the matter. His patient *would* have that injection. "And I'll eat it before I put him on an oral medication," Jim said.

Medicare proved another thorn in the good doctor's side. It cost Jim eight dollars for each Medicare patient that came through the door because he was not reimbursed what he would normally charge. Still, his regular, longtime patients went on the program with his full acceptance and goodwill. They were *his* patients, and he did not mind taking the loss.

A high-handed Medicare watchdog called him one morning, saying Jim had overcharged three patients that had recently moved from private patient status to Medicare status. Jim had not noted the new fee on the billing form and had charged his full regular assessment. He was then baldly informed that he would be fined $20,000 and his books opened for a complete inspection to ensure he had not done this on a regular basis. To pile insult upon injury, he must send an apology letter to the three patients!

All for an honest mistake! Because his busy staff had not immediately caught the status change.

It was ludicrous! "Do you really think I would put my life practice on the line for twenty-four dollars?" was Jim's response. It was a paltry sum on which to risk one's reputation and livelihood.

Nonetheless, he was forced to secure an attorney and an accountant at his own expense for Medicare officials to examine his account books.

Disgusted with the "carpetbagger FEDs," Jim vented his outrage in a letter. Its general spirit can be summarized as follows: "You sit up there in your office with no medical experience, and you're trying to tell me how to treat my patients! How dare you!"

"That was the first time I ever wanted to shut my door," he reflected afterward,

Medicaid was no better than Medicare, but no matter the agency or insurance company calling the shots, their regulative bureaucrats were relentless and arrogant in telling Jim how to handle his patients and practice. He "needed to do" this and "shouldn't do" that.

Jim wanted, *needed*, to be in control. It was the only way to ensure optimal and reasonable, personalized care for the patients in his charge.

Then came Viagra, for which Jim received an absurd rush of requests. This would leave him further aggravated at the disparity and want of judgement inherent in the insurance guidelines and allowances. A man was allowed Viagra for erectile dysfunction with little question, but a diabetic woman for whom pregnancy was a high risk could be denied birth control pills!

Few would meet with a more easygoing fellow than Jim Forrester. But if anything could rouse his bull-dog tenacity, it was the maze of red-tape regulations and impersonal bureaucratic assessments and requirements imposed on physicians, nurses, and patients alike—far removed from the flesh-and-blood patient-physician relationship. The very *heart* of sound patient care was being belittled and violated.

He was fed up! The whole system was bloated, constrictive, intrusive, and inequitable. His disgust would become the major driving force that impelled him to seek a seat in the North Carolina General Assembly.

Ironically, the rules would thwart him even then. A prospective senator, he was informed, was not allowed to work at the health department, a place Jim had already served for twenty years at no compensation to himself. But as the department was supported with state funds, his charitable involvement was now deemed a "conflict of interest," and he must give it up before taking office.

February 2004

President George W. Bush calls for a federal constitutional marriage amendment that defines marriage as a union between one man and one woman as husband and wife.

March 2004

A gay couple is denied a marriage license in Durham County, North Carolina. They immediately file suit.

May 2004

The first legal same-sex marriage takes place in Massachusetts.

County Commissioner

If you want to know if you have the stomach for politics,
start at the county level. That's gutter politics. If you can't
handle that, you'll never survive any higher office.

—Jim Forrester

Jim loathed being referred to as "politician," and he liked to quote comedian Robin Williams, who defined the word as *poli* being "many" and *tic* being "a blood-sucking animal."

He was not the stereotypical political personality. Jim the commissioner, and later Jim the senator, was no different than Jim the man, the doctor, the guardsman.

"He was quiet, mild-mannered, and soft-spoken," his friend and financial advisor Dick Jarman remembered. "He was not forceful in talking about his ideas. He wasn't a political showman or sales personality like others in politics."

Nor did he adopt a showman's ways, being too honest to employ half-truths, embellishment or hyperbole to win people over to his way of thinking. Citizens and voters he met realized this intuitively.

It was his minister, Reverend Charles High, who first asked Jim if he'd ever considered seeking public office. Jim was resistant to the idea at first. Then Charles Alexander "Chappie" Rhyne, a Gaston County commissioner on the cusp of retirement, encouraged him to run for his soon-to-be-open seat, the Riverbend Township. It was then that Jim felt the Unseen Hand nudge him into running.

Mary Frances felt no hand at all and was aghast when Jim informed her of his intention.

"Politics? When are you going to do politics? You don't have time as it is!"

"Dear, it's only one Thursday meeting a month," he assured her. "If people who are smart and capable don't help fix things and do things right, then we have no right to complain." His motives were pure. It was not about ego or attention but another way he could "give back." How could she not approve?

So in 1982, Jim Forrester, a Democrat, ran for Gaston County commissioner for the Riverbend Township and won, launching a twenty-nine-year odyssey through the realm of elected public service, with all its potentialities and perils. The "one meeting a month" claim, however, proved a ploy on Jim's part, as Mary Frances had suspected. The office demanded far more time and energy than that.

In 1990, Jim's eighth and final year as county commissioner, he was elected chairman of that body. But by then, he was wrestling with his party affiliation, and a crisis of conscience had begun to build.

It was the same for Mary Frances, who found it increasingly hard to endure Democrat gatherings. The speakers and members said things she cringed to hear and advanced ideas that were increasingly more liberal and un-American. Enough was enough.

"I changed my name, my church, and my political affiliation for you," she reminded Jim. "But I will not change my values or be intimidated into silence over them. We're not liberals."

Damning the proverbial torpedoes, Jim paid a visit to Governor Jim Martin, the second Republican governor since Reconstruction, and officially changed his party affiliation. "I did not leave the Democratic Party," he announced at a press conference at the Capitol building in Raleigh. "The Democratic Party left me. I'm still the same person with the same values I've always had."

It was a painful switch. One vindictive Democrat senator even threatened Jim with, "I'll make sure you rue the day you did this."

Jim figured it was the end of his career as a public servant. He'd be lucky to serve out his term as county commissioner! Nevertheless, principle trumped politics, and he refused to live as a hypocrite merely for political security.

Besides, he always found an abiding peace in doing what was right. It was its own comfort. So he did not look back but resigned himself to whatever outcome Providence saw fit to allow.

When it came to the marriage amendment, Jim would choose this path again and, in doing so, would realize two clear truths:

First, doing what is right in a fallen world incurs great risk.

Second, a fallen world will hate you for doing it.

Jim, Sister Sheila and Mother Nancy just arriving in America

James Summers Forrester, Scottish golfer of renown

Soda clerk at Futrelle's Pharmacy

A drum major

Mary Frances All and James Summers Forrester, married
in March 12, 1960 in Wilmington, North Carolina

New doc in his office

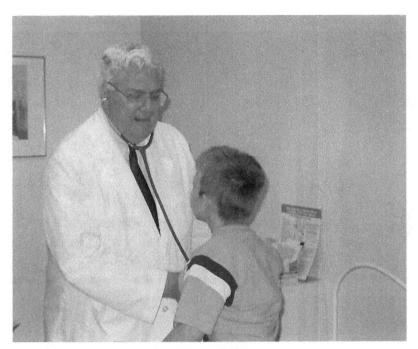

Jim loved his young patients

In Belize, on his way to remote medical clinic

"Doctors' After Hours," Jim is fourth from left

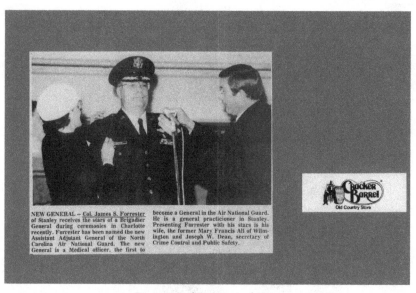

NEW GENERAL -- Col. James S. Forrester of Stanley receives the stars of a Brigadier General during ceremonies in Charlotte recently. Forrester has been named the new Assistant Adjutant General of the North Carolina Air National Guard. The new General is a Medical officer, the first to become a General in the Air National Guard. He is a general practicioner in Stanley. Presenting Forrester with his stars is his wife, the former Mary Francis All of Wilmington and Joseph W. Dean, secretary of Crime Control and Public Safety.

Receiving his General Star

Jim and Mary Frances's thirtieth anniversary dinner in Paris

Giving a veteran a long overdue medal

Flying with cargo to European theatre

After a confetti parade in Bolivia

Veterans' Victory Parade after Desert Storm

At his "busy" Senate desk

With HRH Dom Duarte, Duke of Bragança in
Washington, DC, just prior to Knighting Ceremony

Just following Robing at Knighting Ceremony

Billy Graham

The Worst Weekend

The world will allow you only a few days to mourn and then it
quickly returns to orders of the day and you are left to grieve alone.
—Proverb, quoted by Nancy Forrester

It all began as a normal Saturday morning in late summer of 1988.

Jim was on duty at the Air National Guard base in Charlotte. The girls were working summer jobs to earn money, Gloria as a lifeguard at Cowen's Ford Country Club and Mary Paige as a waitress at Carrie's Fish House in Mount Holly. Jimmy was off on his summer swimming circuit. Gloria and Mary Paige were preparing for their return to Wake Forest in the following weeks, and Jimmy for his first semester at North Carolina State.

Mary Frances had a lot on her mind. Three kids in college at once was proving a financial strain on the family. On top of tuition and other expenses, the Forresters were also supporting Nancy, Jim's widowed mother, and providing medical support to Mary Frances's mom.

"But we'll manage," Mary Frances told herself. "We always have."

But where on earth is Precious? she wondered as she worked. Precious was the family's little Lhasa pPoo. She had not appeared at breakfast, and there was no sign of her now. Mary Frances was worried.

Around noon, the phone rang. It was New Hanover Memorial Hospital in Wilmington, calling to speak with Dr. James Forrester. Through the phone line came the dreaded words, "There has been an accident." A tragic one, wherein a car had hydroplaned across a rain-soaked highway into oncoming traffic and was struck by another vehicle. The three persons in the car were killed instantly: one male and two females.

Mary Frances hung up the phone, heart thumping as she made preliminary arrangements to drive to Wilmington. She would wait until Jim came home to break the awful news. One of the women killed in the collision was Sheila Long, his sister. Sheila's husband, Dan, was also dead, along with a family friend.

Jim was blindsided and shocked upon being told, but there was no time for reality to sink in. They had to get to Wilmington and Jim's mother immediately.

Thus began a two-day surreal blur. Much would be done and little remembered later.

Reaching Wilmington after sunset, Jim and Mary Frances collected a distraught Nancy and headed to Coble Ward-Smith Funeral Services, where the necessary arrangements for a double-funeral ceremony and burial were made. The bodies were too horribly mangled to be embalmed, they were told. It would have to be a closed-casket ceremony, and time could not be wasted in having them interred.

Back in Stanley, Mary Paige finished her evening shift and drove home in a heavy rain, tired and ready for bed. There was a note left on the refrigerator: "Please look for Precious," was all it said. Mary Paige obeyed, only to find the dog's broken and motionless little body near the end of the driveway, some distance from the busy road. Precious's dark head rested on a stone. A car had most likely swerved on the slick road and struck her, throwing her some distance and killing her upon impact.

Tears streaming, Mary Paige called her father at Nancy's to tell him what had happened. He told her, rather brusquely, to "just get the shovel and bury her." He would miss little Precious, but her loss weighed little against that of losing one of the three remaining persons on the continent with whom he shared blood kinship. Losing Sheila was tragedy enough to process emotionally just then. To further shake his mental equilibrium, he had almost lost his mother as well. By some blessed chance, Nancy had opted at the last moment to stay home that rainy night instead of accompanying her daughter and son-in-law to dinner.

So Mary Paige carried out the morbid task of burying Precious, the adored family pet, in the backyard in an uncaring rain.

The Longs' financial situation had not been ideal at the time of their demise, leaving the Forresters with the burden of assuming the funeral costs. Mary Frances arranged with her family to have them buried in the All plots at Greenlawn Memorial Park. Sheila's daughter, Nancy Jane Foster, participated in planning other details.

Sleep came to no one that night. Or the next. Jim and Mary Frances sat up in bed together in the darkness, holding hands and not bothering with useless words. They just took silent comfort and shelter from each other during a storm of helplessness and grief.

The exhausted pair returned to Stanley on Monday following the funeral, only to discover that Fate had dropped exchange student number three on the doorstep: Isabel, from the land of berets and baguettes. Amidst all the death and tragedy, the French girl's coming had slipped everybody's mind.

To wrap up a weekend already under a black cloud, the dreaded Wake Forest and NC State tuition bills were both waiting in the mailbox. The sums due were every bit as daunting as expected. The recent funeral costs had already left a sizeable and unforeseen dent in the family budget.

Still, Jim and Mary Frances found their fortitude, took lots of deep breaths, and emphasized to their children the necessity of "fulfilling one's duty" with regard to their Gallic guest.

"We are *not* going to walk around here like duds and mopes for Isa," Mary Frances said.

So each family member went through the expected motions as cheerfully as possible, never mind the black cloud of grief and worry hovering over the roof.

"If you have to cry, cry in private," Jim admonished.

It would all go down in the collective Forrester memory as "the worst weekend ever."

January 2007

I think he saw himself as a modern Wilberforce to protect marriage.
—Mary Frances Forrester

If you are willing to abandon your principles for convenience, or social acceptability, they are not your principles. They are your costume.
—Anonymous

In early 2007, Jim introduced SB13 Defense of Marriage. Like its predecessors, the bill called for a vote of North Carolinians on a constitutional marriage amendment. But getting the bill through General Assembly was even more a challenge now, considering the increasingly unfavorable ideological makeup of the legislature.

In a January 29 email to Mary Frances and others, dDirector of Government Relations for the North Carolina Family Policy Council John Rustin lamented the uphill battle "with essentially the same leadership in the Senate and a new leadership in the House that had traditionally not supported the marriage amendment, we have our work cut out for us. We need to do all we can to rally the troops and communicate to legislators how important the marriage amendment is for North Carolina."

As previously, there was little hope of it making it out of committee, much less reaching the floor for a vote. Even if it did, the pro-amendment forces still needed a three-fifths majority in both chambers of General Assembly for ratification.

Still, Jim believed the votes were there. "If it were heard in committee, I think it would pass," said Jim, "If it was heard on the floor of the Senate or the House, it would pass."

Those attempting to discredit the legislation were quick to the scene, rehashing all their old objections and arguments. Addressing the *New Bern Sun Journal*, Ian Palmquist characterized the attempt to pass the amendment bill as "more about political posturing and appealing to the Republican base than addressing a real problem for the people of North Carolina."

Senate President Marc Basnight, who voted for the Defense of Marriage statute in 1996, now refused his support for an amendment that said essentially the same thing, claiming there was no need for a constitutional change. He scoffed at concerns that a judge might strike down the DOMA statute by declaring it unconstitutional. "Is there any sitting judge that would even attempt to do that? No!"

Basnight's claim, in light of recent legal decisions that had done exactly that, was an outright insult to the intelligence of North Carolina's electorate.

Jim knew better. The possibility was all too real, inevitable, and imminent that an activist judge would deem the statute unconstitutional. An amendment was the only safeguard. "If you put in in the Constitution, it wouldn't *be* unconstitutional," he said.

Apart from accusations of political motives and time-wasting, the opposition issued frightening warnings to confuse the amendment issue and frustrate public support for it. Palmquist asserted that any change would result in judges denying domestic violence restraining orders to unmarried, opposite-sex couples, claiming this had occurred in other states—also that the amendment wording could result in misinterpretation that prevented companies from extending benefits to same-sex couples.

In fact, there was nothing in the language of the amendment that would prevent private companies from extending said benefits.

Things looked grim for amendment supporters until, through a series of small miracles out of the Carolina blue, it looked as if the 2007 marriage amendment bill might get somewhere.

It began when Representatives Tim Moore (R-Cleveland) and Linda Johnson (R-Cabarrus) managed a recall motion, a rarely exercised parliamentary maneuver, to secure a hearing of HB 493 (the House version of the marriage amendment bill) in the House Rules Committee. Once there, Majority Leader Hugh Holliman (D-Davidson) promptly moved to have the amendment bill referred to the House Judiciary Committee, essentially condemning it to death.

To everyone's surprise, the motion failed. How? At least six Democrats were absent in the room during the vote. Moreover, three of the present Democrats broke party ranks and voted *nay*. Thus, Holliman's motion to send the bill to the Judiciary Committee failed by a vote of 10–14. According to the rules, the bill would now be sent to the House floor for an up or down vote, calendared for the following day, Tuesday.

To avoid this, Rules Chairman Bill Owens (D-Pasquotank) immediately called for a recess, wherein missing Democrat committee members could be rounded up for a second committee vote.

They must have rounded up the wrong Democrats, though, because the outcome of the vote remained the same.

Owens then entertained a motion to send the bill to the House floor "without prejudice." Representative Harold Brubaker (R-Randolph) made the motion, and for a brief time, it appeared as if the amendment bill might finally get a hearing—a chance!—on the floor of at least one chamber of the General Assembly. This had never happened before. Jim and the other amendment advocates felt hope stir within them.

House Speaker Joe Hackney (D-District 54) strangled that hope. "I said at the beginning of the session," he stated, "that we will control the agenda, and that's what we will do." Keeping that promise, he single-handedly referred the measure, after one reading, to the House Judiciary 1 at the end of Tuesday's session without allowing a motion or a vote on it. Once again, it was condemned to die in committee.

"I have always been impressed to believe the Speaker was a man of fairness," Mark Creech, executive director of the Christian Action

League, told the press afterward. "But what he did to the marriage amendment bill was not fair. The legislation is extremely popular with more than 70 percent of the people of this state. He contends the bill is purely a partisan issue, meant simply for political gain. But how can he say that when the bill has more than sixty sponsors who are both Republican and Democrat? The members of the House ought to be able to vote on this."

Jim was frustrated, even discouraged.

"We don't have to continue doing this," Mary Frances reminded him. "You've been there longer that you intended, and we don't believe in a permanent governing class. Maybe it's time to pass the torch."

Jim shook his head. "As long as they send me back, as long as I have supporters, I'm going to finish." He had been entrusted with an important cause, and he would be faithful to it.

Besides, North Carolinians overwhelmingly supported traditional marriage. As such, they had a right to change their own constitution to reflect and uphold that belief. Jim would make sure they got the opportunity. If not this year, then next.

Or the next.

As long as it took.

Following Scottish Roots

*The mark of a Scot of all classes is that he remembers and cherishes the
memory of his forebears, good or bad; and there burns alive in him
a sense of identity with the dead even to the twentieth generation.*
—Robert Louis Stevenson

In the early '70s, the Wake Forest golf team flew to St. Andrews,
Scotland, to attend the Walker Cup Golf Tournament and cheer on
its participating members. Jim, a generous supporter of the school's
athletic scholarship program, and its golf program in particular, was
invited to accompany the team.

He was excited. What could be more bonny than attending the
prestigious Walker Cup match in the very birthplace of the "gentleman's game"? Besides, his father had played there!

But his enthusiasm went far beyond golf. Scotland was *his* birthplace too, and he had long felt a yearning to search out his blood kin
there, kin with whom Nancy had lost touch. Though he was blessed
with his own neat little family, he still longed for the connection and
camaraderie of the wider clan he scarcely remembered and had never
met.

Hope mingled with trepidation. How would his father's relatives receive him? *If* they received him. So much time, distance, and
ill circumstance lay between them all.

Nancy declined the invitation to accompany Jim and Mary
Frances back to Scotland. She had shared with her children few
details about her painful days there as a new widow, or about the
unpleasant aftermath of a world war which robbed her of fortune

and favor in her own homeland. She was especially closed about her Forrester in-laws.

None of this inspired confidence that Jim would be welcomed with open arms and invitations to afternoon tea and shortbread.

Jim and Mary Frances digressed from the golf tournament for a weekend and caught a train to Glasgow. There they got blank looks from taxi drivers when they asked to be taken to Hillfoot Cemetery, where Jim's father, James, was buried. None of them even recognized the name of the place. Finally, they met a cabbie with a grayer head and longer memory than the rest.

"Oh yes, Hillfoot," the man said. "But it was renamed New Kilpatrick Cemetery years ago."

But the aged cabbie remembered more than just the location of the cemetery.

"I know exactly where your father's grave is. Ach! He was very well known."

True to his claim, at Hillfoot he led them to a simple headstone bearing the name *James Summers Forrester* and the dates of birth and death.

It was a solemn time for Jim—and silent. Words are useless and superfluous at a graveside. As in the aftermath of Sheila's death, he just stood hand in hand with Mary Frances, drawing comfort and strength from her.

Afterward, they gave the cabbie an address in Milngavie, on the outskirts of Glasgow, the last address at which Jim's paternal relatives Uncle John and Aunt Nell resided.

Jim steeled himself as the taxi pulled up to the house, having no idea how he would be greeted. "I'm going to go up there and knock on that door," he declared, more to himself than Mary Frances.

"Yes," she encouraged. "And if they don't want to talk to you or they slam the door in our faces, then so be it." He sat in the car for a few minutes more, summoning his courage, then got out and gave the front door a respectable rap.

The door was *not* slammed in their faces. They were cordially welcomed and invited in for tea and raisin sandwiches. It turned out to be a lovely visit. Uncle John braved the attic and found a few of

James's old golf clubs for Jim, promising he would help Jim locate more.

Crossing the lane, they paid a visit to Aunt Jenny and Lillian, Jim's oldest sister, who suffered from cerebral palsy.

But the Forresters were pressed for time, having only a week in Scotland and much yet to see and do.

Cruden Bay, in Aberdeenshire, was the next destination. They explored the place from golf course to clubhouse to castle. But there was one place in particular Jim had to see.

"I need to find Number 2 Serald Cottage," he told the taxi driver.

The cabbie knew the neighborhood, but not the exact house, so he let Jim and Mary Frances out to walk the deserted little street looking for the right cottage. In good Scottish tradition, the day was chilly and overcast, but the brightly painted front doors and window boxes of the gray stone cottages lining both sides of the lane were cheerful pops of color piercing the grim atmosphere. Not a living soul was in sight.

Unfortunately, house numbers were not inscribed on the cottages themselves but listed on a block corner post at the end of the lane. One could not tell which house went with which number!

The two had almost given up figuring it out when they spotted a little white-haired woman who appeared out of the gloom at the end of the lane. They hailed her, and the elderly lady listened with polite attention as Jim introduced himself and asked, "Ma'am, do you know where Number 2 Serald Cottage is?"

At his name, the lady's brow furrowed. "Aye, and why would ye be wanting to know?"

"That's where I was born."

The lady gave a little gasp, and her eyes flew wide. "Ach! Could ye be wee Jimmy?"

"Well, I was *a* wee Jimmy," replied Jim.

"I was your nanny. I'm Elsie!"

Jim and Mary Frances could hardly believe their ears. Providence had brought Elsie Slessor—the one person they had seen!—straight to them. There were goose bumps all around as they visited with her.

Her husky Scottish lilt and gently rolled *r*'s were a delight to the ear, especially when they addressed Jim with grandmotherly affection.

There was a lot of catching up to be done, so Elsie showed them straight to Number 2 Serald Cottage, filling in the gaps of Jim's infancy and boyhood. She recreated the cottage, and Cruden Bay, as they had been thirty-five years before. She told touching and humorous stories of James, and of Jim himself. "Wee Jimmy" was "a little rounder" and "so very inquisitive!"

Jim was spellbound at her words. They solidified his roots and filled in the holes of his memory.

With Elsie's assistance, Jim was able to locate James's caddy, a gregarious and spry eighty-two-year-old still ranging the Scottish hills to "get away from all the women" at his assisted living residence. It was hard being one of only two males. Jim and Mary Frances struggled to keep pace as he conducted a tour of his little borough and expounded on his old friend James's mild nature and giving disposition. The famous golfer had been "well-liked" as a person as much as an athlete.

There were no accommodations in Cruden Bay, so Jim and Mary Frances motored up to the coastal town of Peterhead in search of a place to spend the night.

Peterhead is as far east as one can walk in Scotland before falling into the frigid North Sea. The only lodging the couple could find was a quaint but aged bed-and-breakfast, rich in atmosphere and poor in comfort. Cracks crisscrossed the floor, and the wind off the water whistled through the place like an icy-hearted sea sprite.

"Jim, I'm *freezing*," Mary Frances kept saying. Not even Indiana winters had been this cold!

They tentatively slid between the icy sheets and huddled close for warmth, avoiding even the call of nature for as long as possible. "You found one spot in that bed, and you *stayed* there," Mary Frances later told a friend. "And you blessed the man who invented central heating!"

In truth, the two did not mind the lack of conveniences. They were far too exhilarated by all they had experienced and learned in those few short days. Their time in Scotland had been rich. Jim had found tangible connections to his heritage and paternity. Better still, no small part of his father had been restored to him.

Years later, Jim returned to Cruden Bay for a round of golf with his own son, Jimmy. Traversing the green, both men were overcome with a strange, eerie sense that James was there, playing alongside them in spirit. Jimmy related the experience by saying, "It was a threesome in play and in generation—and with a kindred love of the sport."

Peter Craighead, the P&J golf writer who penned James Summers Forrester's 1938 obituary, described the famous golfer thus: "As big in heart as he was in stature, genial, fair-haired Jimmy was one of Scotland's great sportsmen. He took defeat as he took success—with a smile."

Just like his son.

January 2005, North Carolina

S8 Defense of Marriage is introduced in the North Carolina Senate by Republican senators Jim Forrester and Fred Smith, with twenty-four cosponsors. Four days after its introduction, S8 is referred to the Ways and Means Committee, chaired by Senator Charles Dannelly (D-Mecklenburg), where it is never brought up for consideration.

March 2005

Judge Richard Kramer of San Francisco County's Superior Court rules on March 14 that California's ban on same-sex marriage is unconstitutional. He compares the ban to racial segregation in schools and says "no rational purpose" exists for denial of such marriages. The ruling, if upheld on appeal, sets the stage for California to follow the state of Massachusetts in allowing same-sex couples to wed.

Contemplating Senatorhood

Jim Forrester was conservative when conservative wasn't cool.
—Dr. Mark Harris

In 1990, Jim was prevailed upon to run for Senate District 41, a district comprising Gaston, Lincoln, and Catawba Counties.

At the outset, Mary Frances had one crucial question to ask: "Jim, is there anything you need to tell me before we do this? Any dark secret you've never shared. If so, confess it *now*."

It was a prudent question to put to anyone considering a run for public office. Political campaigns are not for the faint of heart.

Jim's opponent was a high-ranking senator in the General Assembly, Marshall Rauch. Rauch had twenty-four years in the Senate under his belt and all the seniority and clout that went with it, including chairmanship of the powerful Finance Committee. Like many elected officials who hold office for extended periods, he had become estranged from those he represented. He had lost touch.

On the campaign trail, Jim would hold up Rauch's photograph when speaking to voters. "This is your senator," he'd say. "When was the last time you saw him?"

His listeners would mentally ask themselves this question, and Jim's point would be made.

"I assure you," he would add, "when I'm your senator, my door will always be open, and you will recognize my face."

His senate campaign headquarters was a back room in the Stanley medical office. His office staff and patients, some of whom he had delivered, comprised a devoted, tireless campaign crew.

Jim's central campaign plank was simple: there had not been a physician in the North Carolina General Assembly in fifty years and that august body sorely needed one. A full seventeen departments of state government pertained to the growing behemoth of health care. The industry was evolving for the worse, and Jim was concerned over diminishing patient access and increasing costs.

Just as worrisome was the new concept of health management organizations (HMOs), now coming into vogue, such as that proffered by Kaiser Permamente in California.

Jim recognized these as a dangerous remedy to an already bad illness, the first big toe in the murky water of socialized medicine. Limited access, rationed care and resources, and even "patient dumping" were sure to follow. It was the logical and inevitable outcome of collective "managed care."

He had visited multiple countries with nationalized health-care and single-payer systems, all based on rationing. He had witnessed the dysfunctionality of such paradigms. He had noted the absence of the benefits that attend private enterprise, chiefly *patient options*.

Jim wanted to let the free market be *truly* free when it came to health care. As an alternative to HMOs, he promoted health savings accounts. This left some responsibility with the patient for his or her own medical care rather than leaving ultimate decision to the questionable discretion of a nonmedical third party. This would help reduce costs of care and prescription drugs, as well as discourage overuse of the system. Ultimately, the patient and physician called the shots.

It was imperative, Jim emphasized throughout his campaign, that the General Assembly have an experienced physician in its ranks, one with thorough personal and practical knowledge of health care. One who, like himself, was also board-certified in preventive medicine and had served in public health within his community and the military for twenty years.

It was only logical. "If you're going to change farming subsidies or car insurance, you go to farmers and ask them, or to insurance companies and ask them. So why," he would query, "if you're going to change medical care, access, and delivery, would you not ask *doctors*?"

His opponent Rauch spent upward of $250,000 in his campaign, much of it on radio and television advertisements. The sum dwarfed Jim's $35,000, but Jim put in the footwork and organized an efficient "boots on the ground" effort.

Better still, many voters already knew him, from his medical practice and beyond. He was *in* his constituency by sight, by name, and by reputation. His character was proven to be exemplary.

To Mary Frances's worried inquiry over Jim's past, he assured her, "Don't worry, dear. There's no skeleton in my closet."

"Good," she replied. "Because if there is, you can be sure they'll dig it out and rattle it in front of the whole world!"

Raleighwood

Down here experience is worth a lot.
—Senator Jerry Tillman

Close upon Jim's election to senate, a well-meaning friend made Mary Frances promise to accompany him to Raleigh whenever he went. At first, Mary Frances thought it an odd, cryptic overstatement on the part of her friend. Once in Raleigh, she began to understand her friend's implications.

Representative John Torbett (R-Gaston Co.) jokingly describes the intangible, whirling atmosphere of legislative drama, deal-making, and extramarital affairs as "Raleighwood."

The Forresters experienced the slings and arrows of Raleighwood from day one. They felt the condescension and intimidation that a freshman in the minority party was subjected to, not only from veteran Democrat senators and representatives but sometimes from their wives. The Forresters were deemed inexperienced and naive by the standards of the entrenched, and they encountered an attitude of disdain that manifested itself in petty ways.

Jim and Mary Frances both caught a dreadful stomach bug, which they referred to as the "Raleigh crud." One response to their physical misery was a haughty, "That's what you get for being a Republican."

To worsen their general reception, Jim was an "upstart." His surprise defeat of Rauch was fresh and highly resented, which made the new senator and his wife feel like marked men wherever they went. The tension was thick. Pointed jokes and snide remarks were not uncommon.

Only a few weeks after Jim's swearing-in, Mary Frances made her legislative debut attendance at the reconvening of the now century-old Sir Walter Cabinet. The Cabinet is comprised of legislative spouses, as well as all statewide women elected officials, appointed department secretaries, and NC judges and judicial spouses. It's quite an impressive membership list. The group's goal "is to contribute to the good of the State of North Carolina and its citizens, to stay informed on current issues, and to continue friendships established through the years."

Mary Frances walked into her first Cabinet meeting very reticent, knowing only one or two people. But she slid into an empty seat at one of the round tables and right into the midst of a frank discussion between seven other women as to who would be North Carolina's next governor.

She extended a brief but congenial greeting all round but volunteered neither her identity nor her party affiliation. It was soon apparent that all the women were Democrats, which was no surprise.

The topic of the next governor resumed.

"I think Jim Hunt will run," posed one lady. "He's the one who can rid us of these damn Republicans."

"I don't know," another said. "Lacy Thornburg might give him a run for his money."

"Well, anybody will be better than what we've got now," was still another opinion.

With the next question, things got really interesting.

"Has anybody met the wife of the senator from Gaston County that took Marshall Rauch's seat?"

Mary Frances's ears perked up, but she managed a neutral expression.

"Tell me!" cried another. "Where'd they find a Republican to beat him? I still can't believe it!"

"I know." Another woman shook her head in commiseration. "How in the world did it happen?"

They proceeded to malign Jim. Mary Frances sat there and listened, silent but inwardly fuming.

Mary Frances politely excused herself from the table and walked away. Then she spotted a Republican acquaintance named Ruby. She walked over to say hello and requested a favor. Would Ruby mind joining the Democrat ladies' conversation and ask them if they'd met the senator who had beaten Rauch or the new senator's wife? Ruby complied and, in a few moments, was directing the ladies' gaze toward Mary Frances, who stayed around just long enough to see them all turn rosy pink in embarrassment.

A few weeks later, she was asked to be a substitute player for another legislative wife in a Wednesday-morning tennis group. Her introduction to the group was a *backhanded* compliment to be sure. "This is Mary Frances Forrester," said the woman who had recruited her. "We got to know her and like her before we found out she was a Republican."

After a few more subtle jibes, Mary Frances vowed to play her best tennis ever and beat those women! She refused to be intimidated and wanted them to know it. She must have earned their respect, for they all became fast friends as time and tennis passed.

Off the tennis court, she and Jim were at dinner with fellow legislators and their spouses one evening when the topic arose of the difficult adjustment to Raleigh life the new legislators faced. Jim extolled the benefits of having the comforting presence of one's spouse in the capitol and how difficult it would be to return to one's room alone each night, especially when he felt ill or low-spirited after a rough day at the General Assembly.

Mary Frances seconded his thoughts, adding that she enjoyed accompanying Jim to Raleigh during session rather than being parted. "We can look out for each other."

At these words, a lull fell in the conversation, and cynical looks were exchanged between fellow diners. Had they said something offensive? Dumb? A moment later, Mary Frances's tablemate leaned in and informed her with discreet implication, "Well, dear, most people come up here to get *away* from their spouses."

But Raleighwood wasn't just about neglect or infidelity to the marriage bond. It could be rife with other evils, both small and large. To this day, legislators are inevitably tempted to compromise their integrity for some personally desirable political or economic outcome. It can be a challenge to maintain focus and stick to principle, especially for the freshman who may be naive and vulnerable

Senator Kathy Harrington (R-Gastonia), a friend and protégé of Jim, offered her perspective on the difficult transition from local government to state government. "It's a different environment in Raleigh. You encounter pressures you don't encounter in your home district, and you don't have the affirmation. You get negative emails and feedback from colleagues." Furthermore, one is more likely to be confronted on the state level with thorny and divisive social issues one didn't encounter back home at the local level.

As senator, Jim was deeply conscious of the great trust with which he was invested and the daunting public responsibility that went with it. "We're writing laws that ten million people have to live by," he observed to Representative John Torbett, emphasizing the magnitude of their responsibility.

Jim stayed true to the ideals that drove him to the General Assembly in the first place and kept the will and welfare of constituents at the forefront of every bill, every committee meeting, and every vote. "The people that sent you to Raleigh," he reminded Kathy, "are not the people you serve with. They are the people you represent."

Charges that Jim was inexperienced or naive were neatly put to rest in his first term, when it became evident to Republicans and Democrats alike that Jim was competent and committed. He was naturally shrewd, and he had done his homework. Lieutenant Governor Jim Gardener even acknowledged that "he knew the process from the day he walked in the door."

Mary Frances proved her own worth in Raleigh. The crown was her election to president of the Sir Walter Cabinet for the 1999–2000 term. This was remarkable in two ways: One, she was the first Republican ever to preside over the Cabinet. Second, she did so while the Democrats still controlled the General Assembly. No small feat.

When she came home and told Jim she had been asked to preside, his answer was blunt. "You can't say no."

Mary Frances wouldn't have dreamed of it! Nonetheless, she never wore her partisanship on her sleeve, and she treated all Cabinet members equally during her tenure of office.

When the Forresters first went to Raleigh, they had been cynical, expecting the worst. To be sure, they encountered its vices, but they experienced its virtues too. Many legislators faithfully represented the people that elected them with honesty and honor. Some of these colleagues, both Democrat and Republican, who remained above the Raleighwood "fray" became sources of support and camaraderie.

September 2005

The California legislature becomes the first to pass a bill allowing marriage between same-sex couples.

November 2005

Texas voters overwhelmingly approve Proposition 2, a measure amending its state constitution to protect traditional marriage. The victory came on a 76 percent vote. Texas joins eighteen other states in enshrining the traditional definition of marriage in their constitutions.

December 2005

The movie *Brokeback Mountain* is released, depicting a forbidden romantic relationship between two men. It will win both Golden Globe and Academy Awards.

The Maze

The man of character, sensitive to the meaning of what he is doing, will know how to discover the ethical paths in the maze of possible behavior.
—Earl Warren

It's an old joke in Raleigh that the first order of business for a freshman legislator is finding—and remembering—where the bathrooms are located. The joke is funny until one visits the place and desperately needs one.

The legislative building is a maze of repetitive squares, quadrants, and hallways. Even veteran senators get disoriented upon stepping out of conference and committee rooms. Everything looks the same, and one is forced to memorize landmarks such as fountains and artwork to regain his or her bearings.

A conspiracy theorist might suspect this maze is deliberately designed to confuse visitors, solicitors, and constituents. "If they can't find us, they can't annoy or berate us," the politician might reason.

If nothing else, the maze stands as an apt symbol of the vast, convoluted, and impersonal government bureaucracy that confounds and frustrates the average American citizen.

Jim's first office in the maze consisted of two small, narrow rooms barely housing a desk for himself, a desk for his legislative assistant Lois, and two chairs for guests. It was cold and institutional-looking with high cinder-block walls and noisy acoustics.

And it was a hidden gem for Jim. It was situated in a plum spot close to the Senate chamber. The sergeant at arms's office was mere steps away. Also steps away was the exit leading to the Legislative Office Building (LOB), which provided quick access to most committee meetings. Within, the office boasted two floor-to-ceiling windows that afforded an excellent view of Halifax Mall. Better still, Jim and his legislative assistant Lois could observe who came and went from the LOB and when.

Jim's senatorial desk was as sacred as his medical one. Legislative assistants learned quickly that touching it, even to tidy things, drew a swift rebuke. In Jim's head, it was *already* neat and organized, however it appeared to others. Scattered over the top and throughout the drawers were copious stacks of prescription pads, which served as Jim's de facto letterhead and personal stationery. "The man wrote everything on prescription pads!" Mary Frances declared to a friend.

Jim's desk was a pit stop for legislators with the munchies, thanks to the massive jar of peanuts he kept there. If one was really lucky, there would be M&Ms. "If you get a little hungry, go see Forrester," Senator David Hoyle (D-District 43) advised colleagues.

The math of these back-and-forth trips is staggering when one takes the time to add them all up. An approximate calculation puts the total number of miles driven between Stanley and Raleigh at 400, 960 miles and 6,944 hours. The constant back-and-forth was especially demanding for Mary Frances, who usually drove while Jim worked or made phone calls.

The drive would doubtless have been more pleasant if the Republicans were not a lowly minority in the General Assembly with little power. Jim's first Senate chair was stuck on the remotest outskirts of the chamber.

"Jerry, one day we'll get off this back row," he would say to friend and golf chum Senator Jerry Tillman, (R-District 29), before discreetly passing his bipartisan peanut jar around the hallowed chamber for the benefit of colleagues who might have the munchies.

Portrait of a Gentleman

He was hard not to like.
—Senator Jerry Tillman

When you met Jim Forrester, several physical traits struck you right off.

You noticed his walk. Representative John Torbett described it as a "John Wayne" stride. "Not self-made or created but natural. Not hurried, just purposeful." Brigadier-General Fisk Outwater characterized it more as a "dignified Gregory Peck." Mary Frances *refers* to it reflectively as his "drum major stance."

Senator Andrew Brock described Jim's straight, commanding posture as follows: "As if he were always at attention."

Though possessed of an unassuming nature, Jim nonetheless had a commanding "presence" in the words of Jim Blackburn, who remarked that "you always knew if Senator Forrester was in the chamber."

"He just had the aura of a gentleman about him," was Sergeant at Arms Phil King's observation, "the aura of a general officer."

You admired his thick wavy hair, the envy of many a balding comrade. "He had a curl thing going on," John Torbett remembered, referring to an unruly shock of hair that graced the center of Jim's forehead.

You were captured by his perpetual smile and stark blue eyes, which revealed a kind and congenial nature. After the exchange of a few words, you realized that he was very soft-spoken, possibly shy. But then a dry joke would drop unexpectedly from his lips, revealing a matter-of-fact sense of humor beneath the reserved exterior.

Get to know him a little better, and you would discern character traits, such as a consistently mild temper. Jim exhibited few highs and lows and was rarely seen ruffled, much less mad. He was "the most even-keel guy" Senator David Hoyle ever knew. Even Mary Frances admits that, in fifty years of marriage, with its inevitable disagreements, Jim only got angry with her twice. His heart made no room for resentment or spite, and he held no grudges against those who disagreed with him over political issues or personal beliefs.

Colleagues remember him sitting comfortably in his chair on the Senate floor, quietly taking in all that was happening on the floor, turning his head back and forth as speakers changed. An observer in the gallery above might notice him close his eyes periodically and think Jim was nodding off to sleep. They were wrong. Jim never missed a word of debate. Closing his eyes made it easier to focus his mind on what was being said, and helped shut out competing distractions or activity. After session, the same gallery observer might overhear Jim quote exactly what was said in debate when he appeared to be snoozing.

Jim was all of this, but he was not *soft*. He commanded respect always, simply by virtue of being himself. He *demanded* respect when appropriate. He had his boundaries and a deep sense of what was proper and right. He did not shirk from a fight if needed. To Representative John Torbett, Jim was "the most gentle, quiet, demure person—*until* he got his dander up. When he got his dander up, he was serious. He was all business."

A teapot tempest in the legislators' cafeteria one afternoon illustrates this distinction well. A cafeteria manager chided Jim to his face while he was having lunch with a constituent. He bristled at the remark. It was later when he took her aside privately and told her with calm bluntness, "If you have something to say about me, say it *to* me, but don't ever do it in front of another person." Jim had a hunch she would shed a few tears, and he was sorry for that. But he had to say what he said. Her remark had been a petty jibe.

But it was never personal with Jim. "Never once did I hear him utter a cross word about any individual. About the process, yes. About people, no," observed Torbett.

Nor did a person's station in life matter much. "He treated everyone," Andrew Brock would later say, "with utmost respect and decorum, whether it was another member, a visiting dignitary, a legislative colleague, or the custodian."

He had a warm relationship with the Senate sergeants at arms and preferred to be on informal terms. "Just call me Jim," he told Phil King. "Unless we're in the chamber."

"Senator, I'm always going to have to call you *senator*," King replied. That was protocol.

Sergeant at Arms Charles Marsalis, a retired Air Force major who flew combat helicopters and played football for the Cleveland Browns, was also on a first-name basis with Jim when it was appropriate. They enjoyed comparing flight training notes and swapping experiences about military life. Jim had given Charles flight physicals.

To Jim, the sergeants at arms were the hardest-working, least-recognized people in Raleigh; and since Jim showed appreciation through feeding people, he sent them lunch once a year. He did likewise for the legislative clerks. He even sent thank-you letters to the groundskeepers!

Jim's recognition of the work of others was genuine and disinterested, but it also hearkened to the constant maternal refrain in his head: *Son, always remember those who help you.*

In the cosmic scheme, lunches and letters are small gestures. But small gestures have disproportionately large and positive effects on people's hearts.

To Jim, no one was invisible, and every *one* was valuable.

Avoid the Appearance of Evil

Abstain from every appearance of evil.
—1 Thessalonians 5:22 KJV

As county commissioner, Jim had had to face his constituents, the people who elected him, every single day. He was accustomed to accountability, and he embraced it just as cheerfully in Raleigh as he had done in Stanley. A citizen's right and necessary duty to hold their representatives accountable is crucial to a free society. A true statesman appreciates this reality, and Jim Forrester was a true statesman.

Accountability is inextricably linked to transparency and accessibility. If constituents, or any other citizen for that matter, wished to unload, complain, ask questions, or pose potential solutions to issues, Jim believed himself duty-bound to listen with an open ear and respond with a truthful tongue. He appreciated the interaction.

"He always took time to share what was going on in Raleigh," Heath Jenkins, former Stanley police chief, remarked. Jim wished to stay connected with the folks in his district, to understand their issues and concerns fully, and to keep them apprised of all that transpired in the General Assembly.

Dick Jarman, friend and financial advisor, recounted an episode that illustrates Jim's native integrity. In the late '90s, there was a trend for states to deregulate public utilities.

California was one such state, a Republican governor leading the charge, its legislature voted to deregulate their public electrical utilities. The state's utilities and utility management companies were pushing this, including the infamous Enron.

The result of the action proved disastrous, ushering in black-outs, chaos, and skyrocketing energy bills—and hordes of angry citizens.

Some in North Carolina, predominantly Democrats, were taken with the idea and formed a commission to study it as a possibility for the Tar Heel State. They would foment a public groundswell for it; then the General Assembly could pass it.

Dick called Jim and laid it on the line, encouraging Jim to enter the discussion on the proposed venture; for, if it passed, it would be the most profound thing the state legislature did in the next decade to affect North Carolina's economic future. "Jim, you might want to get on that committee and understand this problem better because the ramifications of it are going to be profound."

Things had not ended well for California's last Republican governor. Citizens were outraged over the debacle that had ensued after deregulation. "If you vote for it and it's a failure," Dick warned, "it'll be hung around your neck."

There were other potential complications. Jim primarily served Gaston County, and one of that county's largest taxpayer participants was Duke Energy. If he supported any deregulation venture, there was risk of inviting charges of self-interest or corporate cronyism. Some might view it as a short-term economic scheme to benefit certain people, certain *legislators* like himself.

Dick reminded Jim that he had personal stock ownership in the utilities in question. If Jim chose to get on board with the deregulation venture (or join the commission), he should sell those stocks first. Otherwise, he would be inviting political attacks and accusations of self-interest.

Jim was appalled at the thought of ever being accused of trading the interests of North Carolinians for personal financial gain. Jim ordered Dick to get him out of *all* investments that could potentially conflict with his roles and duties as a state senator. As for deregulation, Jim wanted to be able to assure any jury or committee that he had sold or traded his financial interests in the entities in question before he could profit by them, even unintentionally. There must be no conflict of interest, real or perceived. "I don't want to do anything that could be construed to be wrong or dishonest or taking advantage."

His credibility as a public figure was his greatest asset. He must avoid even the *appearance* of misconduct, lest the people think he had broken covenant with them. They must remain confident in his honest representation.

It wasn't just about political consequences, though. On a personal level, he would not risk his good name and reputation, nor that of his family.

Over the years, there were those who tried to find weak spots in his integrity, a niche in his character wherein a bribe or kickback might be stuck. But such efforts were futile, as the persons in question quickly realized. Jim was integrity to the bone.

Mary, Jim's legislative assistant, overheard two men, probably lobbyists, just outside the open door to his office. They were discussing the state lottery. "You might as well not stop here," one of them told the other. "You can't buy this vote."

Mary hurried out to see who it was, but the two were already lost in the flow of passersby.

"You can't buy this vote"—a compliment indeed, especially in Raleighwood.

Votes *could* be bought in Raleigh, a reality that grieved Jim. The reason might be economic gain, promises, political threats, or some other motivations known only to the giver and recipient.

When the fate of an important or controversial bill is uncertain, and it will turn on one vote, senators can fight like lions over a fresh gazelle carcass. Lawmaking is not always a gentleman's game.

The lottery battle of 2005 was just such a contest. For thirty-four years, conservative and religious groups, such as the Christian Action League (CAL), had fought successfully against a state-run lottery in North Carolina. Each year, the lottery bill was defeated in the legislature.

In 2005, it looked as if it would be avoided once more.

The lottery bill had already cleared the House of Representatives by one vote, but Senate leaders were unable to muster enough votes to pass it, in spite of a marathon twenty-hour session. It repeatedly came down to a 26–24 margin. Prolottery Senate president pro tempore Marc Basnight declared an end to voting and informed everyone that the issue would be put off until May of the following year.

A few days later, however, Basnight abruptly notified senators that yet another lottery vote would occur the following Tuesday, August 30. What inspired the additional attempt at a vote?

Basnight had likely seen a new opportunity that weekend, when it was reported that two senators opposed to the lottery would be absent from Tuesday's session, with excused absences. Without these two votes, the lottery vote would result in a 24–24 tie that would be broken by Democrat lieutenant governor Beverly Perdue, who was also prolottery.

The antilottery forces scrambled to divert this catastrophe, and there was only one way left to do it. They must convince at least one of these senators to "pair" his vote with a senator from the opposition party who would be present on Tuesday and would vote against the bill.

Without that paired vote, North Carolina would find itself with the onus of a state-run lottery.

One of the two outstanding votes was Senator Harry Brown (R-Jacksonville). But Brown was now on his honeymoon and had left no contact information. All attempts to reach him failed, and his paired vote was given up for lost.

The other outstanding vote was Senator John Garwood (R-North Wilkesboro), who was recovering from a leg infection at home. He was the lottery opponents' last hope. If he agreed to pair his vote with a willing Democrat senator who also opposed the lottery bill, the lottery would still be defeated. A close shave to be sure—a 25–24 margin—but it would be enough.

Jim visited Garwood, encouraging him to pair his vote with the Democrat in question to avoid a tie. Garwood assured Jim he would. Mark Creech of the Christian Action League received a similar commitment from the ailing senator.

With at least one paired vote settled, it looked as if the lottery bill would once again be defeated. Lottery opponents breathed a collective sigh of relief.

But word travels fast, and that day it must have flown. Garwood spoke with others that morning besides Jim and Mark. Mere moments before session began, Garwood phoned Jim and said he had changed his mind. He would *not* be pairing his vote after all.

Jim was floored. Garwood had promised him he would!

Mark Creech could not believe his ears when news of Garwood's reversal reached him. Garwood now would not even take his call. Had Garwood been promised some tangible, last-minute incentive for switching his vote? Had he been threatened somehow?

Whatever the reason for his switch, Garwood's decision not to pair his vote resulted in the dreaded 24–24 tied vote. Lieutenant Governor Perdue then cast her tie-breaker, and HB1023, the *North Carolina State Lottery Act*, was approved on August 31, 2005. Governor Mike Easley signed it into law, and the Tar Heel State entered the gambling business.

Jim and Mary Frances were disappointed, to say the least. Up in the Senate gallery, Mark stood with John Rustin, Bill Brooks, and other embattled lottery opponents, shaking their collective head at Garwood's change of heart. Why had he done it? *And for what?*

One little vote. One little last-minute flip-flop.

One *big* outcome.

The drama of the lottery vote would be well-remembered when the marriage amendment struggle came to a head six years later on the Senate floor.

Doctoring the Legislature

He was the medical go-to guy in the legislature.
—Representative John Torbett

In the North Carolina General Assembly, there is always an official "doctor of the day" on call for the benefit of assembly members. However, this individual, supplied by the North Carolina Medical Society, might be a medical genius in any number of specialties, but a dermatologist is scant use to the guy incapacitated by a killer migraine. Or a stroke.

Jim was the "doctor of the moment," in the words of Senator David Hoyle, friend and patient. He was "Doc" in the General Assembly as well "Doc" at the Air Guard, a favorite with fellow legislators who sought relief from minor ailments, required impromptu physical exams, or needed the occasional prescription. There were few medical conditions Jim, being a primary care physician, had not encountered and treated in his career. If faced with something unfamiliar or serious, he would make the appropriate referral elsewhere.

Still, apart from the day-to-day ailments, as in the case of Representative Esposito, emergencies arose, and Jim was called upon to tend to them.

There was a spectator in the Senate chamber gallery who fainted at a January swearing-in ceremony. The sergeant at arms hurried to Jim on the senate floor and said they had an unresponsive person. The man's blood pressure had bottomed out due to medication. Jim revived him, sent him to the hospital, and was back on the floor just in time to place his hand on the Bible and be sworn in.

The incident affected Jim in a positive way albeit through a negative gesture. As they did in the case of every new senatorial class, the Democratic leadership had exercised their prerogative as the majority party by reassigning members to offices according to their pleasure, either by status or otherwise. Jim was to be rudely ousted from his present office, due to a Democrat legislator who had his eye on it, and was now consigned to a remote fifth-floor spot in another building, the farthest point possible from where he had requested to be.

However, after the fainting-man incident, when the Senate nurse and the sergeants at arms learned Jim was to be moved to another building, they approached Senate Pro Tempore Marc Basnight and advised him in the strongest terms to reconsider the assignment. Their concerns were blunt, along the lines of, "If that spectator in the gallery had died and you had access to a qualified physician but had tucked him away in another building, the state could be *liable*."

As a result, Jim got a conveniently placed office in the main building. Apart from its roomier size, it looked much the same as the old one: the same boxy architecture and cinder-block walls.

Mary Frances attempted to inject some charm into it with modestly priced oriental carpets and a stunning silk floral arrangement—an anniversary gift to Jim—which evoked effusive compliments from visitors. Behind his desk, proudly displayed, hung the Stars and Stripes, the North Carolina state flag and his general officer flag from office at the Air Guard. Two of his father's golf clubs, like prized medieval swords in a baronial hall, were crossed on the wall, reminiscent of St. Andrew's cross on the Scottish flag.

Former Representative Pearl Burris Floyd said, "You walked into his office, and you felt like you were walking into a historical museum, but without that 'don't touch' feel."

By far, the most useful thing about the new office was the small side room it contained, which was destined to become Jim's "sick bay" as it lent privacy for any necessary physical exam. It housed all the basic medical equipment—blood pressure cuff, stethoscope, otoscope, thermometer, etc. And of course, a fat stash of prescription pads.

The sitting area in the plaza just outside his office was jokingly referred to as "Senator Forrester's waiting room." Many a Democrat, as well as Republicans, stopped by for blood pressure checks. People falling ill was a regular occurrence, and "sick bay" could get busy.

"Jim, if we don't slow all this traffic down at your desk, somebody's going to come after you for running a damn clinic in here illegally," joked Hoyle.

Jim could not have cared less about a patient's political loyalties. Good medical care was strictly nonpartisan. This was not just an ethical philosophy to which he ascribed, but a mark of his inherent good nature. The Democrat senator who had verbally trashed Jim's legislation that morning received the same sympathy and stellar treatment as the Republican who had championed it. From head cold to heart attack, "Doc" never refused an appeal to relieve suffering and preserve life.

In keeping with its casual wink-and-nod political attitude, the thankful denizens of Raleighwood occasionally responded to Jim's ministrations with a suggestive, "So what can I do for *you?*" or some other implied tit-for-tat offer.

Jim would just smile and shake his head, loath to let the slightest favor cross his messy desk. Such attempts became something of a private joke with Mary Frances at the supper table. "Well, dear," he'd say, "today I guess we could have asked for a new road—and probably gotten it."

As late as the summer of 2011, when Jim was suffering from his own health issues, Sergeant at Arms Charles Marsalis experienced a massive blood clot and lost consciousness. Jim darted out of his committee meeting and rushed to the scene, stabilizing Marsalis until the emergency medical services team could arrive.

Marsalis's own physician was blunt with him afterward. "You're lucky. If you hadn't had immediate medical care, you might not have survived."

Adventures Abroad

The world is a book and those who do not travel read only one page.
—St. Augustine

In the '80s, Jim packed up his stethoscope, his Panama hat, and his smattering of German and headed to Belize on a ten-day mission trip through the Christian Medical Society. Its purpose was to bring medical aid and supplies to that impoverished country's remotest region.

To his delight, serving as the mission team's translator was a woman whose life was the stuff of Hollywood epics. She had been an operative—code name "Toast"—in the Dutch underground during World War II, working alongside Corrie ten Boon, the famous Dutch author of *The Hiding Place.* Together they risked life and limb to conceal Jews from the Nazi occupiers before being captured and imprisoned in a concentration camp, probably Ravensbruck, where they were bunkmates.

Rivers were the only way to get to the villages the team was going to assist, but Jim did not mind this at all. It afforded him hours of listening to Toast's "war stories" as the little outboard motor boat chugged along the watery byways. He hung on every word, fascinated by her history, her experiences, and her remembrances of Corrie and Betsy ten Boom.

But his experiences on land were also profound and eye-opening. Most of the villagers he came to minister to had never before seen a physician. Like Ayo, a dirty and disheveled boy Jim would never forget. After giving medical attention, he gave Ayo a lollipop for being "such a good patient," as he had done with a thousand children back home over the years. To his surprise, Ayo turned around and, without hesitation, passed the lollipop to his little sister. It was just a lollipop, but in the context of such material want, this small act of selflessness made a deep impression on Jim's heart. Ayo would probably never see another lollipop in his life, but that one he gave away in love. Jim, humbled, gave Ayo another lollipop for himself.

Jim's humanitarian efforts were not always made in a medical official capacity.

In early 1992, he received a letter from the International Republican Institute (IRI), an organization that seeks to ensure fair and peaceful elections worldwide. The letter read:

> As you may know, the emergence of Albania into the fold of democratic nations has been remarkable. From the student strikes in November 1990, to the flawed March 1991 elections, and through three governments between April and December 1991, Albania, formerly the most Stalinist country in Eastern Europe, has emerged from forty-five years of isolation. During the last year, the Albanian people have illustrated their desire for establishment of a true democracy. On 22 March 1992, Albanians will once again go to the voting booth, this time, hopefully without fear and after an equitable campaign period.

Elsewhere, it read:

> Over the past decade, the IRI has earned an international reputation for objectivity and professionalism in election observation. The Institute observed elections where there exists concerns over whether the elections will be free and fair, and follows accepted standards in election observation as outlined by international organizations, such as the Conference on Security and Cooperation in Europe. The IRI has been invited

by all major Albanian political parties, including the Democratic Party, the Socialist Party, and the Republican Party, to observe the upcoming elections.

That's where Jim came in, in his capacity as a North Carolina senator. The letter requested his efforts to monitor and adjudicate for the March 22 Albanian parliamentary elections. The first free multiparty elections since the 1920s had been held the previous year, but they had not gone smoothly. Jim, accompanied by other military officers, was the only state government representative in the US asked to go.

Jim had his fill of profound and memorable moments to take back home. The pride and determination the Albanian people had to participate in the government process to make their will and opinion known was humbling. They trekked long distances on foot in many cases and slept outside polling places all night just to cast a ballot when the polls opened. Many cast their vote with tears in their eyes. So many years since an Albanian's vote had meant something. So many years they had had no choice, living in a climate of fear.

The contrast with elections in the US was stark, and Jim grieved over the careless, negligent attitude with which Americans regarded their civic duty and right. It was disgraceful.

Albania was unhealthy, from the collective physical state of its citizens to its stumbling economy trying to gain traction. Years of neglect and human deprivation, along with a lack of infrastructure, had left it in decay.

"If I get sick, don't leave me here," Jim told members of his delegation following an observational visit to a local hospital. His keen medical eye detected disturbing things within its rooms, closets, and corridors.

He wore more than just a senator-adjudicator hat on the trip. He was officer and flight surgeon on the military plane that transported the delegation and acted as the entourage's member physician during their time in Albania. He was happy to save the taxpayers a few bucks by filling those offices himself.

In 1997, at the behest of the North Carolina Department of State, Jim embarked on yet another international mission, this time to the young Republic of Moldova. The trip was one leg of the North Carolina–Moldova National Guard Partnership, one of several similar partnerships sponsored by the United States State Department as a military-to-military outreach to the nascent democracies of the former Soviet bloc.

Like Albania, Moldova struggled to shake off the vestiges of communism and join the world's free nations. The Partnership's overarching purpose was to redirect the nation's armed forces from its purely military function into one of support for civilian government and Moldovan society as a whole. It would now take on a role that more closely resembled that of the National Guard in the United States, including emergency response and disaster relief.

Jim's background in both military and civilian state affairs and his intimate knowledge of the close relationships between the two was ideal. As part of the shift from military state to free-market society, Jim and the delegation sought to open avenues of exchange via trade negotiations and to build the "sister state" relationship between Moldova and North Carolina. The Partnership continues to this day.

Wherever Jim went and whatever his reasons for going, this is one reality that his globetrotting always reinforced to him— Americans have it *good*.

Bills That Were

*Jim was willing to talk about everything and negotiate,
drawing the line at his principles. He was willing to give and
take, but you weren't going to change his philosophy.*
—Senator David Hoyle

It is a shame that Jim is now characterized almost solely for his
efforts opposing same-sex marriage. He was a man of varied interests and concerns, and as such, his legislative career encompassed far
more than marriage amendments and healthcare.

He wrote and sponsored many pieces of legislation that all
North Carolinians can applaud if they took time to examine them.
Getting them through a Democrat-controlled General Assembly was
challenging to say the least.

Naturally, as a doctor, Jim's primary legislative focus was on
issues of medical care and public health, and in those areas he was
extremely influential. "When he stood to talk about a bill," recalled
Sergeant at Arms Jim Blackburn, "everybody listened intently. He
had command and credibility. And they knew his experience as a
doctor."

Jim served on every committee pertaining to medical care, and
there were scores. His expertise on medical issues was invaluable,
arising not from any specialty like cardiology or endocrinology but
from the broad perspective of a family practice physician *and* public health advocate. Some of his bills, health related and otherwise,
were ratified and became law even in the Democrat-controlled legis-

lature. The most significant, with their dates of ratification, include the following:

- *No Blue Lights Allowed (SB23), June 1991.* "To prohibit the use of blue lights by anyone other than law enforcement personnel." This legislation came in the wake of a recent rash of incidents involving the "Blue Light Bandits," criminals who attached a blue emergency light on their car in order to pull unsuspecting victims over for the purpose of assault and robbery. The bill made it a first-class felony to impersonate a police officer in this manner. The bill was the first of Jim's career to pass.
- *Medical Care Savings Plan (SB525), July 1995.* "To require health and accident insurance policies, hospital or medical service plans, HMO plans, and the teachers' and state employees' comprehensive major medical plan to provide coverage for reconstructive breast surgery resulting from mastectomy."
- *Reconstructive Surgery/Coverage (SB714), July 1997.* This mandated insurance to cover reconstructive surgery for mastectomy patients. It was highly contested by the HMOs.
- *No Drive-Through Mastectomy (SB273), August 1997.* This further aided mastectomy patients by declaring that the length of time spent in the hospital following the procedure was to be determined by the doctor and patient, not the insurance companies. The bill was signed by Governor Jim Hunt.
- *Office of Women's Health (SB-626), June 1997.* The bill created the first (as far as can be determined) Woman's Health Commission in the nation to study gender differences in health care. The industry was geared around men, but Jim recognized that women possessed their own unique set of health issues, responded to treatment differently than men, and presented unique challenges to health providers. Norms are not unisex, for example. The bill was signed by Governor Beverly Purdue.

Perdue later tried to take especial credit for the legislation at a meeting of the North Carolina Association of Insurance Women, for whom Mary Frances was then serving as parliamentarian. Seated beside the governor on the main podium, Mary Frances heard loud and clear Perdue's boastful implication that she was primarily responsible for the Woman's Health Commission. Mary Frances struggled to maintain a neutral expression like a good parliamentarian. Inwardly she seethed, knowing perfectly well who deserved credit. But Perdue never mentioned Jim as the bill's primary author. Mary Frances was appalled that Perdue was taking credit for something Jim had worked so hard to bring about. *She knows full well*, thought Mary Frances.

- *Prescription Drugs/Elderly (SB185), March 1999*. "An act to appropriate funds for certain prescription drugs for low-income persons over age sixty-five and not eligible for Medicaid." This measure was approved as part of the budget bill.

- *Insurance/Cover Contraceptives (SB90), June 1999*. In the weeks following Viagra's FDA approval, pharmacists dispensed over forty thousand prescriptions for the drug. Women were coming to Jim, frustrated and discouraged. They had health issues such as diabetes that rendered pregnancy risky, but insurance would not cover their birth control, even though they were unable to pay for it themselves. Jim thought this a ludicrous injustice as insurance covered Viagra for men. SB90 would correct the disparity.

- *Stop Misuse of Laser Devices (SB348), July 1999*. This legislation made it illegal to point one of these easily accessible devices at law enforcement or any other person while it is emitting a laser beam. This was a growing problem as many treated the instruments as toys. The light beam could have damaging effects on the human eye, such as in "flash blindness," wherein a person can temporarily lose sight. The risk of secondary physical accidents could also increase as a result, while the victim is engaged in activities such as operating a vehicle.

- *Encourage Teacher Education/Active Military (SB803), May 2001.* "An act to direct the state university system, the community colleges system, and the Department of Public Instruction to work cooperatively to expand opportunities for military personnel to take teacher education classes prior to discharge from the military."
- *Tanning Salons/Restrictions on Use (SB657), July 2004.* This restricted those under eighteen from using tanning beds without parental approval. Tanning salons were notoriously unregulated with regard to amount of UV radiation and duration of exposure. Jim prognosticated the long-term dangers ultraviolet damage posed to the human body years before statistics proved it, and his tanning salon bill was ratified by the General Assembly long before the effects of tanning beds became a federal issue.

May 2006

SB1228 Defense of Marriage is introduced in the North Carolina Senate by Jim Forrester and nineteen cosponsors. The next day, it is referred to the Rules Committee, chaired by Senator Tony Rand (D-Cumberland), where it is never considered.

October 2006

A ruling by the New Jersey Supreme Court mandates that the state legislature find a way to grant the benefits of marriage to same-sex couples. The 4–3 ruling makes New Jersey the second state in the nation to legalize same-sex marriage.

November 2006

Eight states—Colorado, Idaho, South Carolina, South Dakota, Tennessee, Virginia, and Wisconsin—approve bans on same-sex marriage in state referendums. Arizona becomes the first state to reject such a ban.

Bills That Should Have Been

Justice will not be served until those who are
unaffected are as outraged as those who are.

—Benjamin Franklin

Jim sponsored countless bills that *should have been* ratified to the betterment of North Carolinians. Here are some, to name a few:

- *Prescription Drug Label/Country of Manufacture (SB160), 2007–2008.* Legislation, still desperately needed, that would have required every medication to indicate, on its bottle or package, the place of its manufacture and origin. Because foreign manufacturers have differing and inferior levels of quality control, there can be large inconsistencies from drug to drug. A person might get two identical tablets that are, in fact, very different products, comprised of different materials and/or different strengths. This could have fatal consequences for sufferers of certain medical conditions such as chronic diabetes.

  In spite of harassment from pharmaceutical companies, Jim repeatedly warned of the dangers of improperly or dishonestly labeled drugs.

  It was not the only such bill Jim introduced. For dramatic emphasis, he kept a trash bag of empty medicine bottles he would shake and rattle around when addressing the Senate on medication issues.

- *Physician Assisted Suicide: SB 389 (2001–2002) and SB145 (2003–2004).* Bills that would have outlawed physician-assisted suicide in the state of North Carolina. To Jim, physician-assisted suicide, like abortion, was an act that broke every precept of medical ethics and the law of God pertaining to the sanctity of human life. One of the greatest regrets of his legislative career was that he was not allowed to get a PAS law enacted.

- *The North Carolina Security and Immigration Compliance Act (SB1627), 2006.* "A bill to establish the North Carolina Security and Immigration Compliance Act to provide for the comprehensive regulation of persons in this state who are not lawfully present in the United States." A multifaceted legislation that called for public employer verification of work authorization, created a criminal offense of trafficking a person for sexual and involuntary servitude, enforcement of federal immigration laws, determination of nationality and immigration status of persons jailed upon felony or impaired driving charges (legal status of prisoners), verification of lawful presence to receive public benefits.
- *Ban Partial Birth Abortion (SB 349), March 1999, as secondary sponsor.* Jim was an unwavering champion of the unborn and supported numerous pro-life bills.

Jim also sponsored a resolution that would have designated Reverend Billy Graham North Carolina's Favorite Son. Democrats would not support it, though, and Jim had to settle for Senate Joint Resolution 211 "commemorating the Memory of Religious Leaders in the State of North Carolina and naming Billy Graham as world evangelist."

Later, after the Republicans took the majority, Reverend Graham finally had this well-deserved but belated honor bestowed on him with the passage of SJR 196 in March of 2013.

Jim did not sponsor legislation merely to have more laws. He was not interested in symbolic or nominal gestures that earned media time and had little existential value. His bills, ratified or not, were designed to serve a useful purpose and meet a real need.

The unique foresight and vision they manifested were characteristics recognized even by the opposition party. Moreover, their practicality made them potentially popular among the citizenry. The upshot was that Democrats would snatch one of Jim's bills from time to time, make minor or superficial changes to it, give it a new number and name, and take credit for the idea behind it.

It was an affront to Mary Frances's sense of fair play whenever Jim came home and told her that a bill he had written and proposed—only to see it buried in committee or slightly modified—would magically appear on the chamber floor, championed by a Democrat.

But Jim bore the injustice with admirable grace. "That's okay. It's good for the people," he would say with a shrug. "And I hope it passes."

The Democrats gave his Pledge of Allegiance bill to Julia Boseman, a freshman senator from Wilmington and a lesbian. The bill required the pledge to be said in the classroom each day, though on a voluntary basis for individual students. Jim didn't let it get to him. "I'm not worried about it," he told Mary Frances. "If they give it to her and it passes, fine. It's a good bill."

This was doubly gracious considering Boseman, who often parked in front of the Forresters' kitchen window at their condominium in Raleigh, would catch their eye and give a knowing, too-sweet smile. "Well, there goes the neighborhood," she even remarked once in a subtle chide to Jim, doubtless because of Jim's beliefs about same-sex marriage.

Jim was never a prisoner of his own consequence. He did not demand the credit due him, a characteristic that marks the true servant-statesman, not the politician. Thus, while many of his bills ended up with Democrats, there were others he gave away of his own free will and with his good wishes, often to freshmen Republicans. He wanted them to learn early on how the lawmaking process should work.

It must be stressed that *family* was the ideological starting point and context for every piece of legislation Jim drafted or sponsored during his twenty-year senatorial career. *Everything* affected it in some way. And since the natural family was the crucial axis upon which a healthy people, a healthy society, and a healthy nation turned, every decision or statute passed down from the high halls of government must ultimately benefit and preserve it—or at least do it no harm.

Cultivating Leaders

Keep your vision, focus, and keep your feet on the ground.
—Jim Forrester

Jim believed that one of the attendant duties of being in a position of leadership was to find subsequent leaders to govern the future well.

One man in whom Jim saw great leadership qualities was John Torbett, a longtime acquaintance. Upon first meeting at a parent-teacher event, the two men discovered they shared similar ideologies on a host of things, but particularly regarding education. This like-minded dynamic led to many subsequent conversations about how the school system had "lost its focus" on what should be its overriding concern: the child.

John Torbett, like Jim, served eight years as a Gaston County Commissioner for the Riverbend Township, a seat for which he had Jim's practical support. Jim also supported John during his successful run for a seat in the North Carolina House of Representatives, District 108.

In 2002, along came another protégé. This one he had met before, a little African American girl who had come into his Stanley medical office and told him she wanted to be a doctor. That same little girl, Pearl Burris-Floyd, had grown up and was running for Gaston County commissioner. Now, as she shook hands with Jim as an adult, she asked if he remembered meeting her all those years ago.

"No," Jim confessed with a smile, "but I have a fondness for you. I don't know you yet, but I think we're going to be fast friends."

"He didn't care what color you were or what side of the street you grew up on," Pearl recalled.

He became a mentor and support to Pearl, who had had no previous ambitions to public office and found herself thrust abruptly into the limelight, into interactions with people far more canny in the political process. "He knew I would have some challenges as a female and as an African American entering into politics in Gaston County in the Republican Party," she would later say. "And he wanted to encourage me."

Pearl won the election and became the fifth woman and the *only* African American to serve as commissioner in Gaston County's history.

It is not always easy to be the *first* or the *only* in things. Jim, an immigrant, understood that difficulty and recognized in her a kindred spirit. "He knew what it was like to be in strange place, to be new, and not know how you would be received."

He was a continuous support during her ten years on the county commission and after her election to the North Carolina House of Representatives in 2008. Once in Raleigh, as a first-term legislator in the minority, things could get rocky, and Pearl made many a trip to Jim's office seeking advice or moral support.

"He would always stop what he was doing and sit down and talk with me. He'd say, 'What's on your mind?' 'You need anything?' 'Are they treating you right up here?'"

It impressed Pearl that Jim never told her *what* to do with regard to principle or policy, but only encouraged her to follow her conscience. "Tell the truth and hold on to your integrity," was his admonishment.

Nonetheless, crises of conscience did arise.

In June 2009, in caucus, there was a joint resolution "honoring the life and memory of Senator Jesse Helms." Helms had died the year before, July 4, 2008. Discussion and debate flew back and forth on Senate Joint Resolution 1103. The Black Caucus opposed it, even threatening to walk out of the chamber. Other Democrats just called Helms an "embarrassment."

A member of the Republican delegation asked Pearl to speak in favor of the resolution on the floor. She was taken off guard, inwardly torn in light of controversial things Helms had said in past years.

She confided her uncertainties to Jim and shared a personal story.

Eight years before, as a new Gaston County Commissioner, she had attended the 2001 NC Republican Convention in Raleigh. To her wonder, Senator Helms walked up and shook her hand in congratulations over her election. They talked a few moments, and Helms remarked, "I'm really proud of you. It takes some guts to do what you're doing. But you're a good Republican, and I'm happy to meet you."

"I was very surprised by his candor and warmth," Pearl told Jim, conceding that "everybody has a history."

Still Jim did not try to sway her decision on the proposed resolution.

"He left it up to me," Pearl recalled. "He just said, 'Stand on the strength of your convictions. You'll know what to do when the time comes.'"

In the end, Pearl spoke *for* the resolution on the floor, sharing her story about meeting Helms. Her words nearly brought the House down. The final vote was taken, and Senate Joint Resolution 1103 was ratified. Some members walked out, accusing Pearl of being an "Uncle Tom."

To this day, Pearl refers to Jim as her "father in politics" because "he treated me like his child and wanted the best for me."

Senator Kathy Harrington (R-Gastonia) was another of Jim's protégés. "His door was always open. I could just show up with a question," she said. "He was a patient listener."

By this time, Republicans had finally gained a majority in the General Assembly and would now assume chairmanships over the committees, positions previously barred to them.

Jim, deputy president pro tempore, was to head the Senate Transportation Policy Committee, presiding for the first time and wielding the gavel of chairmanship. It was a position of influence and honor that he had looked forward to after twenty long years of waiting for the political center of the General Assembly to shift. Today that honor had finally come. He took the gavel of chairmanship—and passed it to Kathy, a lowly freshman senator.

"You're going to chair this committee today," he told her.

Kathy was nervous and unsure, thrust into a completely new environment. The room was filled with senators, sergeants at arms, lobbyists, and media.

"You'll be fine," he assured her with quiet confidence. "I'm here beside you."

Jim did not limit his mentorship of future leaders to those of voting or office-holding age. He was an enthusiastic participant in the page program, unlike many legislators who had little time or interest. He wanted to ensure their time as page was the educational experience it was supposed to be. Naturally, he fed them too, taking them to lunch on occasion.

Jim was appalled at the civic ignorance among the electorate, especially younger voters, and did not want the cycle repeated generation after generation. So it was gratifying to see young people take interest in the civic process. He encouraged them whenever possible and willingly took time to talk to high school students who interviewed him for school projects and newspapers. It was an investment in the future, after all.

As for legislators, his general philosophy was handed down to anyone he sought to advise or guide into or through public service and can be summed up in something he told Kathy Harrington: "Don't ever lose sight of where you came from. I have seen so many go to Raleigh and become enamored of the perks and position and lose sight of whence they came. Remember whom you represent and why you're here." A philosophy Jim himself lived by consistently. He kept his perspective and remained unspoiled.

Humor on the Agenda

If we couldn't laugh we would all go insane.

—Robert Frost

Service in the North Carolina Senate was not without its funny moments, a bit of comic relief every so often to lighten the weighty business of government, partisanship and machinations, and long hours.

A bit of comedy surrounded Jim Forrester the day he became the not-so-proud recipient of the not-so-coveted Ox Meter Award. This dubious honor can be awarded a senator for any number of reasons. He might blurt out something dumb or outlandish on the chamber floor. He might give a drawn-out and superfluous speech that has little point or is moot, such as arguing too long for or against a piece of legislation over which the upcoming vote outcome is already certain. Senator A. B. Swindell (D-Nash) received the Ox Meter Award for a long story he told about his mother's potato biscuits and how she sewed him into his flannel shirts before school each day.

As for Jim, he opined a bit too long and laboriously on some bill. So much so that nobody remembers exactly what it was.

But Jim could take a joke even from Senate colleagues. And his Ox Meter Award became a positive when he did a piece on it in his constituent newsletter, getting some good press back home.

"It was supposed to embarrass him, but he turned it around," said former Senator Andrew Brock of District 34.

It wasn't the only time Jim's fellow senators embarrassed him.

The Forresters kept an extra vehicle in Raleigh so Mary Frances would have transportation when there. She certainly needed it to shuttle herself to and from her own committees and commitments—Sir Walter Cabinet, NC State swim meets, and the North Carolina Medical Society Alliance meetings, to name a few.

Enter Mary Paige's old faded red Isuzu truck, generously emblazoned with Wake Forest stickers—a rare and not-so-welcome sight in itself in the heart of NC State country—and other paraphernalia. Mary Paige had left her truck behind when she moved to New York. Its new home was Raleigh, its driver the estimable but busy Senator Forrester's wife.

Mary Frances certainly stuck out in it, as on the morning she parallel parked the shabby truck for a quick dash into Kinkos print shop on Hillsborough Street on the NC State campus. A man standing on the street waiting for a ride saw her, dressed to the nines in a well-tailored suit, step out of the pitiful vehicle.

"Lady, what are *you* doing over *here?*" he remarked.

But by now friends, acquaintances and oft-seen strangers had become accustomed to the incongruous sight of Mary Frances shuffling around the capital in her tailored suits and battered pickup. She didn't care, though. So what if the vehicle was a bit comical? It served her well, and that was what mattered.

Until Jim came home one evening during session and announced, "We have to make new transportation arrangements."

"Why? Like what?"

"Apadaca stood up on the floor today and proposed taking up a collection to get you better transportation because you had been sighted around town in *the truck*."

Apparently, it had been a good belly laugh too often for many people, and the display of Wake Forest loyalty doubtless added to their enjoyment of the joke.

Yes, Jim could take a joke, but his embarrassment spurred him to commandeer Mary Paige's truck and give his wife the Toyota.

Mirth was found in the periodic political stunts that protesters—or some unbalanced citizen who's missed his medication—staged for attention and shock value in the capitol city and at the legislature. "You don't see it from the conservatives," remarked Senator Andrew Brock. "It's generally from the left."

If such stunts weren't funny, canny legislators like Brock learned to treat them that way nonetheless. Humor and a bit of mockery served well to rob stunts and ploys of their intended punch. "Laughing at them," said Brock, "only diminished their argument and rendered their effort counter-productive."

May 2008

Jim introduces SB 1608 Defense of Marriage in the North Carolina Senate. It is sent to committee and dies.

November 2008

California voters approve Proposition 8, which makes same-sex marriage illegal. Activist judges in Massachusetts, Connecticut, California, Iowa, and Hawaii have already struck down marriage statues in their respective states, ruling them as unconstitutional for defining marriage as the union of a man and a woman.

Life Back Home Goes On

In three words I can sum up everything I've
learned about life: it goes on.
—Robert Frost

Life as a private citizen did not stop. Jim still had multiple and varied irons in the fire back home in Stanley. There was still a future to plan and a present to enjoy—as much as a senator/doctor/brigadier general can.

There were children and grandchildren.

Jim wanted all his kids attend an in-state school, far enough to be on their own but able to come home on weekends and holidays, or at any other moment of need. In truth, he just wanted his precious brood close to him. Better still, they were all graduates of his own cherished alma mater. The three girls received their degrees from Wake Forest University, and Jimmy attended medical school there after graduating from North Carolina State.

Miles away, in New York City, Mary Paige was navigating her poor and busy way through life, absorbed in the magical and exhilarating but highly competitive world of musical theater. Perhaps her yearning for the stage—with its smells of theater dust, grease paint, and musty costumes—was partly genetic. Not only had her mother been a dancer, but Jim had taken the lead in *Our Town* his senior year in high school. Jim, though he admired her spunk and determination, missed her and wanted her *home*.

Jimmy was captain of the NC State swim team, which captured the 1992 ACC Swimming and Diving championship title. He was pre-med.

Wyndi and Gloria had married by now, and the first grand-child, William Henry Forrester Maxwell, was added to the Forrester clan. Holiday dinners meant extra places, and Jim and Mary Frances gained the generational titles of "Pop-Pop" and "Sassy."

The Forrester blood, perhaps because of its Scottish roman-ticism, produced a little poet in Jay, Jimmy's son, years later. He penned a set of verses entitled "My Role Model":

> My grandpa meant so much to me,
> Though he died when I was a little me.
> When he would look at me,
> His face would glow and shine with glee.
> His smile is like the sun.
> He was also very fun!
> The stars would smile to him,
> He would smile back to them!
> He would never bother us,
> He would never make a fuss.
> He was a light
> That brought people from day to night!

There were fund-raisers.

The most notable was the one wherein Mary Frances almost went to prison.

Each year, the GOP candidates held a fund-raiser at election time. In 1993, the star guest at this event was Governor Jim Martin.

Halloween was drawing near, and Jim suggested to the Asbury witch that she attend the fund-raiser and sit on the fence outside the venue to greet contributors and other guests coming in. It would be dark, and no one would recognize the woman beneath the heavy green makeup and pointed black hat and wart-studded nose. "People will love it. It's Halloween!"

Jim dropped the witch off, far enough away from the event so that no one would see them entering the complex together. Her secret identity must be kept! She walked down the road to the school, parked her trusty broom, and perched herself on the fence at the end of the parking lot.

Unfortunately, it occurred to neither the witch nor her husband that Governor Jim Martin would have really tight security, casting a professionally suspicious eye on all attendees before allowing them entrance. There they were, standing guard at the front doors, complete in their dark suits and headphones.

After a few moments, she alighted and was moving toward the Asbury School door. The security men immediately stepped in front of her, assessing her strange getup which concealed her true face. To them, she was every inch a potential security threat.

"Ma'am, we need to know your identity and your purpose here."

"I can't tell you who I am. But it's all in fun. I'm just here to add a little Halloween flair to the event."

This wasn't enough for the conscientious security team.

"I have permission," she added, tactfully omitting the fact that it was Jim who had given not only permission but encouragement. To name her doctor/senator/general husband just then would not be prudent.

The stern faces of the security men were unyielding. Clearly they lacked the Halloween spirit, for they insisted on seeing her identification. Alas, the witch had none on her! In her elaborate costume, there was no place to stash a wallet.

Their concerns raised, they proceeded to hustle her into a nearby classroom, sat her down, and threatened her with arrest if she didn't reveal her identity *immediately*.

Still she pleaded her innocence. "You don't understand why I can't tell you. But I promise I'm a good witch! And I have permission." She could not tell them she was Senator Forrester's wife. The mystery of the Asbury witch would be revealed, and she did not want to get Jim or herself into trouble.

The security guys simply would not come 'round to her point of view; nor would they release her, though she begged a blue streak. It was twenty minutes that seemed like forever. She was beginning to sweat from anxiety. Her putty nose and all its warts was beginning to slide slowly downward toward her upper lip. It was all she could do not to make a proverbial "dash" for it.

She didn't even want to join the party anymore.

"Just let me out of here, and I promise I'll go home!" she begged.

Unable to take the stress anymore, she asked them to go find Senator Forrester. Jim had to bail his wife out and claim her as his own wayward spouse. He promised the security that if they let her go without revealing her identity to the other guests, he would speak to the governor about it. The governor knew them both well. The mystery of the Asbury school witch was enjoyed for many years to come with nary a squeal.

There was golf—naturally.

Jim would still play with any two-legged human he could coax on the green. It wasn't that hard because he was *good*, and a pleasant partner to boot.

The only negatives were the frequent complaints from fellow golfers of this or that physical ailment, along with solicitation of his medical expertise, as if Jim were in his examining room in Stanley instead of on the pristine green turf that was his *escape*. Of course, he listened and advised his friends with willing grace, but even friends would take advantage of the situation. Sometimes Jim responded to them with a wide grin and a blunt, "Yeah, the last man I saw who had that died." Anything to gently but effectively shut the person up and allow him to return to his first recreational love. And love it he did.

Former Senator Andrew Brock remembers the day he approached Jim after the senate had adjourned. Jim wore a tie and blazer atop a polo shirt. He was just sitting there, making no move to rise from his seat, mingle with the other senators, or exit the chamber.

"Are you all right?" Andrew asked him.

"Oh yes," Jim responded. "I'm just waiting for everybody to leave." He stuck out a leg to reveal his golf shorts.

He had arrived for session early and wouldn't get up until everyone was gone.

A Full, Empty Nest

He felt now that he was not simply close to her, but that
he did not know where he ended and she began.

—Leo Tolstoy

An empty nest reveals much about the marriage that remains, particularly its negative points. Jim and Mary Frances found they had nothing to worry about wedlock-wise once the kids were grown.

There was also new opportunity for camaraderie and humor, shared experiences, and travel.

In April 1994, the two sweethearts set sail on Cunard's *Queen Mary II* to London. The trip marked their thirty-fifth wedding anniversary.

As the ship departed New York Harbor, Jim's eyes were fixed on the statute of Lady Liberty. It evoked a deep poignancy in his heart. It was yet another moment, like that in front of James's grave, in which words were unnecessary. He and Mary Frances thought the same thoughts.

What a long road back to that statue it had been for Jim. The first time he had seen it, he had held his mother's hand, and the unborn years ahead remained without shape or certainty. Now he held Mary Frances's hand, and most of those unknowns had been revealed.

It was surreal. His feet had then walked over the deck of a humble passenger boat that day in 1946. Now they walked the promenade deck of the grand ocean liner *Queen Mary II*.

Son, always remember to give back—his mother's words returned to him.

Have I been true to her admonishment? he pondered, watching the statue shrink from view.

The *Queen Mary II* was all they could imagine and more, complete with gilded stairways, oil paintings, and crystal chandeliers.

Soon after leaving New York, however, she hit a fog more closely resembling beef stew than pea soup. The foghorn's bellow left a constant echo in the ear as it sounded every two minutes, in keeping with maritime law. Since visibility was nil, the two occupied themselves to pass the time. Jim watched English soccer on BBC television since American football was not available. Mary Frances made new friends and conquered at bridge in the glass-enclosed forward parlor, every now and then looking up to see fog, fog, and more fog.

After three days at sea, the fog finally fizzled into a clear but chilly scene.

On the fourth day, unbeknownst to Jim and Mary Frances, the voyage became an anniversary of another sort. On April 15, the ship approached coordinates 41.726931° N and -49.948253° W, a spot on the nautical map that is forever dark in history's reckoning. The captain's voice boomed over the intercom, informing passengers that they were sailing through Iceberg Alley, passing directly over the spot the "unsinkable" *Titanic* went down.

"This very day in 1912," he reminded them.

The information wrought a macabre atmosphere aboard ship as the Forresters and everyone else recalled the chain of events leading to the loss of 1,500 souls, a small remnant of humanity still lying in wakeless sleep twelve thousand feet beneath their feet.

Of course, there was always the pull of Scotland in Jim's blood, and he returned to his native soil many times. The reasons varied, from visiting family members to hunting his father's handmade golf clubs, from tracing his genealogy to attending the weddings of kinfolk. In 2008, he packed up his own American branch of Clan Forrester and took them to the land of bagpipes, brogues, and Scotch whiskey.

Some things never changed. Whether at home or abroad, sweet and funny moments were still to be found. Nothing brightened the days like an occasional absurdity.

Mary Frances, upon whom "the change" wreaked bodily havoc, had taken to wearing a twenty-four-hour estrogen patch. One morning, she awoke to find that it was not on its designated spot on her backside. She looked herself over but didn't find it. Nor was it on the floor, in the sheets, under the bed, or anywhere else. Suddenly Jim walked over to the bed, lifted his T-shirt, and pointed to the missing estrogen patch stuck on his rib cage. "I think I found it," he informed her in a high-falsetto squeal.

This "girly" voice emanating from her tall, burly husband sent Mary Frances into peals of uncontrolled laughter. Each time their eyes met that day, they lapsed into renewed giggles.

Life was still good.

Knighthoods and Coat of Arms

*"You were a knight," said Merlin. "Somewhere in the world
there is defeat for everyone. Some are destroyed by defeat,
and some made small and mean by victory. Greatness lives
in one who triumphs equally over defeat and victory."*
—John Steinbeck, *The Acts of King Arthur and His Noble Knights*

Iredell County commissioner Ken Robertson used to joke about being at loss when trying to introduce James Forrester, his accomplished and well-rounded friend. He would end up just saying, "Senator/Doctor/General Jim Forrester." He wasn't the only one to stumble over the appropriate form of address at any given time.

Jim, true to his down-to-earth character, tried to make it easy for everybody. "Just call me Jim," he would say.

But his senator/doctor/general status was only the beginning. He gained additional honors from across the pond.

In order to present a petition for a personal coat of arms to the office of heraldry in Edinburgh, once must first submit proof of lineage and accomplishments. A close collaboration with a Scottish genealogist revealed that Jim's ancestors were not only seamen but tradesmen, a status as close to "middle class" as one could get before the twentieth century. The golf champion James Summers Forrester, however, had brought honor and recognition upon his nation, only to die before he could receive the coat of arms he had earned. Jim—and his mother, Nancy—would make sure James gained it posthumously in the person of his son and in his future grandsons.

Thus, in 1991, Jim Forrester, by permission of Her Royal Highness Queen Elizabeth II, was granted his personal coat of arms by the Lord Lyon, Malcom Innes, of Edinburgh, Scotland. The armorial bearing was granted in memory of his father, James Summers Forrester, "a golf professional of renown," as well as in honor of Jim's own accomplishments as a Scottish-born citizen and naturalized American citizen. Its registration was witnessed in the Heraldry Registry Library and subsequently registered in the Armiger Journals of both Scotland and the United States. Jim chose for his personal Latin motto that which was adopted by his beloved North Carolina.

Esse Quam Videri
To Be Rather Than to Seem

They traveled to Edinburgh for an audience with Lord Lyon himself and a history tour of the Royal Heraldry Library before being formally presented with Jim's armorial bearing.

Twelve years later in June of 2003, Mary Frances received an email from one Michael Murphy, who claimed to be the American representative of His Royal Highness Dom Duarte Pio, Duke of Braganza, of Portugal. Murphy was asking Jim, on the Duke's behalf, to participate in the celebration of his noble house's six hundredth anniversary. The Duke was aware that Jim was a registered armiger with distinguished accomplishments, both military and political.

At first Mary, Frances thought it a hoax. She replied to Murphy saying she "needed more information" and then called Jim.

Murphy and his email proved legitimate. Jim was one of only eight distinguished American armigers invited to take part in the celebration. Unfortunately, the General Assembly was in short session, and Jim could not forsake his duty to his state. He asked how else he could participate.

As an American ally, the Duke had been a helicopter pilot in Vietnam. Jim sent a letter to the Duke thanking the Duke for his invitation and complimenting Portugal's assistance during the war in Southeast Asia. Sometime later, Jim received a letter in Portuguese from the Duke's house that Jim was being knighted for his distinguished political, medical, and military service. Gloria translated the letter. "You're being made a knight!"

Mary Frances was agog. To her, she had been calling him her "knight" for forty years. Now her knight would be real. Who would have guessed!

On August 29, 2003, His Royal Highness Dom Duarte Pio, Duke of Braganza, heir apparent to the Portuguese throne, conferred upon Jim an honorary—as Jim was not Roman Catholic—knighthood in the Order of St. Miguel of the Wing (KSMA), with all entitlements, rights, and privileges of the degree including the use of KSMA at the end of his signature.

> Under God's Grace, I, Duke of Braganca, as Judge of the Royal Brotherhood of Sao Miguel of Ala, make it known to whomever sees this letter that I in good faith chose to name Senator James S. Forrester, M.D. Honorary Knight of the Order of Sao Miguel de Ala and honorary Brother of the Royal Brotherhood of Sao Miguel de Ala corresponding to the above mentioned Royal Brotherhood with all its inherent honors.

This order, an "institution of chivalric character," is one of the oldest orders of knighthood in Christendom, founded in AD 1147. No one is admitted to its ranks without due consideration and credentials and confirmation by the Portuguese parliament. Today there are approximately only six hundred knights worldwide in this order.

A year later, an invitation in English arrived requesting the honor of Jim's presence at the "Mass and Investiture of the Royal Brotherhood of the Order of St. Michael of the Wing" at the Church of the Immaculate Conception in Washington, DC. This would be the formal knighting ceremony.

Jim's leg was still recovering from a garden swing accident, and he needed the assistance of a walker.

The ceremony held all the traditional pomp and circumstance that an undertaking of that sort should. There were seals and crests of gold. White capes for Jim and the other knights donned to receive their honors.

At brunch, Jim sat beside Duke and shared experiences of their flying service during Vietnam and the alliance between the US and Portugal. The Azores, a frequent destination for Jim during his flight-surgeon days, was a Portuguese territory, and the American Air Force Base there was still in service.

The conversation turned to other matters, such as the upcoming referendum in Portugal that would allow government-funded abortions. The Duke, as a Catholic and the "defender of the faith," wanted something to encourage citizens to vote against the measure. In his position, he had little governing power, but he was allowed airtime on television for public service messages.

Jim and Mary Frances discussed the matter on the flight home. The next morning, Mary Frances called Focus on the Family and spoke with their chief deputy for James Dobson, the organization's founder. The deputy promised to see "what they could pull together."

A day or so later, the deputy called back. "Are you sitting down, Mrs. Forrester?"

"Well, we're just about to go to dinner."

"I must say that God does work in mysterious ways." He proceeded to tell her that a missionary had walked into the Focus office that very day and brought public service announcement tapes about the dangers of abortion.

"Mrs. Forrester, the messages are *in Portuguese.*"

She was astonished. Surely this could not be coincidence! Jim's conversation with the Duke had been a providential appointment. But as Christian believers, they were all on God's team, so why should anyone be surprised?

Mary Frances eventually got the tapes to a liaison, who got them to Portugal, where they were aired. The Duke was so grateful to the Forresters that he invited them to a private luncheon at his Lisbon palace, which they accepted.

"Through time and history, the knight has progressed to the standard of an officer and a gentleman, a striving for excellence, courage, and loyalty as well as a seeker of virtue and a defender of the weak. It is most often conferred on those who use their strength for good and contribute greatly to society."

A coat of arms and an ancient knighthood do not end up as feathers in the caps of most folk. Jim got them, and it was only natural to acquire yet another nickname or two in the Senate, where nicknames abound almost as must as they do in the military. He now became "Sir Jim" or "Gentleman Jim" to colleagues.

In other men, such accolades and honors can puff up their recipients. Not Jim, who neither rested on his golden laurels nor boasted about them. Three things prevented this:

One, his inherent humility, which eschewed any public recognition of his new title. His attitude was that proscribed in Ethan Hawke's *Rules for a Knight*: "Never announce that you are a knight, simply behave as one. You are better than no one, and no one is better than you."

Two, his good theology, which counted all earthly praise as fleeting.

Three, Mary Frances, who would always be around to ensure he kept his feet on the ground.

Still she would have to be an odd bird indeed if she did not take pride in her accomplished husband and delight in the encomiums bestowed on him—and on her by extension, for she was now Lady Forrester.

Oh, if only Jim's parents could see all that he has achieved, Mary Frances would muse.

If only *her* mother and Aunt Lil could see the knight—the man—she had always known Jim to be!

North Carolina, 2009

Conviction was the core he operated on.
—Tami Fitzgerald

The term "banning gay marriage" is media hype.
One cannot ban something that doesn't exist.
—Mary Frances Forrester

At a legislative press conference on February 24, 2009, Jim Forrester and four other lawmakers joined with NC4Marriage, a coalition of voters, churches, policy groups, and political leaders of both political parties to announce the introduction of a Defense of Marriage bill in both houses of the General Assembly. The proposed amendment in the bill, like its predecessors, held that "marriage between a man and a woman is the only domestic legal union that shall be valid or recognized in this state."

"We are sponsoring this legislation because we firmly believe that North Carolina's marriage laws are at risk of being redefined by activist courts to include same-sex couples," Jim told those gathered. "At any moment, a lawsuit challenging our marriage laws could be filed by a same-sex couple from our state that obtained a marriage license in a state where same-sex 'marriage' is legal. Without an amendment to our state constitution, North Carolina is one bad ruling away from having our marriage laws redefined."

"Our opponents will tell you that North Carolina has strong marriage laws already and that a constitutional amendment is unnecessary," remarked Representative David Lewis (R-Harnett). "That argument no longer holds water as we have seen the strong marriage laws of other states—including states with Defense of Marriage Acts like California and Iowa—overturned by their courts. The indisputable fact is that the only way to protect marriage in North Carolina is through a constitutional amendment, and the people of this state should no longer be denied the opportunity to vote on this issue."

NC4Marriage executive director Tami Fitzgerald and the Family Policy Council had been lobbying for a marriage amendment for five years. Thirty other states, Tami reminded everyone, had already been given the chance to vote on a constitutional marriage amendment and that "North Carolina is the only state in the southern United States that has not protected marriage in its state constitution, which makes us a prime target for same-sex 'marriage' activists."

No one realized then just how much of a national target the Tar Heel state would become.

Jim continued to gather and solidify amendment support among legislators. One was Democrat senator Steve Goss, a Southern Baptist minister and former missionary to Japan, whose office Jim had visited many times to make sure Goss was "on board" and willing to put his name on an amendment bill. "I will be the first Democrat to sponsor that legislation," was Goss's repeated promise to Jim.

Tami Fitzgerald joined with Alliance Defending Freedom (ADF) attorneys to construct new language for the marriage amendment bill, "scrapping" the two or three sentences of legalese used in previous versions. They wanted shorter, simpler wording that would be easier for citizens to understand upon reading at the ballot box, thus making it easier to pass. The amendment was distilled down to one short and sweet statement:

> Marriage between a man and a woman is the only domestic legal union that shall be valid or recognized in this State. This section does not prohibit a private party from entering into contracts with another private party; nor does this section prohibit courts from adjudicating the rights of private parties pursuant to such contracts.

A team of constitutional lawyers concurred with the new version. Jim approved it.

Attempts were made to complicate and misrepresent the issue and to divert attention toward other things. Ian Palmquist, executive director of Equality North Carolina, said, "We believe that constitutions are supposed to be there to protect rights, not take them away. You should never put the civil rights of a minority up for a popular vote." He expressed optimism that the marriage bill wouldn't come up that year for a legislative vote. "We hope the leadership focuses on trying to balance the budget and create jobs, and leaves these divisive issues alone."

The irony and hypocrisy of this statement was astounding to Jim, considering the frequent willingness of liberals to bring up divisive "social issues" themselves.

Representative David Lewis expressed outward concern over inheritance and property rights issues among same-sex couples. Other gay advocates claimed that a marriage amendment would hurt the state's economy. This was a stretch. Considering the overwhelming pro-traditional marriage bent of public opinion, it was just as likely to *help* the state as hurt it.

"I think a business can decide to do what they want," said Jim, in response to additional claims that the amendment would prohibit private businesses from extending benefits to domestic partners.

Arguments continued to fly, but the 2009 marriage amendment, like the one that came before, never made it to the floor of the General Assembly, much less to the voters.

But things were about to change.

The following year, in 2010, a young attorney by the name of Dan Soucek was running for North Carolina Senate District 45, a conservative, largely rural district but for the liberal stronghold of Boone. Soucek's opponent was none other than incumbent senator Steve Goss.

Goss and Soucek faced off in a campaign trail debate. When the amendment topic was broached, Soucek openly questioned Goss about his stand on the issue. Why would any pastor not support a marriage amendment?

Without hesitation, Goss said, "No one has approached me about this."

Soucek was shocked, recognizing this as a blatant falsehood. Jim had spoken of his multiple visits to Goss and Goss's assurances of support for an amendment bill. This backtracking would prove a bad move on Goss's part.

Later on the campaign trail, Soucek stopped for lunch in the farthest, most rural corner of Alexander County. He had barely greeted the waitress when a random stranger approached, saying, "You're Dan Soucek, aren't you?"

"Yes," Soucek replied.

"Well," the man said bluntly, "I'm supporting you because Steve Goss betrayed us on the marriage amendment."

Soucek realized then that the amendment issue was far-reaching and pervasive and that most North Carolinians were aware not only of its existence but its significance. They *wanted* it.

Still a Guardsman

*Ask anybody about Jim Forrester and the first word out
of their mouth would probably be "gentleman."*
—Colonel Irv "Duke" Ellington

Jim's triple-pronged life as senator, doctor, officer converged most strongly in the North Carolina Air National Guard (NCANG). Moreover, as the years passed, his military duties, his medical expertise, and his role in state politics were inevitably and increasingly intertwined.

Like the Army National Guard, this military body falls under the direct command of the state's governor, who acts as its commander-in-chief. Put another way, the NCANG is wholly a state entity and belongs to the people of North Carolina.

It also operates under a different mindset than active-duty or reserve forces. There is an unofficial emphasis on family considerations when enlisting new people. The Air National Guard wants to keep its airmen and medical personnel long-term.

This mindset of family and permanence suited Jim perfectly, and it showed in the legislation he sponsored in the General Assembly. One such bill was National Guard Health Benefits (SB434), which sought to provide health benefits for North Carolina National Guard members and their eligible dependents who didn't have access to comprehensive group health benefits by allowing voluntary participation in the teachers' and state employees' comprehensive major medical plan.

Another was the NCNG Heroes Act of 2007 (SB653). This would create a fund to provide a death benefit for North Carolina

National Guard members killed in the line of duty and would provide a free higher education for their qualified dependents.

Unfortunately, neither bill would pass.

Chief Master Sergeant Terry Henderson recalls Jim's instrumental lobbying efforts for new airplanes, such as the 1993 conversion from the old Vietnam-era B model C130s to C130Hs, otherwise known as the Hercules. When the unit needed new land for expansion, which proved a delicate matter with city, county, and state entities, Jim helped get a deal approved through the General Assembly.

In the military hierarchy of the Air National Guard, Jim became assistant adjutant general for Air, the third highest officer in the state after the governor and adjutant general. This was the highest military capacity in which Jim would serve, and he utilized the position to further meet the NCANG interests and needs.

There was also the federal insurance program TriCare, geared solely for retired military. "Jim was instrumental in getting physicians to accept it and would refer military patients to doctors that took it," remembered Lieutenant Colonel Al Rose. Jim encouraged guardsmen to subscribe to the program as it acted as a safety net, even covering wives, after regular insurance and Medicare are tapped out. If one has neither insurance nor Medicare, TriCare would pay everything.

Even after retirement, Jim served the Guard. Chief Master Sergeant Terry Henderson recalls that even after becoming state air surgeon, Jim would come to the Air Guard clinic on weekends and help the medical teams see patients. "He didn't have to do that, and it furthered their respect for him," said Brigadier General Fisk Outwater. "Plus, it allowed him to feel like he was still a part."

On November 15, 1997, after a total of thirty-four years' service, Jim received an honorable discharge from the North Carolina Air National Guard with the flag officer rank of brigadier general.

"He was one of the most influential people in moving the Guard forward, in making it what it is today," observed Outwater. "He was a voice for the unit and a crucial part of its history."

Still a Small-Town Doctor

He had a touch *with his patients. A compassion.*

—Tammy Johnson

Jim was still a small-town physician, and he continued to see patients as far as time, age, and the duties of statesmanship allowed.

"Even on weekends," Tammy Johnson recalled, "even up to the time before his passing, if a patient needed him, he would go to the office and see them. They knew they could even call him at home if the need was great. Or he would treat them over the phone."

Jim missed delivering babies. He had ended his favorite pastime—second to golf—when he began commuting to Asheville in pursuit of his public health degree back in 1976. Other doctors covered for him, but he could not always reciprocate, which he felt was unfair. But by then, the practice of family doctors delivering babies was being phased out anyway.

Still many of Jim's babies now walked through the doors of the Stanley office and remarked to Tammy that "Dr. Forrester delivered me."

Medically speaking, things around him were changing far too fast and not for the better. Jim had always loved the small, simple structure of his practice, the personalization with patients, and the relatively large measure of professional freedom he enjoyed. But he was tired. The fact that he was considering retirement from medicine revealed just *how* tired.

He was approached by Lake Norman Regional Hospital about purchasing his practice. After negotiation, he proceeded with the deal—and came to regret it. When Lake Norman Regional took over, the practice became a bog of paperwork, numbers, and quotas. Protocol was still good, but overall things were complicated and distinctly impersonal. The additional regulations, requirements, and documentation were choking the life from something he had methodically, lovingly built over the course of forty years.

He resented being told how long he could spend with a patient. That should depend on his or her individual situation!

The new rules also dictated that only so much money could be spent on supplies within a certain time period, which meant only a small inventory was allowed. The upshot was that a diabetic patient might come in, and Jim would have no test strips with which to check blood sugar. Or someone might need a tetanus shot, and Jim was told he could not buy it until a certain date. Before, he had always kept a supply on hand in the refrigerator.

It was rationing—and he would not have that in his own office!

In another effort to cut costs, Lake Norman Regional wanted him to reduce his number of employees. He refused as that would further degrade the quality of care patients received.

His employees hated the new setup, as did his patients, who were being short-changed with substandard service.

"I don't do business this way," said Jim at last. "My patients expect better."

So he bought the practice back.

"How much do I owe?" he asked.

It was a ghastly sum, but Jim paid it gladly.

Apart from death, Jim never really "lost" a patient. He visited former patients in nursing homes, some on a regular basis. One aged lady, a victim of multiple strokes, saw him coming nearly every Sunday. No one else ever came. It was unlikely the lady recognized Jim, and communication was difficult, but Jim went anyway.

His compassion impressed his son Jimmy, who also became a doctor. But Jimmy was also impressed with his father's healthy mix of sentiment and realism. After a deep and poignant conversation about the medical profession, Jim turned to his namesake with a smile and chuckled. "Well, son," he said, "some people are just born with lousy protoplasm."

May 2010

Jim introduces SB1156 Defense of Marriage in the North Carolina Senate. It is sent to committee and dies.

August 2010

Proposition 8 is ruled unconstitutional by a federal judge in California who maintains that the same-sex marriage ban violates the equal protection provisions of the US Constitution.

September 2011

The "Don't Ask, Don't Tell" policy of the United States Armed Forces is repealed.

Bonnie Days

The sun rises and the sun sets, and hurries back to where it rises.
—Ecclesiastes 1:5 NIV

It was a bonnie day when, on Monday, May 10, 2004, Jim Forrester was elected Senate minority leader after fourteen years' service in that august body. He remained a mild-mannered statesman.

"I'm not somebody who's going to bang his fist on the table or something like that. I see a lot of bipartisan support on issues."

It was a bonnie day in 2008 when the First Minister Alex Salmond of Scotland came to visit the North Carolina General Assembly, before Scotland's 2014 unsuccessful vote for independence, *Yes Scotland*. Jim was ecstatic, glorious in his kilt of Forrester tartan. He had good legs and no reservations about showing them. He introduced Salmond and escorted him about with beaming enthusiasm.

It was a bonnie day when Jim found one of his father's handmade hickory shafted golf clubs, etched with his father's name, while poking around in the golf clubhouse while attending a medical conference in Texas. The day got bonnier when he paid only five dollars for it.

It was a bonny day when he first took the train to Raleigh. It was getting difficult time-wise for Mary Frances to drive every week, especially since most of her own pursuits and involvement in the capital were behind her. Jim, a regular passenger during session, enjoyed the quiet, unhurried atmosphere of the train. He could think, work, and rest undisturbed. The attendants grew to like and respect the tall senator who always had a friendly smile and concerned manner toward them.

It was a bonny day in 2010 when it snowed on the beach in Wilmington on Christmas, the holiday for which he never outgrew his "child's delight." All his favorite trimmings were represented—a Scottish trifle, devilled eggs, and a beach house drowning in Christmas lights courtesy of Mary Paige and her fiancé, Thomas Blalock.

Having his *family* around him for the holidays was still his most-loved tradition.

Thomas, now Mary Paige's husband, remembers "the general" quietly and contentedly taking it all in, savoring the magic and love, enjoying the pride he felt in his children and grandchildren.

Almost as if he knew it would be his last Christmas.

Part 3

The Bill

These troubles and distresses that you go through in these waters,
are not sign that God hath forsaken you; but are sent to try you,
whether you will call to mind that which heretofore you have
received of his goodness, and live upon him in your distresses.
　　　　　　　　　　　　　　—John Bunyan, *Pilgrim's Progress*

Jim Forrester did not seek controversy. He was merely a man who stood for something right, and controversy followed. He had no idea the gay-marriage fight in North Carolina was about to be thrust into the national and international spotlight.

In liberal thinking, if a conservative state like North Carolina could be "toppled" on the issue, the rest of the South might follow. Thus, North Carolina became both a test ground and a target.

In November of 2010, history intervened with the election of the first majority Republican General Assembly since Reconstruction. With it came the long-awaited shift in the balance of power. The new majority notwithstanding, there was still no guarantee a marriage amendment bill would pass.

Three-fifths vote of the General Assembly is required to ratify an amendment bill and put it on a statewide ballot. It is hard to get 60 percent of a vote on anything in the General Assembly. Whatever else happened, a floor vote would be close. No one could foresee just *how* close.

But first it had to get there, and that was no simple task.

Dan Soucek, now a freshman senator from Boone, had barely hung his office pictures when Jim walked in, saying, "I'd like you to be a primary sponsor with me on this marriage amendment bill."

Soucek was astonished. *Why choose me!* he thought. He was a novice. *Why should I get to participate at this level?*

But Jim had learned much about Soucek through personal interactions and the previous year's campaign. "He believed in Dan and put great faith in him," Mary Frances remembered. "He was another future leader Jim wanted to encourage and mentor."

"It was an honor," Soucek recalled, especially as Jim had been pursuing the amendment legislation for so many years, along with Republican caucus. It was a cause close to the veteran senator's heart, everyone knew. And now Jim wanted Dan to share it with him.

Soucek, thanks largely to the amendment, would get his legislative baptism by fire. But that was okay with him. It was the right thing to do.

On February 22, 2011, Jim introduced Senate Bill 106, his final marriage amendment legislation.

Leading the charge over in the House were primary sponsors Representatives David Lewis and Skip Stam, who gave the bill its forward push.

But many Republican legislators, though supporting the amendment on an ideological basis, wanted to defer any present action on the legislation. They were overly cautious about bringing a marriage amendment bill to a floor vote. It was not the right time, they believed.

There were several reasons for their reluctance. For one thing, there was a great deal riding on the first few months of that session. The Republicans, in the minority since Reconstruction, had yet to prove their competence and capability for governing efficiently. Those in the opposition party, the media, and elsewhere waited hopefully for the new guys to falter or fail.

If Republicans brought the amendment bill up right off the bat, the Democrats and liberal media would pounce on them like hungry jackals with predictable accusations. "See! All they care about are their darn religious and social issues. They don't care about anything else!"

"They had been a minority for so many years," said Tami Fitzgerald, executive director of the NC Values Coalition, "that they didn't want to blow it the first year by bringing up these social issues that could threaten the hard-won majority." There were always election consequences to consider.

So many Republicans favored pushing the bill back on the calendar, so it could not be abused or used for political mileage against them. They would do the right thing, yes, but would wait for a more propitious time. Why invite controversy at the outset of their first session as a majority party by taking up an issue that might complicate the other more pressing duties and issues before them. "Let's get the hard things done first," was their admonishment, referring to economic and regulation reforms.

In actuality, there was plenty of time for those things. The amendment itself was nothing if not simple, requiring little in the way of time. Besides, as pro-amendment individuals repeatedly pointed out, legislators would not actually be voting for the amendment. They would be voting to give amendment decision to the people. They could tell their constituents that.

Mary Frances suspected that one or two legislators might even have had a gay family member or loved one in the equation, which made them uncertain or reluctant.

It was all a varied mixture of sincere strategic reasons, convenient diversions, or just plain unwillingness to court a controversial social issue. By contrast, Jim and others, though they understood many of the reasons, saw no cause to delay a vote on the amendment bill. Politically, Republicans would get flak no matter when they brought the issue up! Legally, time was an issue in the current court system. Ethically, why delay something that had such overwhelming statewide support! Shouldn't the manifest will of the people be treated with more urgency?

Tami Fitzgerald, in response to an August 16 *Charlotte Observer* editorial "Marriage Amendment a Roadblock to Change," expressed it this way:

> Every state where voters have been allowed to
> vote on marriage (30 in all) has voted to adopt
> a marriage amendment. Conversely, no state has

adopted same-sex marriage by popular vote. In fact, every state where given the opportunity to rescind same-sex marriage that was ordered by a judge or the legislature, same-sex marriage has been rejected by a vote of the people.

Shouldn't the good citizens of North Carolina be granted the same opportunity? The people retain the right to determine the definition of marriage in the laws that govern them!

Whatever camp his fellow legislators fell into, pro or con, Republican or Democrat, North Carolinians themselves were in ideological solidarity with Jim. Overwhelmingly.

"Every poll I've seen," said Jim, "Civitas, Family Policy Council poll, Vaughn–Autry poll, shows that citizens of this state would support this amendment to our constitution. There is only one poll I have seen that negates that, a poll put out by Elon University, where they selected three hundred or four hundred people off the street to vote on this, and it was about an equal poll."

But the amendment bill must wait a little longer. As the legislative session waned toward the end of July, it still had not been scheduled for a hearing.

Whatever the timetable, to say the introduction of SB106 "heated up" the gay-marriage debate is a gross understatement. Now that the party shift in the General Assembly meant a real possibility of a constitutional marriage amendment getting beneath the powerful fingertips of voters, the steady flame of controversy that had smoldered so many years became a full-blown inferno.

And Jim would be burned worse than anyone.

Into the Fire

You have to be thick-skinned in the political world.
—Senator Jim Forrester

Media bias, a cross of frustration for conservatives on any given day, was sure to factor against the pro-amendment forces. Then and now leftists and their handmaidens in the press, always sniffing the wind for juicy "gotcha" moments, harbor no qualms in misrepresenting the words of any public figure on the right and misconstruing the true meaning and intention behind them. The left will politicize a church potluck dinner to rack up political miles!

This sad fact hit home to Jim on September 8, 2010, less than two months before the November election that heralded the majority shift in the General Assembly. At a meeting of Iredell County Young Republicans, he declared that "slick city lawyers and homosexual lobbies and African American lobbies are running Raleigh."

In *context*, Jim was referring to the large and powerful lobbying groups in the General Assembly, such as the Black Caucus, along with high-profile lawyers like John Edwards and Tony Rand. Factions that wielded a large and disproportionate influence on the Democrat Party—the majority party—as well as state government as a whole.

Many a Republican, past and present, recognized the truth of Jim's statement and doubtless muttered a, "Well, it's true," under his or her breath over their morning coffee. Jim had merely verbalized aloud what everyone else had been thinking for years.

But the context of his words and the real essence of what he was saying mattered little to the opposition, who flew into a tailspin and blew the remark beyond proportion. Straw-man accusations sprouted up on cue to obfuscate Jim's meaning. "Senator Forrester hated gays!" "Senator Forrester hated blacks!" "Senator Forrester hated lawyers!" All patent nonsense to anyone who actually knew the man.

"I wasn't trying to be ugly or anything like that, and if it came out that way, I apologize," Jim told the *Gaston Gazette*, "I was just expressing my opinion about the leadership in the General Assembly and the bills that are being passed. North Carolina is a conservative state. Most people are conservatives, and the leadership in Raleigh is liberal." Shameful gerrymandering had largely contributed to this disparity.

Shortly after the event, the *Gaston Gazette* ran a poll asking, "Do you think Senator Jim Forrester should apologize for his comment on gays and blacks?" This question in itself was misleading as Jim had said *nothing* about gay and blacks per se. He had referred solely to the salaried entities that claimed to represent those particular segments of the population.

Even then, 66 percent of poll respondents expressed the view that Jim's comment was "the truth." Only 24 percent deemed it "hateful speech" while 10 percent decided it was "not a big deal either way."

But mischaracterization and exaggeration would remain favorite weapons in the gay-marriage faction's attempt to discredit both Jim and his amendment that year. He was "mean-spirited" and wished to further a "disgraceful form of bigotry." Mary Frances was quick to point out the hypocrisy of the other side by directing them to *Webster's* primary definition of the word *bigot*:

> *Bigot*: a person who is obstinately or intolerantly
> devoted to his or her own opinions and prejudices

It was the pot calling the kettle black!

"He is determined to stomp every gay person into the ground," was the bald accusation of Faith in America founder Mitchell Gold in a group web posting.

Newspaper headlines pertaining to the amendment were worded to reflect the media's own ideological loyalties. Not that this was anything new. Back in 2008, the *News & Observer* had run a story entitled "Same-Sex Couples Left in Limbo," alongside a touching photo of a lesbian couple, one of the two tearful, after being denied a marriage license by a San Francisco city clerk. The headline's phrasing and the language used in the write-up that followed assumed gays as victims, the moral protagonists in the drama. The intended takeaway for the reader: anyone opposed to gay marriage is a jerk.

Another paper ran a story titled "While Conservative Legislators Denounce Same-Sex Marriage, a Lawmaker Discusses Being Gay." A headshot of pleasant-looking Marcus Brandon, a Democratic representative from Guilford County, brightens the page with a friendly smile. The story's implication? How could anyone deny such a nice man the desire of his heart!

So went the lion's share of reporting on the issue, one-sided, heavy with partiality, and infused with a relentless implication that any right-thinking, fair-minded, and enlightened individual concerned with justice would support gay marriage and oppose the marriage amendment. Forget the established and proven wisdom of natural marriage for the past five thousand years of history!

Same-sex marriage was a belief built on faulty foundations, both philosophically and constitutionally. "Love is love" was the new emotional dogma. *Repetition reduces resistance.*

"The truth is that the marriage amendment is not about denying rights to citizens," Tami Fitzgerald, executive director of the NC Values Coalition, wrote in an editorial to the *Charlotte Observer* on August 22, 2011. "There is no right to marry someone of the same sex, just as there is no right to marry your sister, to marry someone who is under 14 years old, or to marry more than one person. Those who oppose incorporating our current state law's definition of marriage into the constitution want to radically redefine marriage, radically redefine families, and radically redefine the natural process of producing and raising children with the safe, nurturing, and successful incubator of marriage."

Apparently, the citizens of North Carolina agreed. On May 17, 2011, Jim spoke at a rally organized by Return America, led by Pastor Ron Baity and held on Halifax Mall in Raleigh. Over five thousand pro-amendment citizens turned out to show their support. North Carolina was in the throes of torrential rainstorms across the state, which worried organizers that this and unfriendly driving conditions would discourage participation.

It did not. Even better, many participants who had driven through downpours remarked that as soon as they arrived in Raleigh and the rally commenced, the skies cleared and the day was perfect. It felt like God giving grace to the endeavor.

The press showed up, naturally, ready to downplay the event and suppress the crowd numbers in their coverage of the event. The rally highlighted the international spotlight the amendment fight brought to North Carolina. Pastor Ron Baity was interviewed by every major network in America and even news teams as far away as Germany and Israel.

But whoever stuck a microphone in his face, the newsperson holding it would frame his or her questions a certain way, revealing a personal bias and a tacit solidarity with the anti-amendment side. A good example is, "Why are you trying to take away personal liberties from them?"—as if the right to same-sex marriage had always been the norm, always been recognized by the culture and the individuals that comprised it. The media's questions assumed it was all a settled matter, and had been for generations.

For the most part, the rally was peaceful. At its end, though, many of the anti-amendment people approached the church buses to show a little "love" in the form of vulgar remarks yelled out to those boarding the vehicles.

Baity became an "object of wrath" when he and his wife, his daughter, two granddaughters, his secretary, and others from their church were leaving Halifax Mall. As they walked along the sidewalk toward Jones Street, a visibly angry homosexual man approached Baity's daughter, saying, "Do you allow your girls to be involved in homosexuality?"

Baity hastened to position himself in front of his daughter, anxious for his family's safety. He had come to expect anything at this point!

"You're depriving them of the best of life!" the man was telling his daughter.

"Sir, you need to leave," Baity warned. He instructed the others to go on ahead, sensing the situation was about to escalate.

The man was now in his face and beginning to hit him with a large piece of cardboard he'd been carrying.

"You don't want to touch me," Baity warned calmly. "If you want free transportation downtown, put your hand on me again, and you'll get it."

The man did not retreat, only hurled lewd insults and suggestions at the pastor.

Thankfully, a policeman across the street saw the confrontation and came to advise the enraged man to leave Baity alone or be arrested for assault.

The Price of Virtue

*The further a society drifts from the truth, the
more it will hate those who speak it.*
—George Orwell

The gay-rights faction did not shrink from employing personal strikes against Jim. They attempted to question his membership in various medical organizations. They even accused him of lying about his membership status with the Academy of Family Physicians. In truth, Jim was one of the first fellows of the academy, an honor accorded him before the organization even began keeping membership records!

An attack on his medical credentials and honesty was the end of enough for Jim. "The gay and lesbian community is trying to discredit me," he said. "I'm not trying to deceive anybody." These were not the only "untruths" he was accused of.

Jim's response to it all: "Well, if you don't like the message, kill the messenger."

Privately, things were tough for the Forresters. They stood behind window blinds as strange cars circled through their driveway at night. Random strangers would stop and take photos of their house or knock on the door with pointless questions such as, "Where did you come from?" or, "What kind of bricks do you have on your house?"

Mary Frances was never sure if they were friend or foe, but she suspected the latter. Such attempts to unnerve and frighten were common, and they worked especially well when she was home alone.

There were scores of nasty phone calls loaded with everything from ominous heavy breathing to screaming insults and threats.

Rachel was on the receiving end of such calls at the medical office. One caller even threatened her with subpoena unless she revealed Jim's present location. Rachel told the caller nothing. Tammy Johnson got her own share of angry calls but was quick to note that "most people agreed with his stance."

The Forrester computers, both the personal and work devices, were hacked multiple times.

Bad health is no respecter of just causes. Jim's physical condition was getting steadily worse. He was constantly tired and pushing himself. He became chronically anemic and required blood transfusions. Mary Frances worried that he might have an internal bleed. His doctors advised a bone marrow transplant from a sibling, but there was no sibling left to whom he could appeal. New drugs were taking a toll with harsh side effects. He often needed a cane to get around. The two stress fractures in his back plagued him, but he refused invasive procedures to repair them due to his chemotherapy treatments and blood infusions, which suppress immunity.

Mark Creech, executive director of the Christian Action League, had always been amazed over the years by Jim's continued passion and determination for the amendment, especially in the face of such opposition. But now he was astounded by Jim's endurance in the face of deteriorating health and pain. There is constant walking through the long halls of the legislature, and in Creech's eyes, Jim was now "just shuffling down the halls. Like he couldn't pick up his feet."

"Will he even live through this?" he would think to himself, convinced the marriage issue was what kept Jim in those legislative halls. "Anyone else would have given up."

"Do you really need to continue doing this?" Mary Frances asked Jim repeatedly, heartbroken to watch his deteriorating condition. Why didn't he retire and come home! "There are others who can forge ahead on this."

But Jim could not pass the torch. *For such a time as this*, Providence had charged him with leading the defense on the marriage issue, and he would shoulder the burden until it was done.

"Sometimes," he said, "you have to weigh the benefits with the risks. And this is one of those times. I'll finish this term, and I'll come home. We'll travel."

No one was more pro-amendment than Mary Frances, but the whole effort was draining Jim, stealing his usual effervescent energy. "We don't have to continue doing this," she persisted in reminding him.

"As long as they send me back, as long as I have supporters, I'm going to be faithful to the task," he would say. "I'll get my bill, and then I'll come home."

It was always the same: *I'll get the amendment, and then I'll come home.*

Hatred and Intimidation

An angry man opens his mouth and shuts up his ears.

—Cato

The introduction of Jim's marriage bill in 2011 launched a backlash from gay-marriage supporters that made the amendment battles of previous years look like friendly turkey shoots. Now that the amendment bill had a viable chance of passing in the General Assembly, a tsunami of protestations and propaganda, local and imported from all across the country, grew and gained force.

Intimidation was ramped up to counter pro-amendment forces. As for Jim, he would find himself the target of day-to-day vitriol and invective, encompassing everything from mild insults to verbal harassment to downright threats.

One morning, Jim, joined by a number of other bill sponsors and lawmakers, held the initial press conference in the legislative building to discuss the marriage amendment bill. The press room was packed wall to wall with people. Besides the media and assorted other visitors, there was a host of pastors from every corner of the state. Attendees spilled out into the hall. A contingent of amendment opponents was also present, seemingly bent on "taking over the meeting," according to Mark Creech, executive director of the Christian Action League.

At some point, while Jim was addressing the assembled from the podium, a man approached it and confronted Jim to his face, talking over him and attempting to shut him down, to *silence* him. Perhaps he also wished to elicit some negative or angry reaction from

Jim for the press to record, snap photos of, and take out of context for the nightly newscast and next day's headlines.

There was no sergeant at arms present to remove the agitator, so his ranting continued.

It angered Mark that the members of the press expressed no disgust for the man's actions and made no move to check them. The conference was for *them*, after all. The press should have been protesting this unruly, interruptive behavior! It was yet another revealing moment about the state of modern journalism. It is neither fair nor disinterested. *Had they even entered the room with the intention to listen to what Jim had to say?*

"Jim never lost his cool," Creech recalled. "He didn't meet hate with hate or rage with rage. He just kept talking, even responding to a couple of the man's confrontational questions and accusations."

Jim remained calm, despite any uncertainty he might naturally feel.

"You don't know the limits of what such a person might do," added Creech. "But there was no fear in Jim, just a resolve. A kind resolve."

"I've never known the LGBT people to be calm," reflected Mary Frances later. "Those who are activists are so full of anger and inner suffering that it comes out in different ways." She perceived a vicious cycle in the mental health and behavior of many of the more radical lesbians and gays. It often begins with some form of abandonment or abuse or the absence of a parental relationship. It births first hurt, then anger. The anger leads to hate, which manifests as defiance—a self-perpetuating circle under which hides a deeply wounded soul.

Nearly every public figure associated favorably with the marriage amendment got his or her shared of cringe-worthy phone calls. But hateful emails, many downright unprintable, constituted the most common form of negative response to Jim's amendment efforts. They were riddled with obscenities, random accusations, and the occasional threat, veiled or not so veiled. The venom in the verbal assaults from gay "victims" confounded belief.

Jim and John Torbett would together shake their heads and wonder aloud together over the irony of the gay-marriage faction's attitude. "It was hard," Torbett later said, "for us to imagine a group that promotes peace and love as strongly as that group did, specifically the people not supporting the amendment, could say and write some of the most vile, nasty, hateful, dangerous-sounding things."

Jim's gentle but honest response to one hateful email is worth mentioning:

> Thank you for your recent emails about Senate Bill 8 (SB8) concerning the North Carolina Constitutional Amendment defending traditional marriage as between one many and one woman. Because of my Senate duties and the fact that I represent over 160,000 constituents, sometimes it takes more than two days to respond to my mail, both electronic and postal, excluding that outside my district. But I am always happy to do so.
>
> Of course you are welcome to visit me and express your views, as are all who feel the need to do so. My door has always been open. Please call my office if you wish to make an appointment.
>
> In regard to your angry diatribe and personal slander to SB8, I am also happy to respond. First of all, I do not hate homosexuals. I love them more. For as a physician, I am frequently saddened by the suffering from the illnesses of my homosexual patients that are directly related to this unhealthy lifestyle. Did you know that the average lifespan of an active homosexual is only 55 years, as opposed to 78 years for a heterosexual? Most often this is because there is no known cure for some of the related illnesses and diseases from this aberrant form of coupling.
>
> As for equal rights, you already have them. They are guaranteed in the Declaration of Independence, that all men are created equal and endowed by their Creator with certain unalien-

able rights that among these are life, liberty and the pursuit of happiness. Anyone can pursue happiness with the right to live with anyone they choose and under whatever arrangement and division of property they so decide. What the homosexual activists are seeking is based on special rights in order to have their particular lifestyle recognized as normal and socially acceptable. This is a lifestyle that every society, every culture and every religion has disapproved for over 5,000 years. "Banning gay marriage" is media hype. You cannot ban something that doesn't exist. Redefining the universal definition of marriage for social acceptance of a minority group, which makes up 1%–2% of the population, is the real issue.

In regard to discrimination, these requested special rights are also a form of discrimination. It discriminates against the universal institution of marriage and family structure originated by our Creator for the procreation, nurture, and social stability of our species since the beginning of time. And its sanctity should be protected.

And finally, since 70 % of Americans and an even higher percentage of North Carolinians support traditional marriage, SB8 represents their desire to have this amendment added to the NC Constitution. However, you also have the right to disagree and your hateful speech is duly noted. Medically speaking, may I tell you that harboring hate is like drinking poison and waiting for someone else to die.

I remain, sincerely,
State Senator James S. Forrester, MD
41st NC Senate District
2011

But the whole charged controversy that year went deeper than mean words and the fear of them.

Senator Kathy Harrington had done campaigns and public events aplenty in her career with little thought to personal safety. Now she felt physically vulnerable due to her amendment stance, particularly during public pro-amendment events and rallies. She could not help but recall Arizona senator Gabrielle Giffords, who was shot at a constituent meeting at a local supermarket earlier that year. One never knew what to expect, and as an elected official, being highly visible in an open public space during such controversy was unnerving.

Tensions were that high. But then the LGBTQ anger was that deep.

Senator Dan Soucek had always been a personable, likable guy with lots of friends and few enemies. Suddenly he found himself an object of loathing. Though he represented a conservative district overall, at its heart lay the liberal town of Boone and Appalachian State University (ASU). ASU was an especially "hostile zone," where he got a healthy share of nasty looks and negative treatment from students and professors alike—especially over the marriage amendment.

"I always had to take a few deep breaths before I stepped on campus."

He couldn't make sense of the hatred. It was so deep, so *visceral*. "I was puzzled that someone that didn't know me could hate me that much *instantly*. I could never hate someone I didn't know"—no matter what they disagreed on.

In a particularly disturbing episode, the amendment fight even followed Mark Creech to the auto shop during a routine oil change. He was twiddling his thumbs in the waiting room when the mechanic working on his car came in with a grim expression. "I want to show you something. Can you come out?"

Mark got up and followed him to the garage, kneeling with the mechanic next to one of his car's front wheels. The mechanic showed him where the tire had been "strategically sliced." The other tire had been altered likewise, with near-perfect symmetry. The incisions were clearly deliberate, intended to bring on an accident. The mechanic explained the trick to Mark. The car rides fine for a little while, but "eventually the tire gives way and blows."

Mark was unnerved to say the least.

"Someone means you harm," the mechanic declared bluntly. "Who'd want to hurt you?"

Mark shook his head. "A whole lot of people."

Allies and Apathy

Repetition reduces resistance.
—Dr. Warner Doles

Equality North Carolina published an anti-amendment pamphlet, the very title of which sounds like an emotional rant: "The Truth About the Discriminatory, Job-Killing, Harmful, Family-Unfriendly, Divisive, Anti-LGBT Marriage Amendment." Behind the title, emblazoned across the cover in a violently repeated motif—"Keep Discrimination Out of NC!"

The national response and support for the gay-marriage side in North Carolina—especially from liberal stronghold states like California, Massachusetts, and New York—was overwhelming. Coffers overflowed with coin wherein to fund anti-amendment efforts.

Still, on the other side of the battlefield the defenders of natural marriage were lined up and ready. At the vanguard was Concerned Women for America (CWA) and Concerned Women of North Carolina. Mary Frances, the organization's state director, asked Senate Pro Tempore Phil Berger, "What can CWA do to help?"

Their charge was simple: reach those legislators who are sitting on the fence or keeping a safe distance on the sidelines.

The efforts of this strong feminine brigade of Concerned Women proved key as they organized an aggressive grassroots campaign leading up to the September legislative vote. Their strategy was simple but *big*.

One crucial Republican senator remained on the fence. So CWA obtained all the zip codes in his senate district and sent over four thousand postcards to their supporters living in it, urging them to call their senator and demand that he support the amendment bill. Statewide, ten thousand postcards were sent, encouraging voters to call their legislators who might be straddling the fence.

This postcard push, combined with phone calls, would reap abundant fruit.

Others who, by all moral and doctrinal standards, should have been supporters of the amendment, took a little coaxing to do the right thing. One particularly bold lobbyist visited the office of Joe Sam Queen, a Democrat from a mountain district who made a point of reminding folks that he was a churchgoing man and Sunday school teacher. He asserted that he could not vote for the amendment because it was "putting down a group of people."

But the lobbyist knew Queen's constituency well, and the good citizens of Haywood County would have tossed Queen out of office in a trice had they known of his opposition to the marriage amendment. So a few days later, the lobbyist returned to Queen's office, along with three pastors from his district, and asked the senator to restate, in their presence, his previous comments about refusing to support the amendment. Those comments were decidedly different this time around.

Garland Pierce, a black Baptist pastor from Laurinburg, went back and forth on his position, noncommittal. The same assertive lobbyist who had outsmarted Queen called a friend, a black Republican who served on the local school board in Pierce's district, and asked if he would schedule a luncheon with all the African American pastors in town. He agreed.

These pastors were Pierce's *peers*, and they were wholeheartedly opposed to same-sex marriage. Three days later at the luncheon, as the lobbyist gave a prepared talk that never once mentioned Pierce by name, the pastors broached the subject of the amendment themselves with one question: "What about our legislators?"

Within days, Pierce was expressing a newfound support for the amendment bill.

Perhaps more disturbing to the Forresters than the hatred they encountered from opponents was the shocking apathy of so many who should have been their natural allies in the moral fight raging around them.

The Forresters observed that the greatest apathy exhibited itself primarily among those of a certain age: under forty. Mary Frances summed up their disposition up with, "They're not so much immoral as amoral." She attributes much of this to a lack of biblical teaching in today's churches. When one is not schooled in the truth, one either believes the lie when it comes along or simply does not recognize its destructiveness. If a certain untruth is heard often enough and in an environment that is increasingly amenable to it, it becomes accepted.

Many church ministers were slow to take a public stand, even among their own congregations. They said things along the lines of:

"I don't talk politics."

"I'm two years from retirement. I'm not touching this with a ten-foot pole."

"If I step my congregation's toes too hard, we don't make our budget."

And the old favorite—

"We might lose our 501(c)(3)."

Only a small percentage of the Forresters' home church was in full and open support of amendment fight. The rest were either in denial or just didn't care.

A prominent woman at church approached Jim one Sunday and said she had a question for him.

"About the marriage amendment, I guess?"

"No," she replied, "I don't care about that. I just want to know if I'm going to get my teacher raise."

Session and Concession

*The difference between a politician and a statesman is
that a politician thinks about the next election while
the statesman thinks about the next generation.*
—James Freeman Clarke

The new Republican majority in the General Assembly was no guarantee of the marriage bill's passage. This was no ordinary legislation but a constitutional amendment bill. Thus, the usual simple majority wouldn't suffice. Passage required three-fifths of both chambers, three-fifths of the *full legislature.*

The battle for ratification began in the House, the tougher ridge to capture, at least according to numbers. There were not enough Republican members there to pass the bill without bipartisan support. Ten Democrat votes were needed to attain the necessary three-fifths majority. Only then could the bill progress to the Senate.

A new champion for the marriage amendment bill emerged in the person of House Speaker Pro Tempore Dale Folwell, who supplied it with new momentum. Folwell, along with Jim, knew that those ten precious bipartisan House votes could only come from more conservative Democrats hailing from rural areas. Many of these had supported an amendment in the past but had never had the opportunity to vote on it. Speaker Thom Tillis began negotiating in an effort to secure their support for a marriage amendment bill.

In the Senate, unlike the House, Republicans had the party numbers to reach a three-fifths majority. *Barely.* They had thirty-one members. Thirty were needed to pass the marriage amendment bill. Jim Blaine, Senate leader Phil Berger's chief of staff, was confident that they had every Republican vote in the Senate secure. There should be no worry in that camp.

Or so everyone thought at first.

House Speaker Thom Tillis, though equivocal in his belief in the efficacy of a marriage amendment, feeling society was moving in an amoral but unstoppable direction, agreed to bring the amendment up in a special session. This would have the effect of placing the whole legislative focus on one issue.

This also presented several obstacles from a lobbying standpoint, which Tami Fitzgerald understood all too well. For one, the pro-amendment faction now had to worry about having a legislative quorum. Second, it was harder to communicate with legislators when they were not neatly congregated in Raleigh but spread out in scattered, far-reaching districts across the state.

But a special session it would be.

Monday, September 12, was now a red date on everyone's calendar.

Skirmishes in the Culture War

Laws do change hearts and attitudes. That's what this is about.
This isn't about marriage. This is about social validation.
This is about transforming society so that [those who practice
homosexual behavior] feel better about what they are doing.
—Frank Turek, founder and president of CrossExamined.org.

In September 2011, Jim participated in a town-hall-style candidate forum at Four Square Church in Dallas, North Carolina. The amendment controversy was at its peak, and the same-sex marriage issue was number one on the agenda.

To put things in perspective, Jim and Mary Frances had recently seen photos of Asheville's latest annual "Go Topless" fair. The group is just what its name suggests and constitutes a national campaign to legalize female nudity under the sanitized rubric of "gender equality."

To the sober observer, the fair reeks far more of a '60s festival of free love and hippie hijinks than any gathering of reasoned "speech" of cultural defiance. Imagine two thousand souls milling and parading in and through Asheville's city square. Hear the ethnic drum beatings and note the tribal garb (though there is little garb of any kind to go around). Smell the occasional whiff of some illegal substance spoiling the clean mountain air. See young children in tow behind participants—witnesses to this defiant display of deviance.

In the course of discussion at the Dallas candidate forum, Jim addressed the larger issue of Judeo-Christian culture and the gay assault on it, stressing the need for an amendment that honored the institution of marriage as it existed for five thousand years of Western civilization. In this context, it was natural to reference "topless"

Asheville as a recent close-to-home example of cultural and moral decay.

"Asheville has become a cesspool of sin," he said.

Asheville has become a cesspool of sin—seven little words that sparked a wildfire!

"What made you say that?" Mary Frances asked her husband upon leaving. "That'll come back to bite you."

"I'm not exactly sure," Jim said. "It just seemed appropriate at the time."

In the audience that night was homosexual activist Robert Kellogg, executive president of Parents, Families, and Friends of Lesbians and Gays of Gaston County. Kellog possessed a mild-mannered facade but acted with radical vindictiveness, which reminded Mary Frances of the divided persona of Dr. Jekyll/Mr. Hyde. Kellogg would subsequently be elected as chairman of the Gaston County Democratic Party and to the Gaston City Council as its first openly gay member in 2015.

Someone that evening wasted no time in alerting the press of Jim's remarks. It would make for useful publicity mileage in the same-sex cause. One could already hear the press's glee in its morning headlines. "Senator Calls Asheville a Cesspool of Sin!" was emblazoned across the *Gaston Gazette*.

Gastonia's mayor phoned her counterpart in Asheville to apologize for Jim's remark. Jim's response to her presumption: "When I need somebody to apologize for me, I will ask them to apologize for me. I do not need the mayor of Gastonia to take it upon herself to speak for me."

Phone calls poured in, accusing Jim of hate in the most hateful ways imaginable. Their accusations might have been laughable if not so blatantly slanderous: the senator had a "hate-consumed heart."

A fresh wave of emails bloated with rage, vitriol, false accusation, and exaggeration flooded the legislative website and the Forrester inboxes. It was a deafening cacophony of all the favorite go-to descriptors of the left—Bigot! Homophobe! Hatemonger! Ignorant! Backward!—all heavily spiced with obscenities and slander.

One of the more eloquent came from someone named Claire:

> Your moronic comments about Asheville and your war against the citizens of North Carolina have given me good reason to consider leaving the state. I'd recently considered moving to my family's hometown of Kings Mountain, but I can't imagine moving to an area where people like you represent the state. It's the 21st century. I hope at some point you'll be willing to leave the Dark Ages and join us in the modern world.

Kelley also made her opinion abundantly clear:

> I would like to suggest that you keep your old, bigoted and country self in Gastonia (wherever that is). I promise I will never leave my home in Asheville to come to your little redneck community. I'm a white female who's married to a while male and we both think that if you were hit by lightening, that is would be no great loss. Where do stupid rednecks like you come from anyway? Someone should have slapped your momma in the mouth for raising you as she did. You are an embaressment to the human race. Stay the f——k out of Asheville. We don't want you. I'm sure Chapel Hills doesn't want your stupid ass either. Shame on you as a political representative for ALL North Carolinians. Again and most sincerely, if you were hit by a bus, I'd pity the bus.

Then Senator Andrew Brock, who attended school in Western Carolina and had witnessed the cultural transformation of Asheville, responded to the tempest with humorous quips. "Is he talking about when I was up there partying?" and, "Well, I guess Chapel Hill's lost its title."

"Jim could not have described things better," Mark Creech said. "But they're going to eat him alive." Still Creech later remarked, "I wished I'd have said it."

The chairman of the Buncombe County GOP at the time informed Mary Frances at a luncheon for Wisconsin governor Scott Walker in Raleigh that "we now have T-shirts that say 'Asheville is a cesspool of sin.'"

Mary Frances promptly googled them on her phone, and they popped right up in a generous selection of colors and sizes.

"Well," she remarked dryly, "the least they could have done was put his name on them."

Juggling Votes

Don't count your chickens before they are hatched.

—Aesop

A frustrating math of counting and *re*counting votes had been going on in the minds of amendment advocates for weeks. But as the final days and hours closed in and pressure mounted, the vote-counting became constant, frantic. Tami Fitzgerald's head was continually adding up *yea* votes—at lunch, in the powder room, in her sleep (when she managed to get any).

Mark Creech also counted votes. "Do we still have your vote?" was his constant question to lawmakers.

There was no assurance of victory, thanks to a small but crucial pool of GOP senators who either refused to state openly how they intended to vote on the bill or vacillated on their position. One day they implied or even promised *yea* only to favor *nay* a few days later.

These wishy-washy commitments made the ongoing prospective vote tally impossible to nail down and solidify, despite the constant, repetitive lobbying efforts of Fitzgerald and others. It was legislative whack-a-mole without the fun. Some moles just refused to stay down. Nothing could be taken for granted.

The Friday before the vote, a problem arose. Several GOP caucus members were balking. These were Republican senators they had already counted on, votes they could not afford to lose.

The knowledge that there was so much at stake made it all the more mentally and emotionally exhausting for the pro-amendment individuals in the legislative trenches. Except for Jim, who was oddly calm considering his long-sought, embattled marriage bill was at last getting the chance it had always been denied. Was it a divine assurance? Or just his characteristic Scottish stoicism?

A compromise was brewing. What if the proposed marriage amendment bill was changed to specify that the amendment would go on the primary election statewide ballot the following May (2012) rather than on the upcoming November (2011) general election ballot? Gay-marriage proponents wanted to avoid putting the amendment on the November ballot, when voter turnout would be higher, because it would increase the likelihood of the marriage amendment being approved. By contrast, a primary election vote gave them a better chance of defeating the amendment at the polls.

The ten pro-amendment Democrat representatives, led by Representative Bill Owens (D-Elizabeth City), were feeling intense heat from the direction of the governor's mansion. Governor Beverly Perdue, worried about her reelection, let drop an unequivocal ultimatum: if any of her fellow Democrats voted in favor of putting the marriage amendment on the general election ballot, there would be consequences.

Representative Owens implied as late as the Friday night preceding the special session that he and the other nine conservative Democrats could vote in favor of the amendment bill *only if it specified the primary election.*

Countdown

Off to Raleigh on Sunday 11th for Marriage Amendment.
Whirlwind two days of special session.
—Diary of Mary Frances Forrester

At eight in the morning, on September 12, 2011, House Speaker Thom Tillis, Speaker Pro Tempore Dale Folwell, and the sponsors of the marriage amendment bill faced a catch-22, for which a crucial decision still must be made. How would the final language of the bill, yet to be drafted, read? Which election ballot—the primary or the general—was to be specified? If they specified the general election, the amendment itself would have a better chance at the polls as more conservative Republican voters would turn out to vote. But if they chose that language, the amendment *bill* would not realize enough votes to clear the General Assembly in the first place! Governor Perdue had made sure of that.

If, however, the bill reflected the Democrats' proposed compromise of including the marriage amendment on the primary election ballot, there was a better chance the bill would pass the legislature, and the amendment would make it to the voting booth.

There was little choice at this point. They would have to go with the primary. Speaker Tillis had the final version of the bill drafted accordingly.

As for Jim, the November general election would have been nice, but he accepted the May primary revision with good grace. Had he not always said, "If I can just get it on the ballot, I know it will pass"? Well, he would not complain about *which* ballot now. If that what was God saw fit to provide, who was he to quibble?

Besides, the date on the election calendar wouldn't matter in the end. He knew and trusted the voters of North Carolina too much. They would turn out in May and do the right thing.

Jim and Senator Dan Soucek had agreed that the latter would carry the bill on the Senate floor the following day, especially as Jim's increasingly frail condition prevented him from giving a robust presentation. Soucek was young, sharp, and savvy to all the legal ins and outs in question. He was the ideal person to speak for the bill and counter debate from the opposition.

And he was more than willing to do so.

The House

If we are not ashamed to think it, we should not be ashamed to say it.
—Cicero

On Monday, September 12, 2011, the marriage amendment bill was heard in the North Carolina House of Representatives.

Representative Paul Stam (R-Majority Leader) presented the bill. He started with basics, citing the Acts of the Albemarle General Assembly, the first two laws passed by the Colonial Assembly in 1669. The second of these laws pertained to establishing how North Carolinians and their forefathers defined marriage.

Stam went on to reference North Carolina's 1996 Defense of Marriage statute, which he made clear reflected the identical policy outlined in the amendment bill at hand. He reminded everyone that, of the twenty-five thousand bills that had been filed since the DOMA statute passed, not one had attempted to change that policy. *Not in those fifteen years that Democrats had full control of the General Assembly.*

"So why are we here today?" he asked. "Because of court decisions and legislative decisions in other states which have forced us to this." He warned that the amendment was the only way to protect the institution of marriage from redefinition by *unelected activist judges.*

He cited Iowa, a politically "down the middle" state, neither liberal nor conservative. "It had statutory provisions limiting marriage to those of opposite sexes. But it had a Supreme Court that decided that somehow in the interstices of their state constitution, imbedded in there from the 1800s was a command that the state of Iowa must have same-sex marriages. We have that same issue in our state Constitution from 1868. It would be very possible for a judge in North Carolina, so disposed, to decide that same-sex marriage has been in our Constitution all along. We cannot upset the settled expectations of our people as to what marriage is and what it's not."

Stam touched on other complications pertaining to the arrival of same-sex marriages from liberal states to North Carolina. "They're going to come South. They're going to bring their same-sex marriages, and they're going to want to get divorced. They're going to have to decide child-custody issues and lots of other things, and we're not equipped to handle that if a court decides to the contrary."

He laid to rest accusations that the amendment would prevent private companies from offering benefits, particularly insurance benefits, to same-sex domestic partners. "It wouldn't have that effect," he explained, "since the basic principle the Constitution deals with the actions of government rather than private parties."

Still, to make things crystal clear, he went on to quote the sentence that bill sponsors had added to the amendment text in the final hours in an effort to allay any such concerns about insurance benefits:

> This section does not prohibit a private party from entering into contracts with another private party; nor does this section prohibit courts from adjudicating the rights of private parties pursuant to such contracts.

After three and a half hours of debate, seventy-five votes were cast in favor of the marriage amendment bill, enough to pass it.

All thought, all effort, now turned to the Senate, where the bill would be heard the following day, Tuesday, September 13. Thirteen had always been a "lucky" number for the Forresters.

There remained one uncertain vote in that chamber, and it would shift back and forth up until the last moments. It was an unknown, a wild card; and for lack of it, the amendment would die.

Jim came home after the Senate's Monday morning caucus. "I know where the vote is."

Tami Fitzgerald was pretty sure she knew *who* it was, for she had done her best to gain the senator's support for the bill, even contacting upward of twenty pastors from his hometown to call him that weekend. She encouraged clergymen from all over to hurry to Raleigh, to try to conduct an "intervention" with him in hopes of persuading him to fight for the proverbial angels.

Mary Frances, in a swirl of anxiety and fragile hope, ducked her head into the office of Senator Phil Berger Tuesday morning.

"Are we going to get the amendment?" she asked with characteristic frankness. "Are we going to get that last vote?"

"We're going to get it," Berger said, choosing to be confident. "It will be there."

The Senate

*Be strong and courageous. Do not fear or be in dread
of them, for it is the LORD your God who goes with
you. He will not leave you or forsake you.*

—Deuteronomy 31:6 ESV

About ten o'clock Tuesday morning, Tami Fitzgerald trekked over to the holdout senator's office. He wasn't there, but Tami found his legislative assistant, a friend of hers, sitting at her desk in tears.

"What's wrong?" Tami asked.

The woman was certain the senator would vote against the marriage amendment bill.

Inside and outside the legislative building, prayer upon prayer rose heavenward like ashes from a hickory fire. So did the chants of anti-amendment protesters, signs held aloft with words written in big rainbow-colored letters:

"Jesus had two dads, and he turned out fine. Evolve already."

"Would U rather me marry your daughter?"

"We're not confused. You're just ignorant!"

At eleven, the Senate Republicans caucused. A circle of pastors stood outside the closed doors and petitioned the Almighty for a favorable outcome. Others milled about the halls, feeling the tension emanating from the caucus room.

Eventually, the doors opened, and the senators exited, heading for their offices or directly to the Senate chamber for the scheduled session.

Jim was already hunkered down in his chair there, saying his own prayers.

Around one o'clock, the session was called to order by a demanding, descending gavel. All nonmembers were banished from the floor, according to protocol, and the big doors secured by the sergeants at arms.

Some senators had chosen to avoid the controversial vote altogether. Senator Fletcher Hartsell (R-Concord), subsequently disgraced in 2016 over misuse of campaign funds, had pleaded pneumonia as the reason for his inability to be present. The GOP party chairman in Hartsell's county had generously offered to pay for an ambulance to convey the senator to Raleigh for the important vote. Hartsell had refused.

Nothing was certain, even now. Historically speaking, persuasive debate or other unforeseen procedural obstacles can change the direction—the outcome—of any given vote. A legislator can enter the chamber with a firm *yea* in his or her head and, by the end of discussion and debate, hit the *nay* button.

It is unwise to harbor absolute predictions when human beings, with their fickle and inconsistent nature, are involved. Add the possibility of last-minute personal circumstances or external manipulation into the equation, and no legislative outcome is wager-worthy. Certainly not one as controversial as the one before the Senate that day.

And everyone remembered the lottery vote.

For Such a Time as This

If an offense come out of the truth, better is it that the
offense come than that the truth be concealed.
—Thomas Hardy

There was palpable tension in the Senate chamber, like a lowering sky ready to burst.

James Summers Forrester rose from his seal-emblazoned chair at the end of his row to address the assembled. He was calm, emanating a quiet confidence. His wife sat in the gallery overhead, a nervous wreck.

Jim's posture seemed frail, his voice fatigued as he spoke. He was dying, but he emanated the power of pure conviction.

"This bill is about democracy, letting the people of North Carolina, not judges, set public policy. There are thousands of North Carolinians, both for and against this amendment, who want a chance to vote on it. This is the eighth year I put in this bill. The past seven years, it's gone to Charlie Dannelly's committee, Ways and Means, and the bill never had a hearing. So I'm very happy to have this bill before us at this time. We have two choices: trust our state's six million voters to make the decision or leave this to activist judges to define it. It's the right thing to do. It lets the voters decide.

"Marriage is a foundation, an institution, in our society that it based upon the complementary male and female union. This provides or creates a wide variety of benefits for individuals and society that no other family form can replicate. This historic understanding of marriage is under increasing attack nationwide. Thirty states, therefore, have included this in a constitutional amendment. We are the only state in the South that does not have this in our constitution. In our state, activists are slowly chipping away at laws that protect marriage and the family through incremental changes. North Carolina does have strong marriage laws, but they are increasingly vulnerable to legal challenges and revisions by the court. Even in states that have passed a marriage amendment in the constitution, judges have said it's illegal.

"The marriage-protection amendment is about preservation, not discrimination. It will help preserve the right of parents to transmit core values about sex, gender, and family to their children. It is necessary to preserve the freedoms of speech and religion in North Carolina. It has a broad and diverse range of support among North Carolinians."

Perhaps the most profound statement he made boiled it down to this:

"Moms and Dads are not interchangeable. Two men do not make a mom. Two moms do not make a dad. Children need both a father and a mother. Please allow the citizens of North Carolina to vote on this important issue."

Senator Dan Soucek rose to speak. "'We the people of the state of North Carolina,'" he began, quoting the preamble to state constitution. "We're asking this body to put this amendment on the ballot so the people of North Carolina can vote on it. Thirty-one of thirty-one states have voted to affirm marriage in their constitution. I don't see why, as the only state in the Southeast, we will not be a state that allows our people to vote on it as well.

"The constitution is the people's document. They have the ultimate authority, and we should give them the ultimate authority on this. There are many complicated issues that our system of government allows legislators: budget issues, complex legislative issues— these are roles of legislators because of their complexity, and trying to put them to the vote of the people would be very difficult.

"This is not like that. This is not a law. This is a constitutional amendment for the people's constitution. They live their daily lives in and around marriage. They see society. They see it in their everyday lives and therefore are uniquely qualified to answer this question."

The floor was opened for debate, and the Democrats, as expected, lashed out with all the expected accusations and grand-standing. They goaded the Republicans like crazy.

The Republican delegation exercised admirable constraint. Soucek and the others were determined not to give the opposition fodder to use in the media, courts, on the campaign trail, or any-where else. They had determined to stay on a wiser path: present the pro-amendment case, take the abuse, and then vote.

Opponents of the bill rose one by one, predicting economic gloom and employing a host of discrimination and civil rights anal-ogies based more on sentiment that fact. Perhaps the most ridicu-lous was that of Democrat senator Doug Berger, who implied that defenders of natural marriage were in the same ideological camp as Nazis.

"Adolf Hitler came to power through the ballot box," he said, referencing how gays and Socialists were target groups in Nazi Germany. Like the yellow star of degradation enforced on the Jews, he claimed, the marriage amendment would persecute gays in North Carolina by "putting a pink triangle into our state constitution."

This was too much for Senator Buck Newton, who had not planned to speak on the amendment bill. He could not let this hyperbolic, slanderous implication go unchallenged. His rebuttal first stressed the importance of the bill at hand and reminded every-one that North Carolina already had a statute defining marriage as between one man and one woman. The rest went like this:

"I've been married for seventeen years now, and it never occurred to me that my belief in traditional marriage—that belief our soci-ety has generally conceded and shared for hundreds of years and predating the foundation of this country for thousands of years—that defending marriage between a man and a woman was some-how akin to Nazi Germany. That somehow this is akin to the crazy racial amendments that were put forward in the '50s. Let's get real. Everybody in this room knows what this is about.

"And let's not pretend this has something to do with business. We have the law on the books. All these employers that Senator Stein cited, all their employees, they haven't fled North Carolina. They haven't run to Massachusetts. This amendment, if it passes the vote of the public, will not change that. I believe the reason why we have a constitution, in addition to what Senator Stein said, is also to protect us from the tyranny of this legislature. It is to protect us from judicial fiat from judges somewhere else, politically appointed, who decide they will impose their will on society about what a marriage shall be. That's what this amendment is about. It is to let the people decide that they will not have some unelected judge, or even an elected judge, decide that today, after two thousand years, we will redefine what a marriage is.

"It is a shame that we have come to this point—it is a crying shame. I agree. I wish this did not have to be in the constitution in order to protect what we all know is a marriage. But we have reached that point when our society has turned itself on its head, and that we have so many crazy judges and crazy lawyers that would challenge this fundamental bedrock of our society. That is what this amendment is about. We will let the people vote. They will decide. I pray to God that the amendment passes the vote of the North Carolina public. And one day, if society has changed its views, as you say, that constitution can be changed again. I pray that day never comes. But let's put all the histrionics aside. Let's focus on what this amendment is about. It doesn't prohibit what Bank of America might give as benefits to its employees. It's not about politics. We've moved it from November to May to avoid the appearance of politics. It's about what is a marriage in our society. I urge you to vote for the motion."

Debate ceased, and the vote was called.

Breath was bated as senators punched in their votes in the five seconds allotted. Soucek counted them down. Five, four, three…

His eye stayed on the *aye* column of the senate screen, waiting for one magic number to appear.

Two, one.

The vote was locked. And there it was—*thirty.*

Thirty precious votes, and history was made.

The unknown holdout vote was later revealed to be that of a Republican senator who represented a somewhat liberal district. Initially against the amendment, he had decided that supporting it constituted the greater good for the state. It was important to show a loyal solidarity with his party caucus at a time when party strength was at a critical and defining stage. The Republicans needed to be seen as strong and unified going forward.

Besides, he had been inundated with so many phone calls and messages from constituents favoring the bill that he chose to support it so the people could have the final say on the matter.

"The bill will be enrolled," stated Lieutenant Governor Walter Dalton.

Up in the gallery, Mary Frances tried to keep body and soul from coming unglued. She needed to burst into tears of relief and pent-up emotion, but Jim's words echoed in her head.

Dear, if you need to cry, wait until you get to the car.

But she was dying to talk to him, to debrief like two soldiers after a dangerous assignment, to relish the aftermath—to celebrate!

Mark Creech kept his eyes on Jim when the vote outcome was announced. He saw Jim lean back in his chair, composed as ever, fingers linked across his chest in his usual way. But Mark also saw him take a long, deep breath and then release it, as though inhaling a long-sought victory and exhaling the heavy burden he had carried so long.

"It looked as if the whole world had come off his shoulders."

Later that day, Representative John Torbett would also sense a huge sigh, albeit a metaphorical one. "I believe to this day," he joked, "that it was coming from Jim's office over in the other building."

And that was it. Jim's fifteen-year campaign to get a marriage amendment on the ballot had at last borne fruit. Naturally, it brought a satisfying feeling of closure, a sense of accomplishment, and the unique gratification that comes on the heels of a moral victory. But he neither celebrated openly nor gloated. Despite how he had been painted by some, he was not insensitive to the feelings and disappointments of the gay community, many of whom were present. He preferred to heal wounds, not salt them.

Besides, the ultimate fate of the amendment now rested in the hands of the citizens, and whatever happened, Jim would honor their choice.

"If people reject it and say, 'No, we don't want this in the constitution,' then I'll live with it," he said. He continued to emphasize that the amendment was never meant to single out homosexuals. "It was just something I thought we needed to do to continue to have a strong family structure here in North Carolina."

It is worth emphasizing that politics is fraught with irony, and sometimes the honest statesman cannot win for losing. Soon after the amendment bill's passage in the General Assembly, Democrats had the proverbial gall to accuse Republicans of putting the measure on the May primary ballot, when voter turnout would be low, in order to "sneak it through" to being approved. The GOP had pulled a "slick trick," they complained to the press.

Republicans were appalled by the two-faced accusations. This was rich!

If the voters only knew the truth, that the concession by Jim and his colleagues to put the amendment on the May primary ballot had been the *Democrats' chief condition for voting for the bill.* Governor Perdue had demanded it!

Well, now the voters *do* know the truth.

Last Days in the Senate

*Jim wants to take a train trip out west. He has really gotten hooked
on trains. He said, "We need to go while I am still able."*
—Diary of Mary Frances Forrester

It is nothing short of a miracle that Jim never became resentful or
bitter in the face of the rage and insults aimed for so long at him (and
Mary Frances) over the marriage issue. While he certainly received
much positive support, both written and verbal, it is generally the
negative that we as humans take to heart and store up. It would have
made most men cynical at the very least, if not downright hard-
hearted, toward his fellow man. Not so with Jim.

Perhaps it was his faith in God that refused to let him be cor-
rupted, together with his innate good nature and a gratitude hear-
kening back to the lowly immigrant experience that had helped condition him to hard knocks and the receiving end of abuse. Whatever
the cause, he had always managed to take circumstances and people
in stride, to keep the good and discard the bad that they brought.
Holding a grudge was wrong and a self-defeating waste of time.

Now that the amendment was on its way to the ballot box, Jim
felt his work was done. He was embattled and war-weary and in need
of a long furlough. His "good fight" had taken a heavy toll. His weak
physical health began to deteriorate more rapidly.

Whatever the full nature and extent of his ailments, he was no
longer capable of sustaining the necessary treatments to fight them.
He had pushed himself—physically, mentally, and emotionally—too
hard over the previous months. His resilience and stamina were spent.

In Raleigh, Sergeant-at-Arms Phil King kept a concerned and watchful eye on him. The senator was becoming more unstable and relying heavily on his cane. Phil feared for him, as the Senate building is no easy structure to exit in case of emergency, especially if elevators fail. He set aside a wheelchair in the Senate chamber near Jim's seat just in case.

Both Sergeant at Arms King and Sergeant at Arms Blackburn had taken to driving Jim periodically to or from the train station in Raleigh, talking and carrying his bags. Blackburn was also worried, especially when he drove Jim to the train station for the last time and realized the extent of Jim's weakness. But the senator's dry, good humor was still in peak health.

"I've got more pints of other people's blood in my veins than I have of my own," he joked to Blackburn.

Did he know he was dying? What did he know about his grave condition, but did not share with anyone? Questions that plague Mary Frances. As a doctor, would he not have recognized the unique physical signs, or at least intuited that his time was short? If so, he remained stoic about it. Mary Frances, fretting, often asked in those remaining weeks if there was something he needed to talk to her about. He would just smile and say "No, everything's okay."

But there was still some work left to do, including the initial meeting of an interim governmental committee on Governmental Operations. His friend and protégé Senator Kathy Harrington was also in attendance.

As the meeting adjourned, Jim called her over. "I'm so happy to see you on this committee," he told her, smiling. "You're doing a good job, and I'm proud of you."

You're doing a good job, and I'm proud of you.

It was the same phrase he used when talking to his grandsons. Solid words of encouragement meant to instill confidence and approval.

Coming to a Close

If you're lucky enough to be in the mountains, you're lucky enough.
—Unknown

The mountains had been a favorite retreat of the Forresters since 1989. Their house near Blowing Rock was as comfortable and familiar as an old slipper, containing a treasure trove of patriotic memorabilia accumulated over five decades. It was where they escaped to rest.

Jim certainly needed rest after the slings and arrows of the amendment fight. So on Thursday, October 27, Jim and Mary Frances, along with her sister Sally, headed up the mountain. It was cold and rainy, the perfect night for supper of tomato soup and grilled cheese sandwiches, a Forrester staple. Toss in a classic old movie, and life was perfect.

Jim was restless that night, but woke Saturday morning to a fresh blanket of white snow reminiscent of his wedding day. Mary Frances made coffee, happy to hunker down with her sweetheart and a good book.

A few hours later, Jim called to her. There was a problem with his legs. It was difficult to rise, even with assistance. The condition worsened throughout the morning until, finally, with the help of a borrowed wheelchair, the three headed back down the mountain toward home.

Dr. Fola Ajao recommended admitting Jim to the hospital and, if necessary, move him from there to rehabilitation if it proved to be an issue with the stress fractures in his back. So he checked in to Gaston Memorial Hospital, the facility he had helped plan and build.

His reflexes were not good, so they kept him Saturday night, intending to do a CT scan the following Sunday morning. A little after 9:00 p.m., Jim told Mary Frances, "You need to go home and check on Lady."

Lady was their little Maltipoo and the canine apple of Jim's eye.

"Don't worry, I'm in good hands," he added.

She promised to be back early the next morning.

"Call before you come," he said. "I may not be—"

"They're not going to take you to rehab before I get here to help," she interrupted him, assuming he meant that he might be discharged from the hospital early. In retrospect, Mary Frances wonders if he were about to say something entirely more profound.

Jim had said, "No, they'll keep me," when they first took him to the hospital.

Did he know something I didn't? Mary Frances would later wonder.

"I'll be back here early," Mary Frances reiterated before leaving.

She went home, saw to Lady, and tried to get some sleep. She called the hospital around 6:45 a.m. Sunday to check on Jim's condition. According to the nurse, he had been restless during the night but was now sleeping well.

"Make sure he gets a good breakfast," she instructed. "He didn't have a real dinner, and he loves his breakfast."

Ten minutes later, Jimmy called. He had just spoken with the hospital staff himself and had been told his father was "unresponsive."

Mary Frances's heart sank. She finished dressing in a rush and was on the verge of leaving the house when she heard a loud fluttering sound on the screened-in back porch. It was a robin. How on earth had the thing gotten inside?

I don't have time to chase birds, she thought.

She snatched up a hand towel and tried to shoo the robin out the porch door, silently pleading with the restless little creature to cooperate. Time was short. She managed to capture him in the towel, and for a moment, the robin seemed oddly content to let her hold him in her cupped hands. But she had to let him go, so she opened the screen door, and the bird flew away, happy to be free.

Jim was in the Intensive Care Unit, intubated, when she reached the hospital. His stillness and pallor were a shock. The doctor advised her to take a deep breath. "Mrs. Forrester," he said, "let's sit down. We need to talk." "We have done a CAT scan, and he has had an irreversible intracranial bleed."

Jim was now on life support, with no brain activity. The world became surreal to Mary Frances. Everything passed in slow motion. *Focus*, she tried to tell herself.

"There's nothing more we can do," the doctor told her. "You and your family have to decide what to do."

The words were a knife in her heart. But she knew what Jim would want. "No heroic measures," she responded. "Just let me get the children home."

With shaking fingers, she called all the kids, scattered across the country, and told them to hurry home. All the while, she battled feelings of guilt—for not staying by Jim's side through the previous night when he was still conscious, for arriving late that morning after wasting precious time on that stupid robin!

In the interim, Mary Frances and Jim shared their last night together on earth. Between spells of disjointed, uneasy sleep, she talked softly to her beloved, her best friend, holding his hand and resting her head on his shoulder as she lay beside him on the hospital bed. Gazing at his pale face, she said all the things one says to a spouse of fifty-one years who is leaving for good. She murmured countless "I love yous" and hoped they were heard, *felt*, by the recipient. Tears fell and prayers rose, both tinged with doubt. Had she done everything she could for Jim?

By late Sunday evening, Jimmy, Wyndi, Gloria, and Mary Paige were all gathered around the nondescript hospital bed. The time for goodbyes had come. Each one poured out words of love and affection, making heartbroken farewells and placing final kisses on their father's brow. Together they sang "You Are My Sunshine" to the daddy who so enjoyed singing it to them.

At 11:50 a.m. on Monday, October 31, the life-support apparatus was disconnected; and James Summers Forrester, aged seventy-four, exited this mortal realm. He died peacefully and, in faith, entered the presence of God. Within hours, Jimmy looked down at his cell phone and saw the notification for his daily Bible verse. It was 2 Timothy 4:7 NIV: "I have fought the good fight. I have finished the race. I have kept the faith."

Mary Frances blamed the robin for her delay in getting to Jim. But Jimmy told his mother that it was most likely a blessing, one that prevented her from seeing something unpleasant or difficult, something Jim would not have wanted her to see or remember.

A stroke, and the resulting cranial bleeding, might have killed Jim, but the amendment fight caused his death. He had pushed himself too hard for too long, solidly committed to fulfilling the will of North Carolinians. Mary Frances, though proud of his accomplishment, is blunt about his sacrifice:

"He gave his life for that amendment."

Memorial

*A general, a physician and a legislator, he was
foremost a child of God, by faith in Christ.*
—Pastor Billy Shaw

November 6, 2011

The autumn air was chilly outside the church, the breeze as crisp as the starched folds of a new Stars and Stripes. Sunshine streamed through the long vertical windows, casting a beneficent glow over the memorial service.

The First Baptist Church of Stanley, North Carolina, was filled to every corner and niche of its seven-hundred-person capacity. Present were those come to pay loving, appreciative tribute to James Summers Forrester. Seats were full but hearts were fuller as fond remarks and remembrances were whispered back and forth. Tears trickled down cheeks unashamed.

"His passing affected the whole town," recalled Tammy Johnson.

The crowd was a fine cross-section of the citizenry. There were Jim's patients, young and old, past and present, along with various medical colleagues. There were fellow guardsmen of all ranks, along with a host of law enforcement representatives. Assorted dignitaries and elected officials of both political parties were present, side by side with private citizens of varying social class, ethnic persuasions, and occupations.

In a sense, America was at Jim's memorial.

Security was an issue. Only a few weeks had passed since Jim's legislative victory over the marriage amendment. Flak still flew in the public arena and social media. No one would underestimate the potential willingness of others to display their hatred for the deceased by disrupting the solemn proceedings. No one knew what to expect. Would there be protesters or some crazed individual intending to wreck the ceremony? Hate can be reckless in its manifestations.

Heath Jenkins, Stanley chief of police at the time, coordinated security, determined to ensure safety but trying to keep all law enforcement personnel discreet and as invisible as possible. "No one sitting in that church would have known we had a SWAT team in the Sunday school room," he later remarked. Ten undercover officers with earpieces were strategically placed throughout the assemblage.

Mary Frances did not want any media there, but had relented enough to allow one news reporter from the *Gaston Gazette* to cover the occasion. The Highway Patrol had requested, and been granted, the honor of attending the casket as pallbearers out of their respect and gratitude to Jim. He had been a friend to them through all his years of public service.

Favorite hymns reverberated through the sanctuary. A bagpiper played "Amazing Grace." Formal eulogies, beautiful and sincere, were rendered.

Longtime friend and ally Sherri Miller of Concerned Women delivered a message from Representative Sue Myrick and, on the congresswoman's behalf, presented to Mary Frances the American flag flown over the United States Capitol in Jim's honor the day he died.

Colonel Phillip Tillman, chaplain of the NC Air Guard in Charlotte, also made remarks recounting Jim's thirty-four years of military service with the 145th Medical Group during war and peace, and how Jim had been the first medical officer promoted to brigadier general of the NC Air Guard and the first to hold the office of assistant adjutant general of Air.

Senator Phil Berger referenced Jim's immigration to America and his mother's long-cherished words. "After a storied life devoted to public service in medicine, in the military, and in elected office," said Berger, "it's safe to say that Jim *did* give back to his community, his state, and his nation more than he received."

An emotional Representative John Torbett talked of the downside of being in the legislative minority for so many years and Jim's impromptu luncheons with him in the legislative cafeteria. "It made for a good day when he would greet me with a simple, 'Hey, buddy.'"

"Because of his lifetime of unquestionable loyalty in service to his country and state," Torbett went on, "Jim was one man on which I could depend to know and live the true meaning of duty, honor, country. He saw the price, he bore the cost. And he knew the sacrifice, having witnessed so many boys, American boys, shed their blood at the altar of freedom."

Jim's children and grandchildren paid their respects.

"My father loved unconditionally," Wyndi told the assembled. "Every child should have a father who tells them the world is a beautiful place and that they are worthy of it. We will see you, Daddy, in the eyes of your grandchildren and great-grandchildren. We will hear you in the memories that are stored in our hearts and that will be told and retold. We will see you as the seasons turn. We have an abundant harvest in your love, and you will be missed."

Jimmy's words referenced the date of his father's death and made it something beautiful. "Pop died on October 31. Halloween. Some may think that a hard day to have a loved one die. There are no easy days to say goodbye, but this is what I think Pop would say: 'As I arrived at the golden gates of my eternal home, in my earthly costume, I rang the doorbell. My Savior answered the door and said, "It's a treat for you today, Jim. Come in. Well done, my good and faithful servant."' And Pop entered his new home. Halloween will now be a day of remembrance. It will always remind me of the blessings and treats to come—a heavenly home with both my earthly and eternal fathers."

"James Summers Forrester was my grandfather," began Tommy Lucioni, Jim's teenage grandson. "As I stand here, I am extremely proud to be his grandson. I was fortunate to have known him as well as I did. I only hope that in my lifetime, I will have the ability to accomplish as much as he did."

But the sweetest tributes are often the simplest, and one of them came from McLennan, Jim's seventeen-year-old granddaughter. "He was my grandfather, and we called him Pop-Pop. There is a reason behind the word choice and why his grandchildren called him that. In my mind, I believed he was such a great man that his name deserved to be said twice."

Jim's casket exited the sanctuary to the piped strains of "Scotland the Brave."

A Good Name

He was a prince of a gentleman.

—Colonel Phillip Tillman

When the North Carolina Senate loses a member, there is a certain tradition that is put into motion. A resolution is brought; and the still-living senators, the family of the deceased member, and all other attendees take their seats in solemn attention. The sergeants at arms lock each pair of tall gilded doors leading into the chamber. One by one, members stand and offer up words of honor and personal remembrances of the deceased.

Senator Austin Allran observed that "he loved the Lord steadfastly."

Senator Bob Rucho recalled "that twinkle in his eye when he spoke of his father" and joked that Jim "took a lot of my money" on the golf course.

Senator David Rouser remembers clearly Jim's admonishments on certain Democrat-proposed bills. "David, this is a tax vote. You need to vote no."

Senator Phil Berger gave a simple but encompassing tribute with, "Though not born in America, Jim was the story of America."

On June 26, 2012, the North Carolina General Assembly unanimously adopted Senate Joint Resolution 958, honoring the life and memory of James Summers "Jim" Forrester Sr., MD.

Praise was heard outside the Senate chamber as well.

"In my eighteen years in the Senate, Jim and I never had a cross word," remarked David Hoyle. "He was a gentleman all the time. Even when we agreed to disagree, it was done in a gentlemanly way."

Even longtime ideological opponents had gracious things to say about Jim's commitment to public service and to his constituents. "It is no secret that his politics and my politics did not always agree," said Robert Kellogg of Parents, Families, and Friends of Lesbians and Gays of Gaston County, who had opposed Jim's gay-marriage stance. Still Kellogg paid respect to Jim "for his service to our state, and I think all Gaston residents should be thankful for his service to this state. I wish condolences to his family and to his wife."

In a joint statement, Democrat Senators Martin Nesbitt and Bill Purcell, who also had had stormy political moments with Jim, declared, "We hold great respect for Jim and called him a friend. We worked with him closely on the Health and Human Services Committee over the years, and as a doctor, he brought a necessary level of expertise to Senate deliberations on health-care matters."

Representative Jason Saine (R-Lincoln) told the *Lincoln Times-News* that Jim's death was a "sad day" for North Carolina Republicans. Party chairs charged with the task of filling the now-vacant Senate District 41 would find that Jim had left "tremendous shoes to fill."

At the height of both ill health and amendment flak, he "never let up, and just kept going," according to Representative Bill Current (R-Gaston), who often carpooled with Jim to Raleigh for General Assembly sessions.

One friend who remembered Jim with fond respect was Iredell County commissioner Ken Robertson, who observed to the *Mooresville Tribune* that in spite of the man's tremendous accomplishments and awards as physician, senator, and decorated brigadier general, Jim was "about as down to earth as a person can be. He was never boastful or had any airs about him. And if someone had a right to be, it was him."

And so it went, a stream of praise and attention that would have embarrassed Jim to no end.

But not all were kind. Jim's more bitter enemies exhibited no qualm about smearing the dead. "A lousy stinking hatemonger who earned his eternity in hell," said Larry Glinzman of Equality North Carolina.

Scott Rose chimed in with, "He was indeed a lousy stinking hatemonger who falsified many of his professional credentials, as I discovered, only to be insulted by him. Good riddance to a very bad bigot."

Even when a highway was named for Jim on the anniversary of his death, such beings simply ignored the man's lifetime of devotion, personal sacrifices, and public service to his state.

Their state.

The *Gaston Gazette* ran a predictable headline: "Highway for Divisive Politician?" Jim was the "architect of NC's gay marriage ban up for honor." The paper could not simply report the fact that the highway designation was happening. Instead, the article was heavily weighted with a revival of the legislative amendment debate. The intended takeaway for the reader: James Forrester doesn't deserve this recognition.

So does hate eat the heart of the hater, gnawing at the deepest part, even after its object is gone.

Swimming Upstream

Some of us are called to swim upstream.
—Reverend Patrick Wooden

The fight for a constitutional marriage amendment battle was not done. All eyes, both pro and con, were now riveted to one outlined date on the calendar: *Tuesday, May 8, 2012.*

No sooner had the ink dried on the amendment bill than gay rights advocates began planning and strategizing, framing their message and raising money. They would outspend pro-amendment forces by two to one. Millions of dollars from across the nation poured in.

The NC Values Coalition and Tami Fitzgerald, now chairwoman of Vote for Marriage NC, the official referendum committee, led the effort to form a solid, and oddly diverse, alliance of religious leaders and groups. These included the Christian Action League, Concerned Women of America, Civitas, Catholic diocese, and a large contingent of African American clergy. Committed individual pastors and churches girded their proverbial loins for this next leg of the struggle for traditional marriage.

Leading pastors became key spokesmen for the cause. One was Dr. Mark Harris, pastor of First Baptist Church in Charlotte and president of North Carolina Baptist State Convention. That body, only hours after electing Harris as president, expressed overwhelming support for the marriage amendment. It is no wonder the press swooped in immediately to cover the story. The convention move was key. One-fifth of North Carolinians, nearly 1.5 million potential voters, identify themselves as Southern Baptist. Their votes were crucial to amendment passage.

Dr. Harris was tireless in encouraging the grassroots efforts of Baptist pastors statewide, encouraging them to pray, contribute, and recruit others. Sermons supporting biblical marriage multiplied in the pulpit and beyond.

Dr. Patrick Wooden, pastor of Upper Room Church of God in Christ Jesus in Raleigh, an influential evangelical leader in the African American community, was another champion of marriage. When opponents said his amendment stance was discriminatory and antihomosexual, he replied, "The amendment is not *anti* anything. It's *pro*-marriage. You can't compare racial discrimination to discrimination based on deviant behavior."

He would not suffer civil-rights comparisons. "When blacks had brains, we were *insulted* when homosexuality and the LGBT community was compared to being black. But we stopped thinking when Obama endorsed them." As for the "born that way" claim, he cited the lack of proof for a so-called gay gene.

"If that were so, there would be no ex-homosexuals," he pointed out. "The only ex-black I know of is Michael Jackson."

Wooden did radio interviews and voice-overs for advertisements to run statewide on black radio stations to "to challenge the African American community to join him in saying no to Obama's assault of marriage."

Wooden endured everything from verbal assaults, threats to burn his church down, and death threats against his family. It was "n——r this and n——r that" from those who called for unity. Some of these voices were white, some black.

A week before the amendment vote, ninety-three-year-old Reverend Billy Graham, a native Tar Heel, took out a full-page pro-amendment advertisement, including his statement on the issue at hand, in the *Charlotte Observer* and thirteen other North Carolina newspapers. "Watching the moral decline of our country causes me great concern," he told the media. "I believe the home and marriage is the foundation of our society and must be protected."

Arguments flew regarding the supposed negative consequences of adopting the amendment. Efforts were renewed to discredit or misrepresent it in the hope of scaring people away from voting in favor of it. Poll numbers on both sides were quoted more frequently than basketball scores.

Some in the business community piped up with claims that this "discrimination" would have negative effects on the state's economic future. Earlier that week, Martin Eakes, CEO of Self-Help and the Center for Responsible Lending in Durham and a member of the Bank of America's national advisory board gave his prognostication. "If you want to figure out a way to push Bank of America from its headquarters in Charlotte to New York, pass this amendment." Was this a veiled threat?

It was certainly not a prediction based on present facts. The American Legislative Exchange Council (ALEC) ranked the economic health of all fifty states and found that nine of the top ten had marriage-defining constitutional amendments while the bottom ten had laws that undermined traditional marriage. Similar data reports and business rankings from *Forbes*, *Chief Executive* magazine, the National Chamber Foundation, and Moody's Analytics consistently demonstrated that adoption of a marriage amendment would have no negative impact on North Carolina's economy. Even the 2011 Corporate Equality Index, published by the Human Rights Campaign, an organization that ranks America's Fortune 500 companies' policies toward gay and lesbian employees, showed that states with a marriage amendment—such as Texas, Michigan, and Virginia—had some of the highest "equality" rankings in the nation.

About a month before the vote, the opposition released a television ad painting the narrative that passing the marriage amendment would prohibit prosecutors from prosecuting domestic violence claims against heterosexual couples. The ad included a Wake County assistant district attorney displaying a stack of files and claiming they represented cases of domestic violence that could not be prosecuted if the measure passed.

"It was a complete fabrication," said Tami Fitzgerald.

Still the pro-amendment poll numbers began to slide downward. So a press conference was held, comprised of district attorneys and law enforcement personnel, chiefly sheriffs, from all across the state who testified that the marriage amendment would *not* make prosecuting domestic violence cases impossible. A video was made of the press conference, which made for a fine television ad refuting the opposition's false claims.

As hoped, the pro-amendment poll numbers drifted back up.

On the other side, the Obama campaign issued a statement declaring opposition to the amendment. Bill Clinton and Erskine Bowles did automated phone calls that rehashed old claims that the amendment would undermine domestic violence protections.

As the weeks and months leading up to May 8 passed, national interest groups poured copious amounts of money into the state. Overall, amendment opponents raised over twice as much money as amendment proponents.

Mary Frances spoke at the final Return America pro-amendment rally on April 20, 2012, at Halifax Mall in front of the General Assembly complex in downtown Raleigh. Capitol police estimated the event drew over three thousand participants.

The anti-amendment "Rally Against Hate" staked out its own territory. With upward of a hundred souls attending, a lineup of speakers lambasted the amendment, sparking the occasional spontaneous chant from the crowd. Flags, shirts, umbrellas, and other paraphernalia sporting the rainbow flag were everywhere, their colors bright as the azaleas blooming in vivid splendor. Gay couples here and there exchanged smooches. Signs abounded with determined slogans, some rife with hyperbole.

"No H8!"

"Imagine No Religion."

"End the Harm from Religion-Based Bigotry and Prejudice."

"Don't Use Jesus to Justify Intolerance."

Accusations of "hatemongering" poured from the mouths of the true hatemongers. To such persons, one issue mattered and one issue only. Truth, honor, and fair-mindedness were virtues unknown to them in the midst of disagreement, and personal attacks a justifiable weapon to achieve their desired end. Pastor Ron Baity, leader of Return America, felt this keenly.

Along with hate mail, there were nasty phone calls and voice mails, which he still gets from time to time. There was a string of threats to his home church, ranging from mild to murderous. Church employees and volunteers did their best to stay calm and let the individuals making the threats know that the church was prepared and had tight security. Usually, it was a threat to disrupt Sunday worship services.

Michelle Lonaberger, the church secretary at the time, remembers an encounter with one woman who called the office to declare, "You're all a bunch of bigots," and announce that her anti-amendment group would be at the church that Sunday morning with signs "to show everyone who you really are!"

"Well, ma'am," responded Michelle, "you and anyone else is more than welcome to come to the service. We don't care about background. We're glad if anyone wants to be here. But the minute anyone starts to disrupt the worship service, we are private property, and we will have to have you escorted off."

"You can't do that. You're public property."

"No, ma'am, we are private property, and we can do that. Again you're welcome to be here but, no disturbances will be tolerated."

"Well, we'll just protest in your parking lot and not let your people in the church."

"Ma'am, *again*, you're welcome to be here, but it is private property, and anything that happens to interrupt the normal service, we will have to call the police to escort you off."

"Well then, we'll get in the public right of way."

"Ma'am, we're on an extremely busy road. There is a large hill in front of us, and there is no place to safely stand. I do not recommend it. If you choose to do so, it's your own risk. But I hope you don't."

The group never showed up that Sunday. Michelle suspected the woman's chief intent was to intimidate them or even to "get a rise" out of someone that could be broadcast as useful publicity.

Nearly six years after the amendment vote and after *Obergefell v. Hodges*, Baity still receives, almost monthly, a card in the mail with a

California postmark. There is no sender name or return address, just a "pleasant" sentiment for him:

> SHAME ON YOU! Your call for persecution is so un-Christ-like that it makes me think you are a DEMON and I rebuke thee. Luke 4:35.

Another missive, postmarked Greenville, South Carolina, went to Baity's house with similar sentiments and even threats to him and his wife. The threats were unspecified, which was somehow more worrisome, as the couple had no idea what to expect or how to take precautions. The fact that their home address was unpublished made things all the more unnerving.

As ever, though, the "colorful" emails took the cake:

> Just out of curiosity what is you "PhD" in? I think the US should round up all the hateful bigots like you and throw some to the lions on occasion to remind you "Christians" just what persecution is about. (Peter Merlin)

> You are a worthless, hate mongering piece of s——t. May you rot in hell clutching your bible. Who are you to decide what is right and wrong. Trying to take God's job! All in the name of Christianity. You can take your hate mongering and put it where the sun don't shine. (ElissaLynn2008)

These were kind by comparison. Others included unprintable things. One particularly blasphemous writer said he wanted to have a homosexual act with Jesus Christ.

"I did not believe it possible for a member of the human race to say or even think such things," remarked Baity.

Perhaps most frustrating was that he did not even recognize half the things anti-amendment people were accusing him of saying or doing. Many of the charges aimed his way were blatantly false, obviously mined from fake news sources. Everything else was taken so far out of context that no vestige of truth even remained! People referenced things they had heard or read, second- and third-hand, which had been run through a mill of misrepresentation and personal resentment on pro-gay blogs. It was like the whisper game played on the school playground, but with much higher stakes.

Shift the scene to Blowing Rock Elementary, where Senator Dan Soucek walked hand in hand with his five-year-old kindergarten daughter. People would drive by, roll down the window, and angrily scream, "Vote NO!" at him.

His children took heat at school. Other kids would walk up and blurt out, "My dad hates your dad," or "My mom wishes you would lose." It got so bad the Souceks had to give their daughter a safe word to use if ever she felt uncomfortable. If the teacher ever overheard the little girl say "I like strawberries," she would know something was amiss.

The Souceks lost no shortage of friends. The most notable was a lesbian couple at the elementary school. The two women shared the rearing of triplets, courtesy of artificial insemination. They and the Souceks, particularly Mrs. Soucek, had always been friendly with one another as their kids shared birthday parties and other school functions and events.

"We always treated them with love and respect," Soucek said. But when the amendment controversy arose, the two women changed abruptly and dramatically, becoming downright nasty. It's possible the couple also poisoned the proverbial well, for many of their mutual friends stopped speaking to the Souceks.

The level of resentment reached an existential climax when the Souceks' daughter wanted to join the school's Girl Scout troupe, organized by the same lesbian couple who despised them. Despite repeated and thorough efforts, it was made impossible for their daughter to join or participate in the troupe. All the Souceks' attempts were stonewalled. Phone calls and emails were rarely, if ever, returned. Applications and required paperwork was never sent home, and pertinent applicant information was somehow never received back.

Dan was furious. He went to the regional Girl Scout director in Raleigh and related what was happening. "Who can I talk to about this?" He got the runaround. The Girl Scouts put him off with excuses—"Oh, well, those are local decisions"—when they did not ignore his attempts to discuss the matter altogether.

Soucek found this treatment mean but also imprudent from a public relations standpoint. This was the personal dilemma of a sitting senator. "You'd think they would at least want to address it, not ignore it," he recalled. "It was discrimination!"

It was also petty as the troupe leaders were penalizing a child.

In retrospect, his experience is not that surprising as the liberal Girl Scouts organization, on the national level, had long since changed its focus to radical feminism and its bloody handmaiden Planned Parenthood.

The Souceks eventually dropped the matter, figuring the organization might be an unsafe environment for their daughter anyway.

It was natural for the Appalachian State chancellor to ask Soucek, who had served eight years' active-duty military, to speak at an outdoor Veterans Day event. Soucek happily agreed. Unfortunately, the amendment controversy was raging; and a host of loud students, armed with signs, showed up at the event to protest him during his speech!

Soucek was stunned and disappointed that students would do this, and he approached them afterward. "I understand your right to protest," he said. "I can understand you disagree with the marriage amendment. But I'm here as a formal army officer honoring our veterans. Why would you come here and degrade and disrespect our veterans because of your view on this other issue which has nothing to do with this? I'm not here as a senator or pro-marriage amendment sponsor but as a veteran to honor veterans. But you've used this event for your own purpose and dishonored them. I'm happy to talk about the amendment with you, but you've chosen the wrong venue. A poor one."

The students' views were by no means representative of North Carolinians in general. A poll of five hundred likely voters taken by Public Opinion Strategies a few months before the amendment vote showed that 61 percent of respondents were "definitely for" the amendment while 23 percent were "definitely against" it.

But not all numbers were favorable. Alex Miller, Equality North Carolina's interim executive at the time, cited an Elon University poll finding that opposition to any legal recognition for same-sex couples dropped from 44 percent in March 2009 to 35 percent in February 2011.

"Attitudes are changing fast," he told the *Charlotte Observer*.

No one, not even Alex, could have any idea just *how* fast.

And the consequences would be dire.

Dennis Prager of Prager University made an apt observation to Fox News host Stuart Varney. "This is the first generation in the West, in *human* history, that is being raised godless. No religion, no God, and the results are the end of Western civilization as we know it." He added that "a wisdom-free generation, a generation that doesn't believe in any transcendent truth, will not survive."

The Soldier Perseveres

I have done all I can do. To God be the glory.
—Mary Frances Forrester

The grieving period was different for Mary Frances than for most widows. For one, there was no time to grieve. That must be deferred, for succumbing to grief would distract her from the work that remained to be done. A soldier's best buddy falls in battle, but he cannot stop. He still must brave the bullets and take the ridge.

The March days lengthened. There was one more trip Mary Frances had yet to take with her husband. Though from that journey, she must return alone.

Upon Jim's death, Mary Frances could easily have finished out his term as she had the encouragement and support of Jim's fellow legislators as well as the Gaston County GOP, which had the prerogative to appoint a replacement legislator to finish out an unexpired term. Most likely Mary Frances would have received that appointment.

But she told the county party officials and Senator Berger that she couldn't do it. For one thing, the timing was horrible. The General Assembly would be convening during Mary Paige's backyard wedding in May, following the primary. There was far too much to do by way of arrangements, and she had to be there for her children in the painful void left by Jim's death. Mary Paige in particular was grieving, for her father would not be there to walk her down the aisle. His absence would make an otherwise joyous event a bittersweet time, and Mary Frances must support them through it. Family came first, after all. That's what Jim stood for.

Besides, she just didn't have the will to take his place.

She could barely tackle the sad job of clearing out Jim's office in Raleigh while holding her emotional self together.

Lord, just let me just get through Thanksgiving. Please.

Mary Frances poured all her remaining energies into the amendment fight.

For five months, she existed on sheer will, commitment, caffeine, and no small amount of adrenaline, traveling to the ends of the state to speak on behalf of Jim's amendment. She addressed political organizations, rallies, conferences, church groups (both black and white), bipartisan civic organizations, book clubs, strangers she met in the supermarket produce aisle, and anyone else who showed an inclination to listen. It was a topic that could hardly be avoided even if she had tried, especially when the person in question knew her relationship to Jim.

She participated in independent candidate forums wherever they were held, including one hosted by the Libertarian Party in Shelby, North Carolina. There were also invitations to liberal group events and forums in which speakers and attendees overwhelmingly represented the anti-amendment viewpoint, such as the liberal African American church attended by Harvey Gantt in Charlotte.

There in the trenches with her was Dr. Mark Harris. They were met with a cool reception and felt the opposition as if it were cold steel. It was doubtful Mary Frances would make a dent with those in attendance on the amendment issue, but she had to try, if only to be a voice that countered the anti-amendment claims.

In her collective efforts, she encountered apathy in some people and sheer ignorance in others, such as an exterminator who came to spray her rental house for pests and declared there was "nothing about homosexuality in the Bible."

"I'm not sure what Bible you're reading," Mary Frances responded bluntly.

The anti-amendment camp changed little, but the degree of its tactics now amped up. The gay lobby was still loud and livid. Intimidation was still used. The media was still one-sided. Hateful calls and emails still rolled in. Jim was still slandered.

And Mary Frances still forged ahead.

It all felt like one surreal and disjointed day that did not end. Her internal clock was shot. She moved in a fog. All she could do was scatter prayers into the whirlwind. "Lord, let me be strong." "Let me say what needs to be said."

Mark Creech was worried. "Mary Frances," he warned, "if you don't take time to grieve, this is going to come back to hurt you."

Her reply to him was simple: "I'm never going to look back and say woulda, shoulda, coulda. I am going to do this for Jim." It was his legacy, and she must see that it triumphed.

Mary Paige's wedding, coming so close on the heels of Jim's death, was indeed a mix of joy and sorrow for everyone. But for the bride, it was particularly bittersweet as she had always longed for "Daddy" to walk her down the aisle and give her away.

Her very last words to him had been, "You'd better be there."

She chose to forgo the wedding gown she had planned to wear, a striking fashion-forward mermaid style in champagne, in favor of the more traditional white gown she was certain her father would have liked. "There was really no choice," she said.

Along with disparate emotions, in the back of her mind lurked an apprehension that her wedding ceremony might become the target of protesters. She had already received ugly emails, and one from a gay friend that read, "It's not fair that you can get married, and I can't."

Thankfully, the wedding came and went without disruption. And Mary Paige *did* feel her father there, alongside her in spirit.

Mary Frances rested in the knowledge that she'd been faithful to Jim's cause, that she had given her all to it even in the face of brutal resistance.

For a time, to google Mary Frances was to be confronted with a barrage of slander and misrepresentation. A search might even turn up a devil caricature of her, complete with horns and tail and born of a childish vindictiveness on the part of whoever originated it. But to this day, she counts the image as a badge of honor. It is, after all, a far better reflection of who they are than who she is.

Arlington

"There," said they, "is Mount Sion, the heavenly
Jerusalem, the innumerable company of angels,
and the spirits of just men made perfect."
—John Bunyan, *Pilgrim's Progress*

Arlington Cemetery.

The very name evokes a flush of reverence in the heart of free-dom-loving Americans. But for those with a loved one buried there, it is far more. It is where they must say goodbye.

Like an illustration from a picture book, March 26, 2012, dawned crisp and sunny and perfect.

Mary Frances walked with slow steps the mile from Arlington Chapel to the waiting grave site. The longest mile she would ever walk.

Before her rolled the horse-drawn caisson bearing Jim's flag-draped casket. Inside, on his lapel, was stuck his American flag pin, an emblem of devotion to his adopted country. A few inches below it, folded and tucked safely into his breast pocket, was a note that read, "Dear Daddy, I love you very much. Love, Mary Paige."

Behind the casket, his general's flag was carried aloft by a color guard, moving to the rhythm of a cadence march played by a parade band. A riderless horse, ever a poignant sight, walked beside the caisson.

Every so often, Mary Frances looked down at the small figure walking at her side and squeezed his hand. It was Jay, her six-year-old grandson. He sensed something important and sad was happening, and it had everything to do with Pop-Pop, who was nowhere to be seen. All the grim people in black, the hushed atmosphere, and low voices were strange. At one point, he turned his blue eyes upward and whispered, "Sassy, is this where Jesus is buried?"

The honor of the occasion and the sacred feel of that hallowed earth affected all present. To look out over the rolling fields of sacrifice and valor wrought a strange mix of pride and mourning—and a lump to the throat. Along the procession's route, visitors to Arlington stopped in their tracks, standing in silent reverence with doffed baseball caps and lowered heads as the parade of eighty or so mourners passed: personal friends, military colleagues, and assorted VIPs.

Heath Jenkins, also present to mourn Jim, had planned a simultaneous trip to the capital city with his young sons, aged twelve and fifteen, along with their two friends. Though it was a sad occasion, it was also a rare opportunity for the boys to witness a military funeral, with full honors, in Arlington Cemetery. To receive a unique and tangible lesson on the high cost of freedom—*their* freedom.

The grave site was located in Air Force Section 64. Words were said over James Summers Forrester and prayers rendered. Four days earlier and four miles away, Congresswoman Virginia Foxx had stood on the floor or the United States House of Representatives and spoken words in honor of her friend and fellow North Carolinian James Forrester.

A sixteen-gun salute cracked the solemn atmosphere. The Stars and Stripes were folded with reverent precision and presented to Mary Frances by the commander-in-chief of the Air Forces.

"On behalf of the President of the United States and a grateful nation…"

Taps was played.

The casket was lowered into the earth as four F-16s executed a smooth flyover.

Back home, in that same hour, the American flag over the Capitol building in Raleigh sank to half-staff in honor of Jim. Governor Beverly Perdue ordered all flags over public buildings also to fly at half-mast. Over the next few days, a host of other flags across the Tar Heel State would be lowered in tribute.

"So, guys, what was your favorite part of the trip?" Heath Jenkins asked the boys on their return flight to Charlotte.

He expected them to respond with the National Zoo or the Spy Museum. Instead, the boys agreed unanimously and without hesitation that the profound and patriotic service at Arlington had been the greatest experience of all. Jim would have been encouraged by their answer and doubtless quoted a patriotic adage close to his heart.

With the funeral behind her, Mary Frances, along with her children and grandchildren, packed up and journeyed home to face the ongoing business of life. Everyone was heartsick, and it felt strange to be leaving Jim, Dad, Pop-Pop behind in Arlington.

But then they were leaving him in the best of company—in the very heart of the land he loved.

Election Day

Marriage between one man and one woman is the only domestic legal union that shall be valid or recognized in this State. This Section does not prohibit a private party from entering into contracts with another private party; nor does this Section prohibit courts from adjudicating the rights of private parties pursuant to such contracts.
—Proposed amendment on the North Carolina primary election ballot, May 8, 2012

The Democrats' hopeful expectations that primary voter turnout would be low went unfulfilled. Ironically, voter turnout was high *because* of the amendment measure. It was a driving force in getting North Carolinians to the ballot booth.

Senator Dan Soucek was working the polls in Lenoir when a middle-aged man approached him in the parking lot and thanked Soucek for his position on the marriage amendment. The man confessed that he had never voted before, but had come to the polls that day to support the measure.

Pastor Mark Harris, working the polls in Stanley County, encountered a woman in her late eighties who had also come to vote specifically for the amendment. It would be the first ballot she had ever cast in her life, but she believed the marriage amendment was too important to fail.

Reverend Patrick Wooden had his own interesting encounter at a voting precinct when he met an elderly African American lady telling passing, incoming voters that the marriage amendment had "tricky language" that would "hurt us."

Wooden approached her with a gentle question. "Ma'am, have you even seen the marriage amendment?"

"No," she replied.

He handed her a copy.

She read it twice, then frowned. "Where's the rest?"

"You mean the tricky-language part?"

"Yes."

"When Reverend Barber and the NAACP told you about the tricky language, did they read the tricky language to you?"

"No."

"Did they read the *amendment* to you?"

"No."

"Ma'am, they were not being honest with you. *This* is the amendment," he said, indicating the copy he had given her. "Ma'am, with all due respect, go home. You're out here fighting against an amendment that you actually do not disagree with. Do you believe marriage is a union between a man and a woman?"

"Yes."

Wooden went on to talk about the second portion of the amendment that stated all private contracts between private parties would not be affected. "Do you disagree with this?"

"No," she replied, her face beginning to show her realization that the amendment and its purpose had been misrepresented to her and many other African Americans.

"Ma'am. I see every day what can happen to a people when this institution is decimated."

Over 2.1 million North Carolina residents cast ballots that day. This translates to 33 percent of voters statewide, a record turnout for a primary election.

Mary Frances worked the polls all day in Stanley, Mount Holly, Iredell County, Lincolnton, before packing up her things and driving to Raleigh to wait out the results alongside Tami Fitzgerald and the other coalition members.

When she heard the election numbers that night, she cried, mentally apologizing to Jim for not being able to contain her tears until she "reached the car."

"I'm sorry, Jim. But this I did for you."

She had been faithful, but it was a happy release to have the task done and behind her.

Naturally, it was the most unflattering photo of her possible that landed the front page of all the statewide newspapers. Her face looked emotional, tearstained, and exhausted. Both her model's self-consciousness over her appearance and her Southern sense of "fit-ness" could not help but be bruised.

The People Speak

The true follower of Christ will not ask, "If I embrace this truth, what will it cost me?" Rather he will say, "This is truth. God help me to walk in it, let come what may!"

—A. W. Tozer

As Jim had intended, the citizens of North Carolina decided the marriage question, and on May 8, 2012, North Carolina became the thirtieth state in the union to constitutionally prohibit same-sex marriage.

The referendum passed with 61 percent for and 39 percent opposed. Only six counties voted against it: Buncombe, Chatham, Durham, Mecklenburg, Orange, Wake, and Watauga—all liberal strongholds.

Reactions from the opposition were predictable. Robert Kellogg, executive president of Parents, Families and Friends of Lesbians and Gays of Gaston County said, "Obviously we are disappointed, but we're not deterred because we will continue to fight for equality and justice in North Carolina. I think it's important for people in Gaston County to realize that while this may be a step back, those of us that fight for equal rights are not deterred. We believe this is the beginning and not the end."

Repetition reduces resistance.

Coopting biblical language, presumably to claim moral superiority, Kellogg, in a written statement, said:

North Carolina now has second class citizens with discrimination written into our sacred constitution. Now we will suffer as North Carolina hobbles along a crooked path with one foot bent toward the bigotry of the past and another one standing firm on the road to redemption. Those who seek to legislate with hate will be met with a firm resolve to fight the good fight until all people in North Carolina are equal under the law.

Governor Beverly Perdue opined, "Folks are saying what in the world is going on in North Carolina. We look like Mississippi." Mississippi Governor Phil Bryant promptly responded to this ignorant pomposity by calling the insult "petty."

President Barack Obama wasted no time in criticizing the outcome of the North Carolina vote and even promised his refusal to enforce the amendment.

Liberal public figures and Hollywood celebrities wasted no time in chiming in on Twitter, indignant over the amendment and corporately turning up their surgically altered noses at the backward voters of North Carolina who believed marriage was providentially designed to be a heterosexual union. To cite a few:

> NC gays, move to Iowa where you are full citizens. Casting *Real Housewives of Dubuque* now. (Kathy Griffin)

> North Carolina, I spit in your general direction. (Matthew Lillard)

> One giant step backward. (North Carolina—born swimsuit model and actress Brooklyn Decker)

> Way to be a bad southern cliché North Carolina. I'm sure your grandkids will look back on this day in horror. (Meghan McCain)

Closer to home, Duke Energy CEO Jim Rogers remarked, "We'll be embarrassed of this as we were of the Jim Crow laws in the 1860s, 1880s. Any time you deny people rights such as wanting to live together, I just don't think it's fair."

It is uncertain just who was being denied the right "to live together"?

And so it went.

With the adoption of the marriage amendment, Mary Frances went "underground" to deal with her deferred bereavement. Finally, she could be alone to collapse emotionally, to put aside her brave face, and cry to her heart's content over her lost soulmate. How she missed Jim! She couldn't even celebrate this hard-won victory with him.

The next few months were a dark valley, and the pages of her diary bled with grief, loneliness, and uncertainty. One prayerful passage reveals the deep and bitter longing left by Jim's death.

> Lord, I still talk to him and it does seem to be comforting. Sometimes I think so hard about it that I try to "think him here." But the feeling quickly passes, and I am still alone.

God's grace and mercy, and her family's support, sustained her. And there were the eloquent, comforting lines of *Pilgrim's Progress*:

> "You are going now," said they, "to the paradise of God, wherein you shall see the tree of life, and eat of the never-fading fruits thereof. And when you come there you shall have white robes given you, and your walk and talk shall be every day with the King, even all the days of eternity. There you shall not see again such things as you saw when you were in the lower region upon the earth, to wit, sorrow, sickness, affliction and death. For the former things are passed away."

Overruled

All animals are equal, but some are more equal than others.
—George Orwell, *Animal Farm*

*You seem to consider the judges the ultimate arbiters of all
constitutional questions; a very dangerous doctrine indeed, and one
which would place us under the despotism of an oligarchy. Our
judges…and their power [are] the more dangerous as they are in office
for life, and are not responsible, as the other functionaries are, to the
elective control. The Constitution has erected no such single tribunal,
knowing that to whatever hands confided, with the corruptions of time
and party, its members would become despots. It has more wisely made
all the departments co-equal and co-sovereign within themselves. When
the legislative or executive functionaries act unconstitutionally, they are
responsible to the people in their elective capacity. The exemption of the
judges from that is quite dangerous enough. I know of no safe depository
of the ultimate powers of the society, but the people themselves.*
—Thomas Jefferson, in a letter to Mr. Jarvis (September 1820)

On October 10, 2014, US district judge for North Carolina's
Western District Max Cogburn, a Barack Obama appointee, struck
down the state's constitutional amendment defining marriage as
an exclusive union between one man and one woman. The ban on
same-sex marriage was nullified—and the people of North Carolina
overruled by one unelected judge in an act of judicial tyranny.

Same-sex marriages commenced in the Tar Heel State.

Mary Frances took no phone calls or interviews. The ruling was a blow, and though she felt personally disheartened, she would give no one the satisfaction of gloating over this defeat.

Then on June 26, 2015, the Supreme Court of the United States ruled 5–4 in *Obergefell vs. Hodges* that states were required to issue marriage licenses to homosexual couples and recognize same-sex marriages performed in other states. This ruling legalized homosexual marriage in the United States, its territories and possessions.

Senator Dan Soucek referred to the *Obergefell* decision as "the greatest voter disenfranchisement in the history of the country."

"Here were thirty states," he said, "tens of millions of people who went to polls to make their will known on something they believed right and important enough to include in their constitutions." It was a *super-supermajority* of voters and elected representative alike, a full 60 percent. But the court has essentially declared to them, "Your votes mean nothing. We don't care what you want or think. We're going to overrule you."

"The Supreme Court may now be the greatest agent of voter suppression," added Soucek, hearing the voice of the man who had never before voted but went to the polls to support the amendment. What would that man say now? *"Why should I ever vote again, when the most important thing I voted for doesn't count?!"*

Chief Justice John Roberts wrote the dissenting opinion, in which he stated,

> This court is not a legislature. Whether same-sex marriage is a good idea should be of no concern to us. Under the Constitution, judges have power to say what the law is, not what it should be. The people who ratified the Constitution authorized courts to exercise "neither force nor will but merely judgment." (*The Federalist* No. 78, p. 465)

Also dissenting, Justice Samuel Alito wrote,

> Today's decision…will be used to vilify Americans who are unwilling to assent to the new orthodoxy. In the course of its opinion, the majority compares traditional marriage laws to laws that denied equal treatment for African-Americans and women. The implications of this analogy will be exploited by those who are determined to stamp out every vestige of dissent.

Tami Fitzgerald, in an NC Values Coalition press release, issued a statement regarding the SCOTUS decision:

> Today's ruling by the Supreme Court will no more settle the issue of gay marriage than *Roe v. Wade* settled the issue of abortion. Forty years later, the majority of Americans are more pro-life than ever, and I believe that history will prove the arrogance of this Supreme Court's new illusory definition for marriage.
>
> Millions of Americans believe that marriage is the sacred union of one man and one woman, and it is an improper abuse of power for the Supreme Court to attempt to re-define an institution that it did not invent.
>
> This landmark decision will bring peril to family structure and stability and will threaten the religious liberties upon which our country was founded. We must guarantee that North Carolinians whose religious beliefs are violated by this decision will have the continuing freedom to act on their beliefs.

Running Leap

*As a former homosexual, when I was involved in the 1980s
promoting the gay agenda, our only focus was to seek tolerance,
whereas today's political activism has moved from true tolerance
into political domination and power. It's an amazing thing to
watch a group that said they were oppressed becomes oppressors.*
—Randy Thomas, "The Homosexual Agenda"

The oft-used slippery-slope analogy has become woefully inadequate to describe the progression of immorality surrounding issues of marriage and sexuality. A more apt comparison is a running leap off a cliff. What was once "extreme" has forced its way into mainstream culture, and "fringe" has hung its sign at the very locus of Western society.

Most of the 1972 National Coalition of Gay Organizations (NCGO) goals have come to pass. They may even appear tame in light of the surreal debates about gender we currently find ourselves having. Certainly not all gay people would acknowledge or approve the NCGO goals. Nonetheless, they have helped open a door through which any sexual abnormality and perversion will now seek to enter.

It is worth repeating that, for the drivers of gay activism, the ultimate end was never merely permitting marriage between members of the same sex. That was only the initial phase in erasing any and all exclusions to sexuality in practice, legal sanction, or self-identity. No, the very concept of "male and female" itself had to be erased, thus marriage as traditionally defined as a one-man-one-woman bond had to go. Redefining parenthood was an inevitable byproduct, and the fact that children reared in homes with same-sex parents are necessarily robbed of either a mother or father is of little concern. The self-fulfillment of the homosexual couple in question takes precedence.

In the five short years since *Obergefell*, while the guns of the "gay rights" wars still lay smoking, the nation has been besieged by a circus of bizarre legal suits that would have been unthinkable a mere decade ago. Leading the circus are the "transgender equality" activists, every bit as demanding and intolerant as their gay rights predecessors. A civilization that has always recognized two sexes is now told to embrace the supposed existence of fifty plus "genders."

The gay-marriage debate convinced many that the sexes were interchangeable with regard to human relationships. Now we must pretend that the sexes are interchangeable with no respect for biology! Thus, we must all rearrange our minds to embrace the idea that gender is whatever a given individual "feels" himself (or herself) to be and reshape our society to accommodate his delusions. Gender dysphoria, what was once officially recognized as a deviant psychological disorder, is now—we are assured by the American Psychiatric Association (APA)—a normal state requiring acceptance and affirmation. The most recent claim is that gender is fluid (can evolve from day to day) or doesn't exist at all.

The prerogative to "identify" one's own gender apart from fixed reality is a direct but natural outcome of the notion that truth is relative—and the possibilities are endless. If I can have a penis and call myself a woman, why can I not call myself a six-year-old or a person of a different ethnicity? Or even a favorite animal or mythical creature?

The level of denial is astounding. Consider the inequities in the realm of women's sports, in which men who "identify" as women are now permitted to compete against biological females. No matter how one mutilates one's privates or how many hormones one ingests, males will always have a physical advantage over women due to greater muscle density and larger cardiovascular system.

The absurdity would be comic if not for the implications of this insidious transgender belief system and the possibility that "gender identity" becomes recognized under federal law. But that is what happens when legal status is not tied to any fixed, natural genetic code and biological design (and inherent biological *purpose*) but rather subjective feeling and outward behavior. By this definition, "civil rights" becomes a political cow whose udders never run dry. The arguments employed for gay marriage laid a neat foundation.

As ever, the radicals want to own the next generation. Propagandizing and carefully crafted language worked with homosexuality, and it will work with transgenderism—from "drag-queen-story hour" at public libraries to gender-transition ceremonies in kindergarten classrooms.

At every level, children in America must now learn, as they learned about homosexuality, about transgenderism and gender fluidity. It is presented as benign, normal, and fun so that young minds become "comfortable" with it. It is given a "human face" at an age when children have not developed the intellectual maturity to distinguish the human from the rightness or wrongness of the human's behavior. If the person wears a friendly smile, then what they do must be okay!

The new gender circus, and its disturbing proximity to children, is more dangerous than people realize or acknowledge. A dark passage has opened up for sexual abusers and predators. As always, women and children are the most vulnerable to the tyranny of political correctness. Repetition reduces resistance.

Even setting aside the most basic right of physical privacy, the allowance of "transgender men" into female venues offers rich, new hunting grounds for sexual predators. The potential for abuse is frightening. Transgender men in many places are already being allowed to invade previously all-female domains or places where the safety of women and children was once sacrosanct—bathrooms, school locker rooms, security checks, hospitals, waxing salons, prisons.

To add to the moral cesspool, the enthusiasm of some progressively liberal activists and parents to push children into transgenderism smacks heavily of pedophiliac grooming. Anyone who cannot see the risks associated with encouraging a ten-year-old boy in flamboyant drag to dance in a club full of men for money is either in denial or evil beyond imagining.

The extent to which the public is being asked to play along with the mental disorder of transgenderism, which needs proper diagnosis and treatment, perhaps takes its most surreal form in the realm of medicine.

For years, medical rules of ethics have been ignored so as not to offend LGBT persons. Heaven forbid they be honestly informed of any risk factors or unpleasant consequences of their chosen lifestyle! For years, taxpayers have been paying for *irreversible* transgender reassignment surgery so individuals can "play-act" at being the opposite sex. Now, just in case you thought it couldn't get more ridiculous—voila!—transgender women (men) can now be pregnant. At least they believe they are pregnant, which is good enough. Never mind that they have no uterus. One cannot but weep over the gender reassignment of prepubescent children as young as five, which requires arresting natural sexual development by pumping their bodies full of hormones.

Make no mistake, all these dangerous and sad absurdities are different heads of the same hydra. So what will be deemed "normal" tomorrow? Polygamy? Pedophilia? The seeds for these vile perversions have already been planted.

Love is love, after all. It is merely the affection of willing parties, we are told.

Repetition reduces resistance.

It is a lethal game that rebellious humanity plays. Reject the Creator's design, and you reject the Creator Himself.

Past, Present, and Future

Indeed, all who desire to live a godly life in
Christ Jesus will be persecuted.
—2 Timothy 3:12 ESV

And I heard a loud voice in heaven saying, "Now the salvation and
the power and the kingdom of our God and the authority of His
Christ have come, for the accuser of our brothers has been thrown
down, who accuses them day and night before our God. And they
have conquered him by the blood of the Lamb, and by the word of
their testimony, for they loved not their own lives even unto death."
—Revelation 12:10–11 ESV

The most disturbing—dystopian!—facet of all this is the casual disregard on the left for religious liberty. It is a crisis few Americans ever thought to see in their lifetime.

What happens to those who stand for right, who refuse to be bullied into violating their deeply held religious beliefs and the conviction of conscience?

Just ask bakers Melissa and Aaron Klein, who refused to bake a cake for a same-sex commitment ceremony. After an investigation, the Oregon Bureau of Labor and Industries "ruled" that they have violated the state's sexual-orientation law and demanded the couple pay $135,000 to the two women requesting the cake. The sum, along with a vicious public smear campaign, put the Kleins out of business. The couple was also ordered to "cease and desist" from speaking publicly about their Christian convictions regarding using their artistic

393

talents to support same-sex ceremonies. Official Brad Avakian stated, "The goal is to rehabilitate. For those who do violate the law, we want them to learn from that experience and have a good, successful business in Oregon." The use of the word *rehabilitate* in this scenario should send an Orwellian chill up any conservative's back.

Just ask Barronelle Stutzman, a florist who declined to arrange flowers for longtime clients to celebrate their same-sex wedding. She had both served and employed gay people in her career. Sued by Washington's attorney general, with the eager assistance of the American Civil Liberties Union (ACLU), Stutzman has been caught in an exhausting legal circus of suits and appeals for six years. The lawsuits targeted not only her business but Stutzman herself, who has been forced to pay a fortune in penalties and legal fees.

Just ask Atlanta fire chief Kelvin Cochran, suspended for writing and publishing (on his own time) a book expressing biblical understanding of sexual morality, including a one-page reference to homosexual sex acts. His monthlong unpaid suspension included "sensitivity training" while an investigation was conducted. Cochran was subsequently dismissed.

Just ask Donald and Evelyn Knapp, proprietors of the Hitching Post Wedding Chapel. Town officials in Coeur d'Alene, Idaho, told ordained ministers they must celebrate same-sex weddings or face fines and jail time under a nondiscrimination ordinance that includes sexual orientation and gender identity.

Just ask photographers Jon and Elane Huguenin, who, according to the New Mexico Human Rights Commission, were guilty of sexual-orientation discrimination for refusing to use their "artistic and expressive" skills to photograph a same-sex wedding. Four years later, New Mexico's Supreme Court upholds the commission's ruling; and Justice Richard C. Bosson, in his concurring opinion, dismisses the religious convictions of the photographers as "the price of citizenship."

Just ask Catholic Charities of Boston, forced to end its foster care and adoption programs in the wake of Massachusetts' decision to recognize same-sex marriage due to its unwillingness to place children with same-sex couples. "We have encountered a dilemma we cannot resolve," said a joint statement of Rev. J. Bryan Hehir (president) and Jeffrey Kaneb (chair of the board of trustees). "In spite of much effort and analysis, Catholic Charities finds that it cannot reconcile the teaching of the Church, which guides our work, and the statutes and regulations of the Commonwealth." Denying hundreds of children the opportunity for a family merely because the adoption agency in question chooses to place them only in traditional homes that include both a mother and father—yes, the gay lobby is that vindictive. Better the agency be run out of business than same-sex sensibilities be offended.

Just ask the embattled Jack Phillips, a cake artist who told two gay men he could not design a cake for their wedding, though he expressed his willingness to custom-design other cakes for them. The Colorado Civil Rights Commission declared that he *must* design the cake and even demanded the "reeducation" of Phillips's staff as well as the submission of mandatory "compliance" reports every quarter for two years.

Thankfully, the courts ultimately ruled in Phillips's favor. Of course, this is unacceptable to the intolerant "gaystapo" activists who have made Phillips a particular target of their wrath. Subsequent, contrived attempts to force him back to court included an attorney for the opposition asking him to bake a cake celebrating a transgender transition as well as requests for cake messages with satanic themes. These bullies appear determined to break Phillips through intimidation and ongoing litigation.

Just ask any of the other dozens who have faced social and financial ruin because of their refusal to kowtow to the new dogma! All the individuals and organizations mentioned above were the focus of derision, threats, harassment, and costly lawsuits intended not only to drive them out of business but to create precedent and make a public example of conscience-bound dissenters. A clear message is being sent: "Comply, or we will destroy you."

One of the bitterest aspects of this collective travesty is that the controversy often begins with an unelected, unaccountable government commission or entity whose purported *raison d'etre* is the just treatment of minorities under antidiscrimination laws, laws that are increasingly vague, subjectively interpreted, and ever-expanding in their scope of victim categories. Via these entities, far-left bureaucrats wield an excessive amount of influence. Add the collusion of appointed leftist judges, and you have a neat poison with which to kill all freedom of conscience.

The controversy will not stop with artists and service providers. The left is not coming merely for your compliant actions but for your beliefs themselves. Whoever gets in the way will simply be deigned guilty of "discrimination" and "hate speech" as broadly defined by liberal progressives and the laws they pass to enforce conformity of thought.

From public schools to college universities, from retail establishments to churches, officials and administrators are already swift to enforce the new rules. Pronouns of choice must be honored, or there will be consequences for the one who misspeaks. It is the old strategy of intimidation and ruination, the same tactics employed for the gay-marriage debate and the same willingness to run roughshod over any opposing voice.

They are coming for you, Christian pastor, if you continue to preach that homosexuality is a sin or that true marriage consists of one man and one woman, no matter how kindly you put it or how much compassion you feel for gay individuals. They are coming for you, Christian educator, if you refuse to teach indoctrinating curricula touting a gay lifestyle. They are coming for you, Christian professor, when you declare the notion of "gender fluidity" to be a farce. They are coming for you, Christian student, when you decline to participate in campus gay-pride events or use a forbidden pronoun. They are coming for you, Christian physician, when you are forced to ignore basic biology (as if one can!) to affirm a patient's mental delusions.

They are coming for you, O church of the risen Christ. And losing your tax-exempt status will be the least of your concerns.

It is time for American Christians, individually and collectively, to ask themselves some hard questions. Are we a nation under judgement? Have we slumbered too long and awakened too late? Will those who profess Christ remain true in the face of a godless, intolerant culture? Or can the pendulum still swing back to Judeo-Christian values? The God who created them "male and female" still reigns over His creation. But sometimes He first judges those whom He means to restore. Is this what He intends for the United States of America? Since the *Roe v. Wade* decision of 1973, she has openly worshipped the spirit of Molech. She is now an unabashed Sodom. Biblically speaking, these inseparable twins of idolatrous rebellion signal an end to grace.

Yet we are not privy to the secret counsel of God. We *are* responsible for obeying the dictates of His Word, whether in freedom or persecution. Nor are we without hope in either state. Doing the right thing, no matter the outcome, is a triumph in itself when the cosmic victory is already won. Jim Forrester knew this.

Following the *Obergefell* decision, Reverend Patrick Wooden observed, "They can make same-sex marriage legal, but they can't make it right. We were still right."

"Aren't you concerned about being on the wrong side of history?" someone countered.

"No," he said. "I'm only concerned about being on God's side of history."

A much-anticipated lunar eclipse took place early on the morning following the Supreme Court's *Obergefell* ruling. The celestial event had been all over the news in the week leading up to the decision.

Still struggling with a bitter moral defeat and its heavy implications for the future, Mark Creech stepped out onto his back porch in a crisp breeze to witness the eclipse with his own eyes.

The full moon was a white, stunning beauty. Mark stood there, transfixed in wonder and fascination as the dark shadow of the earth passed in front of it, blotting out its brightness.

But eventually the moon returned to its full celestial radiance, and the shadow was driven back into the void. In that moment Mark was overcome with a clear, analogous truth: darkness may eclipse the light for a time, but the light is still there—and it *will* return.

For the light can never be vanquished.

Epilogue

It is perhaps a curious twist of geometrical fate that the grave of James Summers Forrester lies directly on an invisible line which runs between the Air Force Memorial and the Pentagon. From his little plot of earth, one can see both structures clearly.

He is a little more difficult to locate each time Mary Frances visits due to the constant additions to Arlington Cemetery. Thirty per day. Row upon row. Cross upon cross. Every inch of his grave site, however, she has memorized, especially the deeply etched letters on the marble headstone.

JAMES
SUMMERS
FORRESTER
BG
US AIR FORCE
VIETNAM
JAN 8 1937
OCT 31 2011
LEGION OF MERIT
SENATOR
MD

A robin is usually there to greet her. She sits on the grass under "his tree" and thinks, often to the comforting strains of hymns being played during a burial service nearby. The robin seems to be listening with her. The bird is a small bit of divine grace, she believes, a token of assurance that all is well with her husband.

She closes her eyes and thinks about Jim and their life together. She contemplates the heavenly realms now unveiled to his sight, and "Well done, good and faithful servant" echoes in her mind, along with the strains of the old hymn—

It is well. It is well with my soul.

Author's Note

Know that this book is not an apologetic or legal defense for traditional marriage, nor is it a scholastic rebuttal of same-sex unions. It is not a political work but a personal one. It is tribute paid and honor bestowed. It is an exemplary sketch of how one principled, determined man can champion a righteous but risky cause. May this hero of the not-so-distant past inspire and impassion the heroes of the future, though overwhelmed, to persevere and not despair. *For the future is at hand, the war goes on, and our nation needs heroes more than ever.*

Jim liked to quote the famous pledge from the World War I diary of Private Martin Treptow, a soldier killed in action in 1917:

> America shall win the war. Therefore I will work.
> I will save. I will sacrifice. I will endure. I will
> fight cheerfully and do my utmost, as if the whole
> issue of the struggle depended on me alone.

Anyway

Mother Teresa

People are often unreasonable, illogical and self-centered;
Forgive them anyway.
If you are kind, people may accuse you of selfish, ulterior motives;
Be kind anyway.
If you are successful, you will win some false friends and some true
    enemies;
Succeed anyway.
If you are honest and frank, people may cheat you;
Be honest and frank anyway.
What you spend years building, someone could destroy overnight;
Build anyway.
If you find serenity and happiness, they may be jealous;
Be happy anyway.
The good you do today, people will often forget tomorrow;
Do good anyway.
Give the world the best you have, and it may never be enough;
Give the world the best you've got anyway.
You see, in the final analysis, it is between you and your God;
It was never between you and them anyway.

About the Authors

Mary Frances Forrester, an influential public servant, holds many leadership roles in civic, historical, medical, and political organizations and has received numerous awards as a champion of Judeo-Christian conservative ideals. Most proud of being founder (1999) of the state chapter of Concerned Women for America (CWA-NC), the largest women's public policy organization in the nation, she remains a leader and advisor for CWA-NC. An avid historian, she was a guest lecturer at the University of Rome's United States History Class on the Electoral College after the 2000 presidential election. Mother of four and grandmother of eight, she considers her family to be her raison d'être.

Rebecca Anthony is a freelance writer and editor of both fiction and nonfiction. She has submitted articles for various periodicals including *Pointe Innovation, P31 Woman, and Learning through History* and will be releasing her first work of historical fiction, an epic trilogy set in ancient Rome, this fall. When not tapping out literary masterpieces on her laptop keyboard, she is decorating her house and annoying her friends by correcting their grammar.

CPSIA information can be obtained
at www.ICGtesting.com
Printed in the USA
JSHW031238230322
24155JS00002B/2